Thank Goliath

A Memoir About an Italian Mother,
a Rebel Son, and Life's Noble Teacher

Domenic Aversa

Copyright © 2023 Domenic Aversa

All rights reserved. No part of this publication in print or in electronic format may be reproduced, stored in a retrieval system, or transmitted in any form or by any means, electronic, mechanical, photocopying, recording, or otherwise without the prior written permission of the publisher.

The scanning, uploading, and distribution of this book without permission is a theft of the author's intellectual property. Thank you for your support of the author's rights.

Distribution by Bublish, Inc.
ISBN: 978-1-647046-36-1 (eBook)
ISBN: 978-1-647046-35-4 (paperback)

Edited By and Special Thanks To David Aretha

CONTENTS

Weeds 1

Two Cakes 7

That Kid 13

St. Jude 19

My Son Will Work for You 39

Two Guns 77

Who Is Responsible? 97

Things at Night 111

Sacrifice 139

Once Again 163

Not What I Had in Mind 199

Searching 213

You're Nobody to Me 243

Miracles 267

Amen 293

About The Author 313

Each day, for 40 days, Goliath would present himself at the edge of the village.

Goliath was a giant. Not only was he double the size of most average men, but he and his people had trained to be the most skillful and lethal warriors in all of the lands.

Each day, at the edge of the village, he would invite a challenge to the death. He proclaimed that if he were slayed, his people would become servants to those in the village. If not, they would seize everyone and everything in sight.

The villagers were terrified. They saw no possible way to defeat this menace.

On the 41st day, a young boy, a shepherd named David, approached the leaders of the village and said, "I can defeat the giant."

Older and much wiser, the leaders laughed and dismissed David. "How could a simple boy that guides lambs and goats slay a giant warrior?"

David stood tall and courageous. "I will show you the power of God." David had protected his lambs and goats from lions and bears. Now he would protect the people of the village.

David walked to Goliath, announced his intentions. The giant laughed and mocked the young boy. Determined and full of might, David put a rock in a sling and launched it directly to the middle of the head of Goliath.

The giant fell to the ground. He was vanquished and eliminated.

The villagers rose to celebrate David. He would become their new leader. He had slain the giant and showed the power and glory that resided in each one of them.

1

WEEDS

It was 1975. I was eight years old, and I was picking dandelion greens on a Saturday morning, along the railroad tracks, with my mother and my four-year-old sister in tow. My father was at his garage working on a customer's car, or else he would have been alongside us, looking for other things to pick. It was spring; wild asparagus could most certainly be easily found.

My mother was 20 feet away from me, hunched over, nimbly working a small kitchen knife around the root of the dandelions as she picked them one by one.

I called to her.

"Mom."

I was bored and getting tired.

"Mom."

I didn't understand why we were the only people out there by the railroad.

"Mom."

"What is it?" she answered.

"When can we go home?"

She ignored my question. "Shake the dirt off before you put it in the bag."

"Mom."

"Shake it good or it will get all over the kitchen."

"Mom."

"Keep picking."

"Mom, it's Saturday."

"You can watch television when we get home."

"You always say that."

"Domenico, keep picking." I knew she was upset when she used my full Italian name.

"Mom, I'm tired."

"How do you think we can afford things? Be grateful."

"I should be grateful for grass?"

"For food."

"Mom, these are weeds."

"It's food. And, you should be grateful it's here."

My mother liked this particular stretch of land along the tracks because it was rich soil. It was clean and there were thousands of dandelions. For most people, these were just weeds that should either be cut or killed with pesticides. Cars that drove by while we were picking honked their horns, pointed, and laughed at us. At times it was confusing and embarrassing to me. I didn't know why we just couldn't go to the grocery store like "normal" people. However, my mother was unfazed by any detractors. For her, this was just another way to provide for her family. These weeds were free, and they would feed us for several months.

Now, 40 years later, in 2015, my mother and I were no longer picking weeds by railroad tracks, but we were still negotiating endlessly with each other. Our discussions were pretty much the same, but now she rarely called me by my full given name. Somehow, it got shortened as I got older.

"Dom."

"Mom, look at this grass."

"Be a good son—go get me a drink."

"Mom, seriously, look at this grass. Not one weed in it."

"Just a small one. Maybe some Sambuca or even Kahlua."

"Do you think they have a family of Italians pick their weeds?"

"Hurry up before your father comes back."

"He said you can't have any alcohol."

"It's because he's stingy."

"The doctor said you can't have any."

"Your father worries too much."

"How much do you think they'd charge us for a bowl of their grass?"

"Be grateful. How do you think you got here?"

"Because Jesus loves me."

"I'm your mother. Be nice and go get me a drink."

"Would Jesus want you to have a drink?"

"And get me a piece of chocolate if they have them."

"If you were an alcoholic, they would call me an 'enabler.'"

"I'm not an alcoholic. I'm your mother."

"You're acting like an alcoholic. How about I get you some flowers to eat? Would you prefer roses or lilies?"

"Lilies are for dead people."

"You have that drink and we might be having your funeral."

"Stop joking around. I have one drink a year, it's not going to kill me."

"I think you had three drinks last year."

"Why can't you let me have some fun?"

"Am I taking the *fun* out of *funeral*?"

"Just a little one. Hurry. I'm your mother."

I was still bantering with my mother, but now I had a bit of the upper hand because I had money. I didn't have to pick weeds in order to eat. However, her razor-sharp mind and her willingness to endure always kept her one step ahead of me. She knew that I wouldn't say "no" to her. It had been a long, difficult, surprising, and at times excruciating road that we had taken to get here, but now we were here, and it was genuinely gratifying.

As we talked, we stood on polished marble, on a balcony of a five-star hotel, looking out at the impeccably pristine lawn and garden. To those with wealth, this was just brunch. However, for my family, it was an arrival. My parents and their parents had made tremendous sacrifices to get to a place where they had some sense of financial freedom. For my mom and me, it was arrival of a different sort. We knew better than to feel completely settled. This arrival was more of layover. A moment in time when neither of us was struggling with a wide range of challenges.

For us, the tale of David and Goliath was more than a story of a boy taking on a giant. For us, it was a way of life. We knew that adversity was inescapable. It presented itself all through our lives. We knew that Goliath could and would show up at any moment in any form. Rather than run from adversity, we decided to develop a relationship with it. We thanked Goliath and made him noble because without that adversity, we wouldn't have known what was inside of us. While others cried, we moved forward. We learned that adversity was noble because it didn't take from us; it gave. It was the most generous and benevolent teacher we would ever encounter. Without adversity, we would have never learned how strong, creative, and resilient we were. Without adversity, we would never have seen the weakness, corruption, and criminality in humans. Without it, we would have never learned to forgive. As Goliath grew, we grew.

The challenges became bigger, more complicated, and more persistent. And, each time, we learned something deeper about our lives and our souls. We never gave up. We came to know that with each challenge, each setback, with every moment of sacrifice that we could overcome, we grew closer to serenity.

2

TWO CAKES

My mother was born with a twin. They were premature. At birth, they were weighed with a kitchen scale. They weren't much more than 1.5 pounds each.

Being the fourth and fifth children of the family, Benedetta and Luigina had the odds stacked against them. In their small town in central Italy, life was difficult. World War II was in its final days, there was only so much food to go around, and the fields still had to be worked, now more than ever. The work needed to be done before fall and another wet winter.

Their mother would carry them with her in a basket. She had them next to her as she patiently cut wheat with a scythe. Months passed. The fields were cleaned of anything of value, and the grains were processed and sold. The yield was promising, but Benedetta and Luigina were struggling to put on weight.

Luigina would pass one month after the war in Europe officially ended. For Benedetta, this meant more time, attention, and food was available to her. The struggle within and around her home would subside, and the coming years were filled with great health and joy. She grew into her dimples and shared a wide, bright smile with everyone she met. Eventually she would be joined by another brother and sister. Now, totaling six, they lived a charmed life filled with love and support from their parents and each other.

Life moves on. Young kids grow, and eventually it is time for them to start their own families. Benedetta's father felt it was best that they begin new lives in America. At the age of 11, with her three sisters, two brothers, and parents she arrived in Long Island, New York, to begin the next chapter of a delightfully explored life.

The years of charm and laughter would continue to be kind to Benedetta. Her smile became brighter and her skin glowed. At five-foot-five and weighing 95 pounds, she was slender and elegant, her thick brown hair always nestled perfectly under a pillbox hat or silk scarf. Now 17, she worked alongside her sister at Lord & Taylor. As a tailor, her sister always knew the right outfit for her. Not too tight or too short. She typically had her wear a delicate pearl necklace and an A-line dress. It was 1964, and she looked like she could have walked down the red carpet of a Broadway premiere and been mistaken for Jackie Onassis.

Her father knew she was a gem. He loved all his girls, but he also wanted them married and out of his house. Two were gone, and now it was Benedetta's time to leave the nest. The only problem was that she loved school. Books and learning were far more interesting to her than boys or men. Marriage was out of the question.

Her father was a determined man. She would be married, and it would be soon. She needed to focus on being a wife and mother; there was no need for more schooling. If Benedetta wouldn't find a suitor, then he would find one for her.

Sure enough, he found one.

He arrived at their family home with two cakes: one vanilla, one strawberry.

He was a much older man, at least 20 years her senior. He was short in stature with dark hair and even darker, brooding eyes. He wore a tailored suit but appeared uncomfortable in it.

Benedetta sat in the kitchen, staring at the two cakes. She was having none of this, neither the cake nor the man. Her father insisted that she try to spend time with this man. He was older and established, and he represented that he owned multiple businesses. He claimed to have significant wealth, enough to keep a learned and beautiful woman happy for her entire life. All she had to do was say "I do" and move to Australia.

The more her father talked, the angrier she became.

She rose from the kitchen table, walked into the living room, and approached the dark, older suitor. "I'm not sure what my father told you, but I'm not interested in you. I'm not going to marry you and I'm not moving to Australia. Thank you for the cakes."

Offended and flustered, the small Aussie man walked to the kitchen, picked up the strawberry cake, and left their home.

Naturally upset, Benedetta's father also left their home.

She knew she'd won the battle, but the war for marriage would carry on as long as she lived with her parents. Nonetheless, she would return to her books and sit quietly, reading in her room.

Later that day, her older brother, Mario, was visited by some friends from Canada. They had known each other while growing up in the same town in Italy but hadn't seen each other since they immigrated to North America; one family went to Windsor, Ontario, a small manufacturing-based city located across from Detroit, Michigan, and the other to Manhasset, an upper-middle-class, colorful town on Long Island, New York. In this group of friends were Carlo, Gino, and Giacinto. They had made the 11-hour car ride to New York to visit the World's Fair. They sat at the kitchen table and reminisced about their childhood in Italy.

Taking a break from her studies, Benedetta came to meet her brother's friends. She knew them as well. They had grown up in the same small town in Italy, but she had first met them on a brief visit to Canada with her parents the previous year. As they spoke, she quietly sized up the shy, handsome young man at one end of the kitchen table. Giacinto was tall and strong but with soft brown eyes and a warm demeanor. In that moment, she realized that the vanilla cake was still in the middle of the table and had been there for hours, untouched. Still fuming about her marriage duel with her father, she said to the young men, "Would anyone like a piece of cake?"

Gino and Carlo declined, but Giacinto accepted.

Benedetta cut a piece and served it to him.

As she watched him eat the cake, she realized, *OK, he'll do.*

Two years later, they married.

In those two years, most of their correspondence was through payphones and letters. They only saw each other in person five times, but the distance and time were small obstacles that were easily overcome by their love for one another.

Giacinto was a kind, caring man who worked as an auto mechanic at a non-union shop. It was an honest career but not a lucrative one. In his world, there was no spare change. Every nickel and dime was accounted for. To make ends meet, he lived with his parents and his younger brother.

Despite the limited time together prior to their marriage, despite the financial limitations and having to live with her new in-laws, Benedetta packed her bags, with the blessings of her parents, and moved to Windsor. She knew that this was the person she wanted to be with.

What she didn't know was that while on their honeymoon in Italy, Giacinto would be fired from his job, and she would get pregnant.

In the blink of an eye, Benedetta's life changed dramatically.

She was 21 years old, pregnant, husband unemployed, and living with her mother-in-law, father-in-law, and two brothers-in-law, one with a wife and two young children. And her best friends—her sisters, brothers, and parents, the people she had relied on her entire life for support and companionship—were a million miles away.

3

THAT KID

Several nights a week, no less than half a dozen adults would gather around the dining room table in my grandparents' home. It was a comfortable and solid home, thick walnut wood and plenty of windows, built in the 1920s. It was two stories high with a big basement, perfect for making wine and prosciutto. Kitchen and living room on the main floor. Twenty stairs up, four bedrooms and a bath. Friends and relatives lived close by—all the lots of the homes in the neighborhood were only 30 feet wide. Everyone could talk or visit each other without having to walk too far. They drank wine or coffee, sometimes water with a wedge of lemon in it. They'd eat walnuts and hazelnuts and homemade cookies. Some smoked cigarettes, some played cards, some just shared stories from their day. Regardless of the activity, there was never any real arguing. Perhaps debating but nothing of actual substance. The environment was always cordial and fun. But occasionally, there was one problem—"that kid."

"That kid" was me. I was upstairs and they were downstairs. I was supposed to be sleeping but they were having fun. I'm not sure if I wanted to join the party or if I just had a lot of energy, but one thing was for certain. I wasn't sleeping.

I didn't cry. I didn't yell. I just rocked my crib.

I rocked my crib from one side of the room to the other side of the room...and then I'd rock it all the way back. I would do this all night long. It was a big crib made of solid wood and metal. It was two feet wide by four-and-a-half feet long. I rocked the metal feet against the wooden floors as if I were on an ice rink. All my rocking made a lot of scratches in the floors, and it also made a lot of noise. On my active nights, the frustrations and sometimes humor of the adults below would grow. "What is that kid doing?" "Will someone go see what that kid is up to?" "Please, go take care of that kid!"

And there began the tone of the relationship with my mother. She was living in someone else's home. She was young, insecure, and wanting to make everyone happy. She was also very aware of the hierarchy in my father's family. Respect went up; commands went down. Just like the military. My father was the middle child. He had a younger brother and sister. He also had two older brothers, who were married. In the pecking order of women, after my grandmother, my mom was third in line. In general she was treated well, but often she was told what to do. Knowing this, the last thing she wanted was to cause any disruption with her new family. So, on the nights that the complaints grew, she would come up and try to get me to stop making so much noise. She knew putting me to sleep was impossible, but she'd settle for me not playing bumper cars with my crib.

She tried her best, but I never stopped. Over time, her patience diminished and her anxiety grew. For a few years, a couple of my older cousins lived in the home with their parents at the same time we were there. It was a full house; three families, 10 people in total. It could be noisy, but for her it felt like someone was always commenting on "that kid." To some, my behavior was seen as a reflection of her poor parenting. There were always one or two people who thought they had a better parenting solution. They'd offer my mother sage and straightforward advice such as "just hit him." In their mind, a few smacks and a good old-fashioned beating would teach a child in a crib how to behave.

Fortunately for me, my mother had not been hit as a child. My mother had lived a happy life with her brothers and sisters. Their parents adored them and openly expressed their affection. My mom smiled wide and made friends wherever she went throughout her youth. There was no reason to hit anyone at any time. However, at this time, she was growing weary of her child being viewed as troubled and out of control. My father offered up a solution.

The next day, my dad came home with eight wooden blocks cut from a two-by-four piece of wood. In his pocket was a handful of three-inch metal nails. He put the baby crib in one corner, put two blocks around each foot of the crib, nailed them together, and nailed everything to the wooden floor. "That should do it. It's not going anywhere now," my father proclaimed. My mother smiled and breathed a sigh of relief.

That evening, she put me to bed as she had every other evening. The adults gathered at the dining room table. She felt that now she was finally in control and could simply be one of the crowd rather than the focus of the conversation.

It took me less than 20 minutes to shake those nails loose from the wood floor.

My mother was exasperated.

The only better solution was to get out of her in-laws' home and into her own home. That certainly would minimize the scrutiny and scorn on her and her child.

It was a good plan; unfortunately, it would be another five years before that would happen.

My father's pay was increasing, but in 1967, as an auto mechanic, he was barely making $100 a week. Our family believed debt was the worst possible thing a person could have in their life. Anytime my father thought of buying a home, the fear of having a mortgage choked him. Not wanting to live in fear, they stayed with his parents and slowly built up a nest egg to minimize any future debt.

My mother sat me on her lap, facing her. She gently rocked me forward and back as she sung an Italian children's lullaby.

Fa la ninna, fa la nanna
Nella braccia della mamma
Fa la ninna bel bambin,
Fa la nanna bambin bel,
Fa la ninna, fa la nanna
Nella braccia della mamma, fa la ninna, fa la nanna.

She learned that this was the only way to calm all my curious energy. Many nights, she rocked me to sleep as she sang in hushed tones with a gentle pacing.

Goes the lullaby, goes to sleep
In the arms of your mother,
Goes the lullaby, lovely child,
Goes to sleep, child so lovely,
Goes the lullaby, goes to sleep
In the arms of your mother, goes the lullaby, goes to sleep.

My mother and I were together all day. I was never out of her sight or reach. She'd help me color and build with blocks. She would fill big bowls with pasta shaped like stars and feed it to me. At times, she held me so tight, it felt like she was clutching a life preserver. She was trying her best to mold me into a creative and courageous human. She was willing to try anything for me. In the summer, she'd take me to the beach on Lake Erie. I was afraid of the water. It was dark, and I thought things could be hiding under the surface. I would plant my feet in the hot sand and not want to move. But, there was my mother. Despite not knowing how to swim herself, she'd stand in the water and gently call me to come to her. She didn't want me to be afraid of the unknown, and she was willing to walk into the darkness every step of the way with me.

Despite this loving bond, the bliss in her began to fade. She wanted to be happier, but as the years passed, she grew wearier and more frustrated. Gone were the days of chiffon dresses and pillbox hats. She now spent days in an apron, her hair wrapped in a handkerchief, cleaning, washing, and cooking from morning to night.

4

ST. JUDE

Each week, my father would hand his paycheck over to my mother and, in turn, she tried to save as much as possible. For her, saving was easy because she didn't spend much on anything other than food. And, even with food, she found every way possible to save money. What she didn't grow or pick from the yard or farm, she made herself, no matter how difficult.

It was Saturday, I was now five, and my mother and I had just returned from our weekly bus ride to the farmer's market. We were in the basement, and I had the wings of a chicken pinned back under my feet. My mother had her feet on the chicken's legs, her left hand around his neck and a chef-sized knife in her right hand. To save money, my mom would buy and butcher her own chickens. On this day she decided to make soup. She felt that capons made tastier and richer soup. Capons are male chickens that are larger than the average chicken. My mother was no longer the dainty girl from Long Island. She was still petite, but she was now strong and in no mood to deal with this feisty bird.

"Mom, hurry."

"Just hold it."

"I have it. Just do it."

"Make sure your feet don't move."

"I have it."

"Are you sure?"

"Mom, hurry."

"OK, OK...just..." She tried to calm him as she pressed the blade into his neck.

"MOM!"

My foot slipped.

"MOM!"

"OH GOD!" she screamed. "GO GET IT!"

I was paralyzed. The chicken's head was on the floor and the headless body raced away from us as my mother yelled for me to get it.

I had never seen such a thing. It was like I was watching a cartoon. I couldn't move. I didn't know if it was really happening.

I had heard the expression "like a chicken with its head cut off," but I didn't think it was a real thing. But it was. The capon ran across the entire room, smashed into the back wall, fell over, got back upright, ran back toward us, got halfway, made a sharp left turn, smashed into another wall, made another left and then my mother threw herself at him.

"COME HERE," she yelled.

As her knees hit the floor, the chicken jumped up on to the kitchen table. My mother picked herself up and said, "What a disaster."

The chicken jumped off the table and ran toward the stairs. My mother yelled for me to "GET HIM." I felt so bad for my mother. There was blood everywhere. It spurted and squirted out of this chicken's neck non-stop. I had to help her. I ran toward the chicken and cornered it on the bottom step of the stairs.

My mother came rushing in. "Come here, you disaster." She grabbed the wings, brought him to the sink, and held him there until the very last kick of his legs.

I'm not sure how much money she saved by doing all of this herself, but the stern look on my mother's face told me she definitely wasn't happy with her life.

The years of living under someone else's roof and under the constant scrutiny of other family members without support from her own family wore her out. My grandparents were always kind and respectful to her, but my father's family was big. Anyone who has ever been raised in a big family knows there are always one or two voices that try to command over everyone else. There's always one who has to have things their way and criticizes others for being different. My mother and I paid a heavy toll for the years of constant instruction from others on how to live and how to think.

By 1972 my parents finally bought their own home. We moved to a suburb on the edge of the city that bordered endless miles of fields for farming corn, soybeans, tomatoes, and wheat. The home was newer but still modest; a raised ranch style, three bedrooms, one bathroom, a basement, and a yard big enough for a large garden and a swing set, all for the price of $29,000.

We didn't have a lot of furniture, but what we had was either the color of mustard or moss green. We also didn't have a garage, a dishwasher, a clothes dryer, or air-conditioning. My mother still cleaned, cooked, and kept busy from morning to night. Despite the heavy load, she was happier. She was still stern, but she was more patient.

"Mom, can I have pancakes?"
"You can have pancakes."
"Can I have them with chocolate sprinkles?"
"You can have sprinkles."
"Can I have them with walnuts too?"
"You can have walnuts too."
"And butter?"
"And butter."
"And syrup?"
"There's a jar in the fridge. You can get it."
"Can I help you stir?"
"You can help stir."
"Can I flip one?"
"You can flip one."
"Can we make them now?"
"We can make them now."
"Can I have chocolate milk?"
"You can have chocolate milk."
"Can I have a chocolate chip cookie?"
"After you eat the pancakes."
"Can we make them now?"
"Go get me the mix for the batter and the bowl."

My parents had moved out of my grandparents' home, but they hadn't moved far away from the rest of the family. A block in each direction were my dad's brothers and their families. A few more blocks out from that were cousins, second cousins, and friends from my parents' hometown in Italy.

Family aside, I was simply happy to have a bigger yard to play in, and my school was only one block away from our home.

On the first day of school, my father walked me to the street corner, where he stopped and kneeled. He looked at me and said, "Remember, don't start fights with anyone. Leave people alone and be nice. But if someone starts a fight with you—you fight back. You don't run away. You defend yourself and you fight. You understand?"

Seemed like clear instructions to me.

I nodded. *Yes, Dad.*

For all intents and purposes, my father was a pacifist. He never physically disciplined me or my sister. He thought the notion of hitting children was reckless and dangerous. However, he also knew some of the ugly realities of the world. When he first arrived in Canada, like many other immigrants, he was subject to scorn from bullies. It was not unusual for him to have to fight his way out of the grade-school playground. Now, years later, he was just trying to prepare me for what might eventually come.

My mother took a different approach. She still wanted me to stay on a straight and narrow path. Despite never having had a hand laid on her as a child, she openly told my teachers, "If he steps out of line, just hit him. And then call me, so I can hit him again when he gets home."

I'm not exactly certain when my mom first hit me. What I do know is that the chorus in her ear of "just hit him" reached a crescendo and she broke. Eventually, she did hit me and would continue hitting me for about the next eight years. My sister was born four years after me, but my mother never laid a hand on her.

For whatever reason, I was treated differently. She loved me and made it clear every day. Not an hour would pass when she didn't caress me, hold me close, and look at me with warm, albeit tired eyes. She gave me everything she could give. Nonetheless, she was determined that strict punishment was the only solution that would keep me in line and out of trouble. What she didn't know was that the repeated beatings would eventually push me toward trouble, not away from it.

Today, reading this, combining my mom's actions and the teachers' willingness to accept instructions for beatings comes across as a world of perpetual child abuse. But in those days, in my neighborhood, at my school, I was not the only one who had a parent delivering a strong message to teachers.

My new neighborhood consisted predominately of European immigrants who had arrived in Canada after World War II. They were strong people of humble means who worked long hours. It didn't matter if they had come from the losing side or winning side of the war; everyone in this group had suffered. Everyone had witnessed chaos, destruction, and loss of life. Years of exposure to war made many people hard. People were friendly and generous, but the moment something was out of line, anger rose quickly, and discipline was required, especially when it came to children. Corporal punishment and the notion of tough love was real. It was commonplace and it was encouraged.

Despite living in this difficult environment, for the first few years at St. Jude Catholic Elementary School, the only fights I had actually been in were with my mother. They usually revolved around her wanting me to wear a particular piece of clothing that I did not want to wear. The discussions were quite basic. She would say

"You're wearing this," and I would say, "No, I'm not," and then she would smack me over the head until I either gave in or her hand got tired. I usually gave in before that point because if her hand got tired, she would grab a big wooden spoon and then hit me over the head with it.

By grade three, there was one piece of clothing that proved to be a persistent nemesis.

My mother loved to knit and crochet. You could find her handiwork anywhere in the house. Even in the bathroom. There was a crocheted doily on top of the water container for the toilet, and on top of that was a spare roll of toilet paper—which was also neatly encased in a crocheted cover.

One morning, my mother came to me and said, "I have a new hat for you. I made it last night." She then presented a little, spindly hat that looked exactly like the one covering the spare roll of toilet paper. It was the exact shape and color. One row of forest green and one row of dull beige alternated throughout the entire hat, and at the bottom, frilly bell-shaped things were sewn into the rim.

"Come here. Let's see how it fits," she said.

I was somewhere between grossed out and frightened. "Mom, I'm not wearing that."

Her blood started to simmer. "Why? It's a nice hat."

I shook my head. "It looks just like the cover for the spare toilet paper roll."

She dug in her heels. "So what? That's the only yarn I had. Come here because now for sure you're wearing it."

There was no way I was going to wear this to school. I couldn't risk the humiliation. If one of my friends came over, used our bathroom, and then saw my hat, it would invariably take mere minutes before someone started calling me "Toilet Paper Head." Or worse: "Shithead." Sorry, I was not going down that road. That would be a name that would stay with me forever.

We did our usual dance. No. Yes. No. Yes. Eventually, I took a beating and wore the hat.

Once I turned the street corner and was out of sight from my mother, I took the hat off and put it in my pocket. When I got to school, I couldn't risk anyone finding this hat in my pocket, so I threw the hat on the school roof.

When I got home that afternoon my mom asked me where my hat was, and I told her I didn't know. "I must have lost it. Sorry." My mother squinted her eyes, nodded her head, and said, "OK."

By the next morning, she had crocheted me another hat—again, looking exactly like the spare toilet paper roll cover.

I wore the hat, turned the street corner, stuffed it my pocket, walked to school, and, like its predecessor, I threw it on the school roof.

This went on for six days. I threw them on the roof as fast as she could make them. Eventually, she ran out of that wool. My mother was stubborn and incredibly determined, but she also was a pragmatist. There was only so much money she was going to waste on yarn that would eventually disappear.

Fighting with my mother would eventually become just warm-up for what was at school. Although, for some reason, taking a beating in the playground seemed like it was more fun.

I'm not sure if other schools played this game, but at St. Jude we played it every year throughout the winter. The origins of the game are believed to date back to 1930 in England. It's a simple but brutal game called British Bulldog.

Thank Goliath

The game is as such: Find a stretch of land that's about 50 yards wide and 0 yards long. Two people are randomly chosen to be the "bulls." They stand in the middle of this patch of land, and the other participants stand at one end. The number of participants varies with each game, but the more there are the better the game. For us, it would not be unusual to have 40 kids playing.

The object of the game is to run past the bulls and make it to the other side. The bulls, in the meantime, try to stop you from going to the other side. Generally, they physically tackle you. Once down, you join the bulls in trying to stop others. The participants keep running from side to side, trying to get past the bulls without being taken down. The goal of the game is to be the last person standing on one side.

As you can imagine, the game becomes intensely more difficult as the number of bulls in the middle accumulates. The longer you are running, the more people you have chasing and trying to tackle you. It would not be uncommon to have 20 people punching, pulling, kicking, and piling up on you until you hit the frozen ground. Of course, the real excitement came if you miraculously managed to be the last person standing. Enduring that much pain gave you bragging rights for at least one day. Rarely did the same person win two days in a row. No one could withstand that type of punishment for more than one day. It wasn't exactly ping-pong or volleyball, but it was fun. It was also vicious, and it hurt.

Outside of the playground, the tone was a bit different. At times, it was sinister.

If I stepped out of line in class or around the school, I would get sent to the principal's office to get the strap. "The strap" was a thick piece of leather that was most commonly used for sharpening a barber's shaving blade. At St. Jude, for several years we had a principal who took immense pleasure in punishing and strapping young kids. At six-foot-four, he was a tall and imposing man. He would bring you near the front of his office so other kids could see what was happening through a glass wall. He would make you stand in between two filing cabinets so other kids couldn't see your face, but they could see your outstretched hand and they could see him swinging the leather strap. Most kids started crying before the first strapping. He'd grab their hand, straighten their arm, cock back the leather strap as high as his long arms could reach, and then he would bring it down like a whip, as if he were taming a lion. He didn't hold back anything. He hit extremely hard, and he'd smile every time he heard a child cry.

The first time I got the strap it was because I had committed the cardinal sin of throwing a snowball at another student. We could punch and kick the living daylights out of each other in a game of British Bulldog, but God help us if we threw snowballs at one another.

As I walked toward the principal's office, I didn't have a worry in the world. This was an ordinary day for me. I just happened to hit another student in the head with a snowball. Typically, if you got hurt, you lived with the pain and said nothing. However, in this instance, I believe that snowball stung him hard, so he complained to a teacher and the teacher immediately sent me out to be disciplined.

I walked in, and without receiving instruction I put myself between the filing cabinets and waited for him to come out. When he did come out of his private office, I saw that he was angrier than usual. He liked children to cower in fear, and he could see that I was unfazed. He approached me and I stretched out my hand toward him. He didn't like my little brazen act of courage.

He grabbed my hand tight and swung the strap hard. He didn't take a second to catch his breath in between swipes—he just kept swinging. He was determined to hit me until I cried. What he didn't know is that I had already been beat into the ground for years. I was already a stone. He could swing that strap all day and not get one teardrop from me.

Eventually he tired and stopped. My hand wasn't bleeding but was deep red in color and inflamed.

For good measure, at the end of the strapping, that principal made me call my mother to tell her what had happened just so he could hear her scream and know that I would receive another beating when I got home. The last thing I remember from that day was my mother yelling through the speakerphone on his desk, "Why is it always *you*? Why are you always in the middle of things? Why?" I wasn't afraid of the principal. He was a big man, but he sat there with a smile on his face as my mom's voice screeched through the phone. He couldn't make me cry, but he took joy in the humiliation my mom made me feel. I was only a child, but I felt like a man. This principal was my enemy, and I was engaged in a battle with him. In my mind, I was winning. He couldn't break me. But, in an instant, there was my mother, yelling at me, reprimanding me, making me feel—once again—dumb and small. She just handed my adversary a victory with her incessant questioning. "Why? Why is it always you?"

She kept asking those same questions for most of my youth. The reality was that it wasn't always me. She just felt like it was. She wanted a perfect son, but she kept telling me that I was a troublemaker. She said it so many times that eventually other adults said it, then kids said it. Mothers in the neighborhood would tell their kids, "Stay away from him—he's trouble." Over and over, this was said to me and about me, so what else would be the answer to my mother's question "Why is it always you in trouble?" I thought the answer was obvious: Because if I was "trouble," where else would I be?

Since my mother worried about my behavior, not only did she have my teachers on high-alert, ready to notify her of any of my missteps, but she also had an entire spy network through the neighborhood, monitoring my every step. I'm not sure if she wanted a network of vigilante homemakers reporting on her son, but there were many days when it felt just like that. There was a group of moms who were convinced I would corrupt their sons and daughters. They had to keep my mother aware of all my actions so she could beat me into obedience and decency.

This homemaker spy network was a simple but effective structure. A typical scenario might go something like this: Once school ended, I might be "horsing around" with some friends. We could be playing with a soccer ball, a football, a Frisbee, or just nothing. We would push each other, trip each other, kick each other, and then most likely end up wrestling each other on the ground. It could start off with two guys and then maybe grow to 10 guys. Someone would push or pull too hard and then someone else would throw a punch. One punch became two punches, which quickly became boys fighting. We'd fight until someone said, "Enough!"

For me and my friends, this was normal behavior. However, to the untrained eye and overly nosey neighbor, homemaker, aunt, or friend, this behavior was troublesome and required immediate attention.

Our horsing around would happen on the front lawn of the school or across the street in the public park. Both areas were visible by many people. Invariably, someone would see this horseplay and interpret it as a melee or a riot...and they would phone my mother to give her an update "Your son is in a fight—again." Of course, this would upset my mother. Not only was she concerned about my well-being, but she also was upset that her son and her mothering skills were being called out into question—again.

These hawkish phone calls to my mother were bad, but they were worse when a cousin was involved in the horsing around. Not only would the overly nosey and intrusive vigilante homemakers phone my mother, but they would phone my aunt as well. Then, my aunt would phone my mother. "Why is your son getting my son in trouble—again?"

On those school days, by 3.45 p.m., after a handful of phone calls with the same message, my mother would have an echo in her ear: "Your son is trouble." Over and over and louder and louder this message would play in her head. As the message repeated, she became rattled, anxious, and frustrated. She would then stand at the screen of the back door to our home. She'd put one hand on the door handle and wait for me to turn the corner. The moment I saw her, I knew what was coming. It was the same every time. In her mind, she didn't know what else to do but to hit me.

Some days I just let her hit me, but many times I would run once I saw her standing at the door. Once I ran it was like watching Marlin Perkins' *Wild Kingdom*. There were days that I felt like a squirrel or gazelle being chased by a bobcat. I did anything I could to survive.

Sometimes, I would run to the other side of the yard and jump the neighbors' fences and keep running and jumping fences until I was at least five houses away from ours. Other times, I would climb the first tree I came across. I was nimble and very fast. I always felt safe 20 feet up in a tree, hiding behind branches and leaves. At other times, if it was raining or snowing, I would take my chances and try to run past her to get to the bathroom because it had a lock on it. The other option was to dive and slide under my bed because it made it difficult for her to swing and hit me when she was kneeling.

Despite my best attempts to avoid capture, my mother was persistent in trying to shape me into a proper, well-behaved boy. She would continue hitting me with anything in the kitchen she could get her hands on; wooden spoon, a broom and even a wooden clog from her feet. Over the course of several years, she broke three wooden spoons on me and a couple of brooms across my back. All of them hurt, and I learned to tolerate the pain. However, one thing I never got used to was the wooden clogs. They never broke. They were solid and made to last. She would hold one clog tight in her hand and just pound me on the head until she was exhausted. It would have been simpler if I just fell to the ground and cried the first time she hit me. If I had done that, she would have stopped sooner. But I wouldn't cry, and I wouldn't give in. I didn't like the feeling of being weak. I could accept being labeled as "trouble," but something inside of me refused to be weak. If I was going to be a threat, I was going to be resilient.

"When do I do it?"
"Soon."
"But when?"
"Soon."

"Just tell me."

It was Sunday morning, nearing 11 a.m. Mass was being held in our grade-school gym. It was an interim place of worship while a new church was being built. In attendance were about 70 people from our neighborhood and five other friends were serving as altar boys. I really didn't care for mass, but I became an altar boy because on occasion, the priests and teachers would take us on a field trip. It was usually to a church or shrine of some sort, but it was a day away exploring, and it was also an opportunity to steal something. I'm not sure why I stole little bottles of holy water or tiny, painted crucifixes, but it was entertaining to me.

I had no problem sitting still for an hour. No problem wearing a very ugly long white gown with a red stripe down the middle. But I had a real problem knowing when to ring the bells during the blessing of the Eucharist. Holding and ringing the bells was a form of prestige among the altar boys. For devout Christians, the bells signified the real presence of Christ. However, for the less faithful, the ringing bells were a signal that mass would soon end. Nonetheless, I could never get it right.

I couldn't stand being in church. All I heard was, "We are born sinners. You have sinned. Confess your sins. Don't sin again. But you will sin again because you are human, and humans are sinners. If you keep sinning, you will go to Hell. However, if you confess your sins before you die, Jesus will give you a free pass to Heaven and all your sins are wiped clean" ...or something like that. It was just noise in my head. So, I asked my friend Dave for help. Dave was very smart. He was also a good thief. He didn't need to steal because his parents were rich, at least richer than my parents. Dave was sharp and cunning and a practical joker.

The priest, Father Michael, held up the Eucharist and said, "Take this and eat this, all of you..." And Dave nudged me. "Now!" Nervously, I shook the handle on the four copper bells that were welded together. *Kling, kling, kling.* Father Michael spun his head toward me, darted his eyes, and smirked. I had screwed up again. I shrugged my shoulders and mouthed to him "sorry."

He continued, "For this is my body and will be given up for you." Dead silence. Father Michael again spun his head toward me. I thought, *Jesus, why is this so difficult?* Again, I mouthed "sorry." Dave could not contain his laughter. He buried his head into his altar boy smock. I wanted to punch him, but the entire congregation, including my parents, were looking at us.

Father Michael continued, "Take this and drink of it, all of you. For this is the chalice of my blood." I thought "blood"—this must be the time. I shook the bells. *Kling, kling, kling.* Dave burst out laughing. A few people in the mass started laughing. Father Michael dropped his head down, looked at the ground, took a deep breath, and continued: "...which shall be poured out for you and for many. For the forgiveness of sins. Do this in memory of me."

I had no clue what to do next. I wasn't going to ring anything. I knew they had to be rung three times. I screwed up twice; I wasn't going for number three. Father Michael dropped his head and shook it back and forth. Apparently, I missed my cue, again. He raised his head one final time, exasperated, and said, "Amen." By then, I had learned that "Amen" meant "so be it," but I didn't know if he was blessing everyone or just accepting that I was a complete screw-up.

Mass ended. I was the joke of the day. The altar boys retreated to the dressing room to change out of our smocks.

In typical manner, the entire congregation left mass quickly. Dave and I stayed in the dressing room longer than usual. We were laughing and kidding around. We hadn't noticed the time but when we came out, everyone was gone. Everyone, including my parents, teachers, our friends, and Father Michael. Here we were, two 10-year-old boys, locked inside our grade school. Most boys that age may have taken out a few basketballs and shot hoops for an hour or so. However, Dave and I decided that this was a prime opportunity to explore and, of course, steal.

First target: the fridge with milk. We always had a gallon of milk at home in our refrigerator, but somehow, this stolen quarter pint of milk was better. Second target: supply room. No luck. It was locked. One last place to explore: the classrooms. Why? Colored pencils. This was 1977, and Crayola was a symbol of status. The bigger the box, the wealthier you were. They came in boxes of eight, 12, 24, and the Rolls-Royce—64 distinct colors *and* a built-in pencil sharpener.

My mother never bought me 64. She felt 12 was enough. She couldn't understand that the kids with 64 were doing way better artwork than me and that I always had to ask them if I could borrow different colors from them. But not anymore. Today, I was going to take not just one box of 64 but three of them. And Dave was going to take three more. Dave already had a box of 64, but he just thought this was fun.

We filled two bags, and each of us went home to hide them.

Maybe the priest was right; we're all sinners. But I didn't care. I had almost 200 colored pencils. I was rich.

The next day, Monday, back at class, it took the teachers about 15 minutes to figure out that a larceny had been committed. Apparently, the thieves had a liking for milk because they found two empty containers in the otherwise clean trash bin next to the refrigerator.

It took them an additional three minutes to figure out it had to be someone at mass.

And, several minutes later, Dave confessed his sins because he didn't want to burn in Hell, and he felt that neither should I.

We had a new principal by this time. He was a nice man. No more strapping in the school. However, he had a responsibility to inform my mother of what had transpired. Her son, the altar boy, had stolen from other children, on Sunday, shortly after mass, after receiving the blessed sacrament.

It was a long, slow walk home. I didn't even know what to think about. I just stared at my feet as I walked. My legs grew heavier with each step.

I turned the corner of our house, into the backyard.

As I expected, she was already waiting for me. I felt like she could have killed me with her dead eye stare that looked right through me. I knew this was going to hurt more than other times.

I didn't even consider running this time because I knew that what I did was very wrong. And, even if I ran, eventually I was going to face the noise for stealing from other kids.

She had the door half open with her left hand and with her right hand she pointed at me and said, "Get in here."

"Mom, I'm sorr..." Before I could finish, she had one of her clogs in her hand and she began hitting me on top of my head. As she hit me, she would repeat her mantra: "Why, why, why is it always YOU? WHY? Why do you have to steal? Why? At church? WHY? Why does the entire neighborhood now know that you are stealing?" She didn't pause for a moment. She kept pounding on the top of my head with this three-inch-thick wooden heel from the clog. I just stood there. I didn't move. I didn't say anything. I didn't wince. I didn't cry. But I felt my soul rise from my body. I looked down at the two of us and saw the sadness and folly of what was happening.

At that moment, it hurt so bad. I felt like a piece of lumber that was being split in two. When she finished, I was not the same person. She had finally broken me. The feeling of joy left me and seemed to never return. From that moment on, I was different. Outwardly, I still laughed and played, but never again did I feel completely free and lost in wonderment. Instead, what remained were two identities that were at odds with each other. One part of me wanted to make everything perfect and everyone happy so I would no longer have to be hit and live in a world of chaos. The other part of me embraced the tough love and violence. I felt that if this was the actual world we were living in, then so be it; I would learn to survive in it as it was.

5

MY SON WILL WORK FOR YOU

y father arrived from Italy with his family when he was 15. Since he was unable to speak English, the school administrators put him two years back from where he had been in his home country.

He enjoyed learning, but school was not a pleasant experience for him. It wasn't teaching him what he needed to learn in order to get a job. The entire purpose of the long journey by boat was to create a better life. For my grandmother, a better life outside of the fields and farms meant learning a skilled trade. If you were credentialed in a trade, you could travel the world and always find work. Trusting his mother's guidance, my dad completed the eighth grade of school and then enrolled in the licensed auto mechanic program. After a couple years of studying, he was able to get a job as an apprentice mechanic in an auto garage and gas station.

Five days a week, each morning, he would take a public bus for several miles, then transfer to another bus for a couple more miles and then walk a half-mile to get to the garage. In the afternoon, when his day ended, he would have to hitch a ride from a friend, family member, or kind stranger because one of the buses did not run past a certain time so he would be otherwise stranded. Every two weeks, he was paid $12 for about a hundred hours of work. The bus pass cost him $3.50 per week. After paying for transportation, he was left with $2.50 per week for all other expenses.

Given his limited income, my father, like many poor people before him, learned to live with little. Nothing was wasted, and everything could eventually be useful.

Over the years, my dad continued to learn his craft and trade. He was grateful for the kindness showed to him by employers so he would do likewise with others he encountered. By the time I was 10, my father took ownership of the gas station and garage he had been working at for the past decade. The previous owner decided to retire, so my father and one other mechanic stepped in. They would be equal partners in the garage. No money was exchanged. His boss had always been generous and continued to be that way in retirement. The building and property were owned by someone else, so there wasn't much to buy other than some machines and the rights to sell gas. Either way, it was a step up.

My father's Sunoco station was not located in the best part of town, but it didn't bother him. He was happy to have his own freedom and be his own boss. He did get frustrated when his tools were stolen, but he would turn the other cheek and just buy himself a new set and keep moving forward.

I loved going to his garage because it was filled with strange and crazy people. People of all walks and all colors. Many of them were poor. Some were criminals, but most were just average people hoping not to get swindled by a mechanic. My father was honest, talented, and generous. Often, too generous. It was not uncommon for him to give customers his own car to use while he repaired theirs. Once, he gave customers our family car the night before we were scheduled to leave for vacation. My mother was equally charitable so it didn't bother her. However, my sister and I were so upset. Our vacation would be delayed for two days. Two days in a child's mind is the equivalent of two months.

He was the owner of the garage, but he still didn't make a lot of money. He had a kind heart and felt bad charging people full price for his work. Often, he would just charge customers his cost for the parts, not even taking pay for his hours working on the repair. Naturally, this kindness attracted a lot of people—people who couldn't afford to pay anything. At least once a week, he would be paid with something other than cash. He would come home with bottles of wine, jars of tomato sauce, gallons of ice cream, skinned rabbits or plucked chickens, homemade sausages, or freshly caught fish. He would hand them to my mother. She'd shrug her shoulders and, good or bad, we would eat it. Nothing was wasted or unappreciated.

In this same neighborhood, kids roamed the streets. Many of them had single parents or parents who were absent, drunk, high, or even in jail. For a few years, my father befriended several of them. Each morning, my mother packed extra lunch for my dad to take to this group of kids. It usually consisted of apples, cheese, and sandwiches. In exchange for healthy food, my father would ask to see their homework and their report cards. Just as he encouraged my sister and me, he did the same for these kids in the neighborhood. It got to the point where the kids would race to his garage to be the first to show him their good grades.

My father didn't like us being around the garage because he didn't want us exposed to that rougher, darker side of life. He wanted us at a safe distance, far away in our suburban home. Nonetheless, if he needed something, my mom would stop by periodically and we'd be in the car with her. I always got out of the car and roamed around to explore this greasy, colorful world. Eventually, I asked my dad if I could come to work with him. He initially said "no," but when I turned 11, he agreed to have me come to work by his side.

On the first day, we arrived by 7.45 a.m. and he gave me my own set of coveralls. He rolled up the legs and sleeves so I wouldn't trip and then had me follow him around. At each stop, he taught me something new. We began with pumping gas, wiping the windshield, and putting air in tires. As the week progressed, he taught me how to use the big hoist to raise cars into the air and how to properly lubricate cars and change oil. When I wasn't doing that, he taught me the importance of keeping the garage, your tools, and your hands clean.

Each day, some new character would come into the garage. Occasionally, I couldn't understand what people were saying. I thought they were speaking English but I couldn't make out a word. My father would then tell me they couldn't be understood because they were very drunk. Around his garage, people drank at all hours of the day.

One day, a skinny, frail man, wearing no shoes or shirt, only ragged shorts, came running across the lot, into the garage, and jumped through an open window on the other side of the garage.

The entire time, he was screaming at the top of his lungs. My dad, unfazed, looked at me and said, "Just ignore him. The police are probably after him again." Another day, my father was out of the garage, road-testing a car, when a massive, boat-like, burgundy and silver Cadillac pulled in front of the car. Two giant men got out of the car. I was only 11, but they looked like they were seven feet tall.

One of them wore a white fedora, a black silk shirt, and red polyester pants. He looked down at me and said, "Jack around?" "Jack" was the name my dad used with Canadians because they struggled to say "Giacinto." As I shook my head, my father pulled up. He got out of his car, walked over to the two men, shook their hands, and said, "You lost? What are you doing here?" Before they could answer, one of them opened the trunk of the Cadillac. The entire trunk was filled with anything imaginable. Jewelry, clothing, portable TVs, radios, coffeemakers, rows and rows of sparkling gold, and what appeared to be diamonds. There was more stuff in that trunk than I had seen in actual retail stores.

My dad walked to the car, leaned over, and scanned the goods. At that point, the man with the fedora said, "Come on, Jack, why don't you buy something for that pretty wife of yours?" My dad smiled and said, "I can't afford it. You guys are too expensive." Fedora man quipped back, "Name your price. Pick anything and name your price." My dad said, "I don't need anything. I don't have any extra money." And fedora man continued, "We'll give you a good price. Just name it." Without hesitating, my dad started laughing and said, "OK, I'll give you what you paid for it." I was a kid but even I knew all those things were stolen goods. The two giant men burst out laughing and got back in their Cadillac. "We catch you next week, Jack."

Not everyone was scandalous, but they still were interesting. My dad would send me around the neighborhood to pick up parts, deliver mail, and pay people. Most were kind and always had a smile on their face when I told them I was "Jack's son." He left a favorable imprint on whomever he spoke with. The biggest impression was with the owner of a local deli. I would get iced tea from the deli and one day my dad treated me to a corned beef sandwich. Each day, the stoic but warm old man would say something kind about my father. I listened attentively but I could not take my eyes off the numbers he had tattooed on one of his forearms. It was many years later that my father explained to me that he had been in a concentration camp during World War II.

At the end of this first week, my father pulled me aside and asked me if I had enjoyed the week. I told him that I had a lot of fun. He then reached into his shirt pocket and handed me an envelope. I opened the envelope and there were six $10 bills. He said, "That's for you. It's a lot of money, but you earned it." He then looked at me and said, "You did a good job, but you can't come back here again." What? I was so confused. "What did I do wrong? Why can't I come back here? I thought you said I did a good job."

My father leaned over, stretched out his arms, and opened his hands. "You see my hands. My hands get dirty so yours don't have to."

I was still so confused. I thought that I had done something wrong and disappointed my father. I was so happy working with him. I was finally in a place where no one thought I was "trouble." I wanted another chance to prove myself, but my dad patiently explained to me that I had been a good employee, but it was important for me to go to school. He wanted me to have a job that didn't involve working on cold cement my entire life. In his eyes, formal education would give me the freedom to choose to do whatever I wanted in life.

Clearly, he and my mother had spoken about this in advance. They knew I was showing way too much interest in the garage. My dad was always of the mind to remove the mystery from things. He let me experience working with him so I could learn about the realities of working on cars in a garage. He felt that if he let me see and smell his dark, greasy, cold world that maybe I would stop glorifying it. It had the opposite effect on me. I liked the diversity and the unpredictability of all of it even more. But I had little say in the matter. My parents did what they thought was best, and I did as they said.

I was again back at home, trapped with my mother. My father was a much easier boss. My mother had her own list of tasks for me. First and foremost was reading. Not just reading anything. She wanted my sister and me to read the encyclopedia—all of it. I was always looking for some place to go but she would barely let me out of her sight. The one place that she would let me visit was the public library. But, one day, all of that changed. She announced, "You don't need to go to the library. I'm bringing the library to you." She would not spend an extra penny on toys, games, clothing, records, or any food from a restaurant—but she would spend it on books. Somehow, she managed to save up enough money to buy the best set of Encyclopedia Britannica.

The day it arrived it felt like an entire new universe had just entered our home. Each book was thick and weighed several pounds. They were bound with soft leather and had pages that felt like silk that were lined with gold paint.

My mother filled and entire bookshelf with all that set. A few months later she bought a different type of encyclopedia. This set focused on science and technology. Shortly later, she purchased a set that was created by National Geographic and focused on nature. In a brief period of time, we had filled bookshelves in every room. We didn't have air-conditioning, a clothes dryer, or a dishwasher—but we had the most beautiful, comprehensive educational books you could find.

Surrounded by books, it was inevitable that reading would become a significant piece of my life. I enjoyed it. Every time I opened one of the books, I was being transported to someplace else in time and space. I couldn't physically escape my surroundings, but these books allowed me to travel into every imaginable and unimaginable world. I felt like one of the great explorers sailing the oceans to lands unknown. Every day and every night, I would open one of these giant books and read about places and people that were different than the world I knew. Kings and queens, cars and countries, pioneers and planets. It was an amazing and unending, fantastic voyage. I loved all of it and couldn't wait to go discover on my own.

I read incessantly, but eventually I got to a point that I needed to go experiment and explore on my own. After years of being physically hurt and verbally ridiculed, I developed a high tolerance for pain. I grew less fearful. There wasn't much that could frighten me. I didn't think anything could be worse than what I had already experienced. With this mindset, I began toying with things and situations that should have easily killed me.

I was not yet a teenager, but around that time, a couple of my cousins, some friends, and I had become a worrisome menace to the family and neighborhood. We were obsessed with burning things, blowing up stuff, and playing pranks on people. We didn't want to harm or hurt anyone, but we unquestionably found great excitement in surprising and explosive moments.

We decided to not play tennis in the ordinary way. We thought that soaking tennis balls in gasoline for a few days and then lighting them on fire would make the game better. It was significantly more entertaining when a ball of fire was headed toward you.

We learned that if you mix sulfur and sugar with saltpeter, it makes really cool and colorful smoke bombs. Saltpeter was typically used for curing meats, but it's also used in making gunpowder. It just happened that we could buy tubs of the stuff at the local pharmacy. On occasion we'd get a strange look from the pharmacist, but no one ever questioned us. We would take scoopfuls of saltpeter and put it in big pieces of aluminum paper. We'd buy dozens of boxes of matches, cut the tops of the matches off, and put those in the mix in the aluminum foil. We then would attach a string or piece of paper as a fuse, light it, and run for shelter as fast as we could. Each time, the bombs got bigger and bigger. Eventually, you could see the smoke from several blocks away.

When we grew tired of burning things, we became more sophisticated. We learned that if we took a piece of metal and stretched it across the railway tracks at just the right place, we could bring down the crossing bars, make the bells go *ding, ding, ding,* and backing up traffic for an awfully long time.

Some kids threw eggs at houses and places of business, but we were a little more creative. We would get old cassette tapes, take out the tape, tie a rock to one end, and throw that rock over an electrical line that crossed a road, then we would remove the rock and replace it with a raw egg. We would hide behind bushes or in a tree, maneuvering the egg up and down, depending on what we wanted it to hit. We lowered it for cars, raised it for trucks and buses. In the bright sun, you couldn't see the egg or the tape. People would drive right into them, stop their cars, and could not figure out where it had come from.

When we grew bored of this, we then rummaged around garbage bins, ditches, and alleyways. What were we looking for? Anything we could build or put together for free. One summer, we crawled around several big garbage bins that belonged to a plastic injection molder. They were making toys for Star Wars, and they threw away broken or disfigured ones. When we would reconstruct them, they had little resemblance to the original design, but we didn't care. In other instances, we'd find broken bicycles and make our own strange-looking bike. It didn't matter how odd it looked to others; for us, it only mattered that it was free.

The most fun we had was making elevated wooden ramps and jumping them with our bikes. These were the days of Evel Knievel. There was no one else like him on television. Everyone wanted to be like Evel.

We started by jumping a simple ramp. Then we moved on to jumping over things like garbage pails. Then, to make it more exciting, we started jumping over each other. We would put pails near the ramp, and then we'd lay down on the ground at the very far end, hoping the guy jumping wouldn't land on us. Sure enough, a couple times we'd land short, and you were getting a bike tire either in your mouth or on your stomach. It hurt, but somehow we managed not to get more severe injuries.

For my mom, all of this was just insanity. She desperately looked for ways to keep me out of trouble, but by this time in my life, I just couldn't be kept in a box. Her answer had always been to discipline me by hitting me. However, this phenomenon was nearing its end because I was growing, and I was bigger in size. It was only a matter of time before I would tower over her and she would be defenseless. Eventually, it would have to stop.

One of the last times she hit me, I actually felt like I had it coming to me.

On Saturdays through part of the year, I would attend Italian school at a cultural club that my parents belonged to. After one class, a group of us found a big box filled with leftover matches from a wedding. We each took a couple packs of matches and immediately started flinging lit matches at one another. There were no rules. Burning matches in the eyes and hair were fair game.

After 15 minutes of dodging matches, I got bored and then decided to light an entire pack of matches on fire. I threw it at a friend. It missed him and fell inside of the big box of matches. Everyone started laughing. I ran over to the box, and by the time I got there, other matches were on fire. Instead of trying to put it out, we all ran.

By the time I got home, my mother had already received the message that the fire department had been called. One wall was burned, and the club's bar was entirely filled with smoke. The club manager informed her that the other boys said it was me who had set the box on fire.

I didn't try to explain or run away. I knew what I had done was very wrong. It was stupid and could have burned down an entire building that belonged to the Italian community.

She hit me in the head a few times with her hand, and as I went to move away, I turned my head into the wall just as she struck me. I didn't break my nose, but blood came out all over the wall and floor. Blood streamed down my face and neck.

With my mother at wit's end, all motion stopped. We just stared at each other. She had hit me for years, but this was the first time I shed blood. Taking a deep breath, she said, "I'm sorry." She then grabbed a towel and began to clean the wall and floor. She told me to go wash my face and lay down.

As I left the room, she asked, "Why do you make me do this? Why can't you just stay out of trouble?"

At that age, I didn't know the answer, nor did I care. Maybe I was "trouble," maybe I wasn't; either way, I just wanted to be left alone. We were taught not to hate our parents, but anger and confusion were definitely growing in me. My mother cared for me and protected me every day, but she could lose her temper and become unhinged. I wanted to fight back, but I couldn't reconcile hitting my mother because I knew she loved me. It was an image I couldn't create in my mind. The only solution I thought possible was running away. I spent many days and nights dreaming of running far, far away. But I never arrived anywhere. I just ran toward an endless horizon. No matter how many dreams or plans I made, I couldn't figure out where to go. The conclusion was always the same; I couldn't escape, and there was no way she was letting me out of her reach.

It was now 1980, the middle of a hot summer, and my cousin Pete and I were under house arrest, again. Pete was a couple years older than me. He hadn't achieved the designation of "trouble," but he certainly was on the "junior trouble" team. He lived a block away, and on "arrest days," that one block was the entire distance we were each allowed to travel. I stood in front of the screen door and stared at the backyard as my mom washed dishes. I was so bored. I had listened to Pink Floyd's "Another Brick in the Wall" so many times, I felt like a brick. I couldn't get the song out of my head. I was humming and singing it all morning: "doo to doo...we don't need no education...doo to doo, HEY TEACHER, leave them kids ALONE." I was alone and so bored.

"Mom, can I go to the park?"
"No."
"Can I go to the pool?"
"No."
"Can I go for a bike ride?"
"No."
"Can I go bowling?"
"No."
"Can I go play tennis?"
"No."
"Can I go to the movies?"
"No."
"Can I go to Dave's?"
"No."
"Can I go to John's?"
"No."
"Can I go to Mark's?"
"No."
"Can I go to Joe's?"
"No."
"What can I do?"
"Go pull weeds."
"I already did that."
"Go water the garden."
"I already did that."

"Go sweep the garage."
"I already did that."

Long silence.

"Mom?"
"What is it?"
"What can I do?"
"Go read the encyclopedia."
"Mom, it's summertime."
"I spent a lot of money on those."
"Can I call Pete?"
"Call Pete."

Before I dialed, I knew Pete had already had the same conversation with his mother. Although I'm sure it was a shorter list, my aunt had even less patience than my mom.

Everything in our parents' yards was cut, trimmed, watered, and cleaned. We were tired of board games. Playing cards wasn't interesting. And, pretty much everything that was visible we had already set on fire or blown up at least once.

When we absolutely didn't know what to do with our time, we opened the newspaper, and with a pencil in hand, we would change the words in articles to make them rude and funny. We'd redraw faces on people, and we'd make up our own answers for the crossword puzzle. On this particular morning, this is what we were doing—playing with the newspaper.

It was close to noon when we heard a common phrase that most mothers say to their children. "I'm just going to the store. I'll be back in a little bit. Behave."

My mom grabbed her car keys, went out the door, and started the car. By the time she got to the end of the driveway, Pete and I looked at each other. We didn't say a word but in the silence both of us thought, *We should do something.*

In a matter of a few minutes, we were standing at the kitchen counter with a clean piece of paper and a pen.

With pen in hand, I began writing.

> *Dear Mrs. Aversa,*
>
> *Your nephew, Peter, and your son, Domenic, have been kidnapped.*
>
> *We are very dangerous people. We mean business.*
>
> *If you want to see them again, you will leave one thousand dollars in a lunch bag under the rose bush in the front yard.*
>
> *You have ONE hour.*

I put the pen away and placed the letter on the counter near the rack for keys. At that moment, Pete and I start laughing hysterically. Uncontrollably. Laughing and laughing. Over and over, we said to each other, "This is the best. This is going to be sooooo funny. It's the best."

We then climbed the side of the house, onto a windowsill, and then pulled ourselves up to the roof of the house, overlooking the kitchen window. We were in prime listening area to hear my mom's reaction. We were convinced this was the absolute best thing we'd ever done. We took a seat on scorching hot roof shingles and waited for what was certain to be an afternoon of laughter.

Sure enough, right around 12.30 p.m. my mom pulled up in the driveway. Pete and I couldn't control our laughter. "This is going to be GREAT!" We then started to "shush" each other. "Quiet. Be quiet. Don't ruin it."

She walked in the door. We heard keys land on the counter and then a long silence. We were waiting. Waiting. Waiting. And there it was. "OHHHH GOD, OH GOD, OH NOOOOO!"

We burst out laughing. Punching each other. Laughing and laughing. "This is the best! The BEST."

And, as we laughed and tussled with each other we heard a very distinct sound: *shitititida, shitititida*. I turned to Pete and said, "That's the phone. She's on the phone."

There were only two possible numbers she was dialing—and one wasn't 911. She was either calling my father or Pete's mom. And, if she was calling Pete's mom, we would have wished to be kidnapped.

Somehow, in our adolescent minds, we really hadn't thought this prank through. We hadn't thought about the consequences, but now there was no mistaking what was going to happen to us—especially when Pete's mom got the news. My mom could be driving force, but she was no match for my aunt. My aunt Vittoria had the ability to cut through people like a buzz saw. When she made rules, you didn't dare break them.

Pete looked at me and said, "What are we going to do?" I looked at him and said, "Let's run." And Pete said, "Where?" I shook my head. "It doesn't matter. Let's just run." Pete was frozen. I pushed him trying to get him moving but he wouldn't get up. He just pushed me back. Then we heard my mom say, "Vittoria..." And she paused. She heard us rummaging around on the roof. She continued, "Never mind. I'll call you back later." She slammed the phone down and ran outside, looked up at us, and said, "I'M GOING TO KILL YOU."

At that moment, I absolutely believed that she might kill me. I knew I had to do some fast talking to calm her down.

"Mom, it was a joke."

"You're an idiot. Get down here."

"OK, but you have to promise not to hit me."

"I'm going to KILL YOU."

"It was a joke."

"That's not a joke. You scared me half to death."

"I'm sorry."

"I'm going to show you how sorry you're going to be. GET DOWN HERE."

"I'm not coming down."

"The longer you stay up there, the worse it's going to get. GET DOWN HERE."

I just kept shaking my head. There was no way I was getting off that roof. She had us trapped. I looked at Pete, and all the blood had left his head. He wasn't afraid of my mom; he was working through every angle of the beating he was going to get from his mom when she found out.

This was not the best scenario, but I knew my mother couldn't climb walls and the ladder wasn't tall enough for her to reach the roof, so in my mind I was safe if I didn't move.

My mother returned inside and then, every 30 minutes, she would come outside and yell, "GET DOWN HERE. I'M GOING TO KILL YOU." Each time she got angrier. On her third visit outside, she transformed into a dangerous cartoon character, and she stopped making sense. "Come down here. Come down because I'm going to kill you like you never imagined I would kill you." I thought that maybe if I talked with her, I could get somewhere. "Mom, what do you mean kill me like I never imagined? Why would I imagine you killing me? It doesn't make any sense." She then stopped shaking and trembling at the mouth and looked at me. "Get down here...because when I kill you, it's going to make perfect sense. GET DOWN HERE."

Clearly, my negotiating skills were not yet fully developed.

So, we sat on the roof, boiling and burning under the summer sun and, of course, worrying about our fate.

By 3.30 p.m. the blood had returned to Pete's face. It was now time for him to go home. His dad finished work around that time, and they always ate dinner early. He figured he was in the clear because my mom hadn't told his mom what had happened. I was confident my Aunt Vittoria would have laid most of the blame on my mother for our very dumb prank. Aunt Vittoria was older than my mother and married to the oldest in the family so she outranked her. If she said you were at fault, there was no questioning the decision.

Pete stood up and said, "good luck." He was taller than me. He went to another side of the house, hung on to the gutter, jumped, and ran as fast as he could. He was gone, but I knew I could not come down from that roof. I only had one chance at survival, and that was my dad. I had to wait for him to come home. I figured that even if she told him, at a minimum, I could use him as a shield from a beating.

At 5.30 p.m. I saw my dad's car turn onto our street. This was the moment of truth: Would I be caught or would I escape? I hung on to the gutter, worked my way to the window, and then jumped. As I jumped my mother came running out of the house. I ran as fast as I could to the far end of the backyard, planning one of my typical escape routes—jumping the neighbor's fence and the fences of seven other neighbors until I reached the cornfield. But that wouldn't be necessary. As I approached the fence, my dad turned the corner and saw that my mom was racing after me. He smiled and said, "What's going on?" My mother stopped running and said to him, "Ask your son what he did today. Go ahead, just ask him." My dad looked at me soberly. "What did you do?" My eyes darted between him and my mother. I knew lying wasn't the way out of this. "Nothing. Me and Pete played a joke on Mom and now she's mad."

My dad was too tired for this conversation. He shook his head and walked inside the house. My mother followed him. And I followed her. She showed him the note. He shook his head in disbelief but tried to de-escalate the anger in my mom. "It's OK. They're alive. Nothing happened. What are you going to do now?" To my mom's credit, she held true to her convictions as she responded to my father, "If you would hit him, he wouldn't be like this." My father didn't answer her because he knew there would be no chance in changing her mind after the scare we had put in her. He would wait for a calmer time.

All things considered, the day ended well—no kidnapping and no murder.

Three days later, my mom came into my bedroom at 7.30 a.m. "Get up." I was still under house arrest, but she usually didn't bother me this early in the morning. "Mom, why do I have to get up? It's early." With little hesitation she said, "Get up, we have to go." I was confused. "Where do we have to go?" Quickly she was losing patience. "Get dressed, wash your face, come eat breakfast, and hurry up."

I sat there eating toasted bread, drinking tea, and wondering why she was packing a lunch. After a few minutes, we got in the car and she drove toward the countryside. I was still groggy from sleep, so I didn't ask any additional questions. I figured we were going to visit someone, but then I remembered my sister was home alone, still sleeping.

We drove several miles, and she pulled into a driveway. It was a small, brick home with an above-ground pool on one side of the yard. In the back of the home were many acres of tomato fields. She parked and then told me to grab the lunch bag and come with her. She knocked on the side door of the home. A portly man in a white T-shirt, eating an apple, opened the door. The homeowner said, "Hi, Signora. Sorry, if you're looking for my wife, she's not here, but she'll be back in a little bit." My mother responded, "I know your wife. We go to church together and I've seen you, too, a few times. Do you remember me? You know my husband, the mechanic, Giacinto Aversa?" He said, "Oh yes, I remember. You're Benedetta. Nice to see you."

And then there was a long pause.

He took a bite of his apple. Looked at me. Looked at my lunch bag. And then looked at my mother "How can I help you, Benedetta?"

Casually she said to him, "It's not for me. It's for my son. He would like to work for you."

I was very confused. What work? No one told me about this.

The portly man smiled as he took another bite of his apple. With his mouth full he said, "But Signora, what work? I don't have work for him." Without pausing she responded, "You still have your tomato fields? Don't you need help picking the tomatoes?" He nodded and said, "I do. I have a lot of tomatoes, but I don't have any money to pay someone to pick them. I do it myself and my wife helps." My mom shook her head and said, "That's OK. You don't have to pay him. He just wants to work. If you can give him some money at the end of the week, that's nice. If not, don't worry. He likes to work."

He took a final bite of his apple and nodded in agreement.

My mother then added, "I will have him here every morning by eight and I will pick him up by four o'clock in the afternoon." She then turned to me and said, "Behave."

My mother was brilliant. One way or another, she found a way to "kill me." I wouldn't be shoveling manure, but it was backbreaking work.

So, there I was, in the middle of a 10-acre field, by myself, no radio, no watch, hunched over, picking tomatoes, one by one.

I already knew how to pick tomatoes because every year, as a family, we picked and canned our own tomatoes, but that was a family project and more social. In this situation, I was alone and in the quiet. In the far distance, I could hear other kids playing in pools and yards, but mostly I just heard the sound of bees that would fly around my head and eventually sting me. I was so upset. But I had no choice. My mother was a bull, and she had clearly won this battle. She had tried every way imaginable to keep me out of trouble, and this was her next solution—in the middle of a field, alone, working eight hours a day.

I was angry. I thought I might protest and just do nothing, but that only made the days longer. I learned that it was easier just to do the work. As you pick tomatoes, your hands become increasingly dark green and brown from the pigments in the branches of the plant. The only effective way to remove those stains is from the acid of a tomato. At the end of each day, you scrub up by crushing tomatoes between your hands and rubbing them vigorously. It took me many decades to understand the irony that the very thing that made you dirty would also clean you.

After two weeks of picking tomatoes, it was time to go back to school. In the end, the farmer did decide to pay me. He paid me 30 cents per bushel, which worked out to an average of $5 a day. I know there had to be child labor laws in place, but somehow they didn't apply to me.

The following year, I was determined to not go back to the tomato field. I began trimming hedges, bushes, trees, essentially anything that grew. My mother's father and one of her brothers were gardeners; I learned a few things from them. I enjoyed it, and it made the days pass without drama. My mother saw how it kept me busy, so again she started volunteering my services to everyone she spoke with in the neighborhood, in our family, and in her circle of friends. Everyone she came across, she would ask, "Do you need help with your yard? My son will work for you. You don't have to pay him. He enjoys it."

I enjoyed it, but I still wanted money. I couldn't buy candy and ice cream with pruning shears. I wanted something for my effort.

Fortunately, many were kind and did manage to pay me what they could.

It was a busy summer, and it passed quickly. When the next year came, I was determined to get a job that actually paid me consistent money. I was 14 going on 15, and I wanted money to buy clothes for school. I grew tired of wearing hand-me-downs from my older cousins and clothes my mother had picked for me. I wanted my own identity and sense of not feeling like I owed anyone anything.

Thank Goliath

To my mother's credit, she helped in the process. She went from business to business getting applications for me to fill out. She went to more than two dozen separate places. It was 1981, the country was in an economic recession, many people were being laid off. Companies were closing. Jobs were hard to come by. But she was persistent. She'd get applications, fill them out at the kitchen table, and then turn to me and say, "Sign here." When they were filled in, she'd drive me to each place and have me go in to drop it off with the manager or owner.

Soon a job opened at a restaurant where several of my older cousins had worked. The position was for a busboy. The pay was $1.85 per hour, plus tips. It wasn't a lot of money, but it was more than zero. "I'll take it."

Milano's restaurant was a high-end, fine dining, Italian establishment. Three separate dining areas were divided by long, green velvet drapes. The tables had crisp white linens, wine glasses and wax candle that sat in a chandelier-style holder. The bar was adorned with brass and unique cordials and whiskey from around the world. All the employees were in a uniform. Busboys wore a red suit-style jacket, white shirt, black bowtie, and black pants. Being clean-cut and clean-shaven was mandatory.

On my first day of work, my mom drove me to the restaurant at around 4:30 p.m. on a Friday. It was like walking into a freeway of human beings. People were moving quickly and hardly speaking to one another. Everyone knew what to do and had been doing it for a very long time. Another busboy came to me and said, "You're going to shadow me tonight. Everywhere I go, you go." Seemed simple enough. I nodded in agreement.

By 5 p.m., customers started pouring into the restaurant. We poured each of them water and cut fresh bread for each table. That was easy. We watched them as they ate their meal and refilled the water and bread when it emptied. That was easy. If they smoked, we would replace their ashtrays with a clean one after each completed cigarette. That was easy. When they completed their meal, we had to remove their dishes and unused glasses, put them on to a tray, carry that tray over our shoulder with one hand, through a crowd of humans racing back and forth, across a slippery tiled floor, through a swinging door, and do this while looking graceful and not dropping anything. That was hard.

I watched my fellow busboys zip around with loads of dishes on those trays. They carried 20 pounds of dishes and glasses as if it was a teacup and saucer. They were nimble and quick, and I was very uncertain I could do what they were doing. My trainer kept telling me, "Don't worry, you'll get the hang of it. Wanna try?" Each time he asked me, I shook my head and said, "Not yet."

One hour passed. Two hours passed. Tables came and went at a frenzied pace. I watched at least 75 trays hoisted by busboys and servers… "OK, I'm ready. I got this one." I was convinced that this was going to be like weightlifting. I had watched weightlifting in the Olympics on television; first up to your shoulders, then up over your head, and finally sitting back down on your shoulders—no problem.

I grabbed the big tray. It was filled with half-empty dishes of pasta, veal parmesan, chicken cordon bleu, salad, bread, dirty ashtray, wine glasses.... I hoisted it up to my shoulders and then one more quick move up over my head and then back...and... "Oh shit!" Way, way back. So far back, the entire tray sailed over my shoulder, behind me, and the entire tray of dishes and glasses came tumbling down onto the ground of the main dining room. I guess it was lighter than I thought.

I was so embarrassed. Nothing like making a big, noisy mess in front of a hundred people on your first night of a job.

Within seconds, three other busboys were there. They grabbed everything off the floor, re-stacked everything, and wiped the floor of any residue like a pack of restaurant-cleaning jackals. They laughed and work resumed like nothing had happened. Having been reprimanded every time I had made a mistake, in that moment I assumed the worst would happen to me. My entire body tensed up and I began to sweat. I thought for certain I would be fired. It was my first real job; I didn't know how things were supposed to work. The only thing I knew up to that point was that when you made a mistake, someone was yelling at you. But, in this case, they laughed. They didn't dismiss it, but it was an important moment for me in my life. It taught me that everyone makes mistakes, and that life moves on. Just clean up the mess and keep moving. And that's just what I did.

I worked that entire weekend, learning as much as I could. Mostly, I learned that when you made people happy, they gave you money. I was paid only $1.85 per hour, but getting tip money seemed endless. I watched how every senior waiter, bartender, coat checker, and busboy interacted with people. I watched them light cigarettes for guests and get tips. Bring a bottle of aspirin on a plate with a doily for a guest with a headache and get tips. Run outside, start cars for guests in the winter, warm them up, and get tips. There was no end to the list. It was a simple premise: Whatever the guest wants, get it for them. When you were really paying attention, you'd get them what they wanted or needed *before* they asked. I never heard the words "capitalism" or "customer service" before that first weekend, but I fell in love with both of those two thoughts. Make people happy and they give you money—so much easier than picking tomatoes.

The maître d' was responsible for scheduling all the front-end staff, which included the busboys. I quickly asked him to schedule me for as many days as he could. I decided that I would come to work every day. Where else did I have to be? If I was at home, my mother would be giving me a long list of things to do—and not paying me a cent. Whereas at work, people told me what to do, but I got paid for it. Work seemed like the easier of the two.

I worked 10 of the first 14 days of my employment. I was so excited when I picked up my first paycheck. I stared at it for 30 minutes: $111.32. All I could think about was how many French fries I could buy with this money. A small order of fries cost about 35 cents at McDonald's, but at the school cafeteria I could get a huge plate for 90 cents. In my mind, I searched for all the places I ate fries and what was the best deal. In the end it didn't matter. I concluded that I was rich—I could eat wherever I wanted. I could even buy fries for all my friends.

I was so excited to tell my parents how much money I had made. I came home and told my mother, "Mom, I don't need you to buy anything for me from now on. I have my own money. I made $111.32 this past two weeks." I was both proud and smug. I could smell the freedom from begging my mother for pocket change to buy an ice cream or bag of potato chips. Now, I could buy whatever I wanted, and I didn't need to ask anyone for money or permission.

My mother looked at me and said, "That's great. Where's the check?" I looked back at her and said, "It's in my pocket." She put her hand out and said, "Let me see it." I was a bit confused, but I figured I was proud of this—it was like looking at a report card—so I handed her the check. She looked at it, nodded her head, and then quickly put the check into her apron pocket.

"MOM! What are you doing? It's my check. Give it back."

She shook her head and said, "I have bills to pay. How do you think bills get paid around here? I have to buy food, pay for electricity, water, gas, insurance, clothing."

I was so upset. "I'll buy my own food and clothes. Just give me my check."

She smiled and said, "Yes, you're going to be buying your own food and clothes and a little of everything else—with money from your job."

"MOM! You never told me I had to give you MONEY!"

"I never told you that you didn't have to give me money."

She then put her hand on my shoulder and said, "OK, we're going to make a deal. Every two weeks, you give me your paycheck, but whatever money you make in tips, you can keep that for you. OK?"

I was angry, but I thought I'd better not complain, or she'd take all of it. I also was a bit relieved because I knew if I hustled, I would make a lot more money in tips than on my paycheck. I hadn't told her what I made each night in tips in those first two weeks because I was too busy buying French fries for me and my friends.

For the next year, I went to work taking the bus, getting rides from my parents or friends, and then being driven home by colleagues. It was fun and I appreciated everyone's patience and kindness, but it was time for me to get my driver's license.

I practiced for a couple months with my mom. We started in the parking lot of a big mall by our home, and then I worked my way up to driving on the highway. The night before the driving road test, I asked my mother if we could go practice one more time. But this time, I wanted to practice around the neighborhood where they did the actual testing. She agreed, and we drove there. For about an hour, all went well. I wanted to practice parallel parking just one last time before going home.

I lined up to the right side of the parked cars. It seemed a bit tight, but I thought I could make it. Carefully, I angled my car into the spot. As I tried to align the car better, I nudged the bumper of the car behind me. Just a nudge. There was no sound; it was just a nudge. My mom looked at me and said, "That's OK. It happens. It's fine." Not convinced of my parking skills I told her, "I want to try one just one more time." My mom agreed and pointed farther up the street. "OK, go down there and find another spot."

I drove out of the spot and worked my way up the street, reaching a stop sign. I looked up in my rearview mirror and saw a car driving extremely fast. It was racing toward me. It looked like an old Volkswagen Beetle. I then realized it was the car that I'd "nudged." My mother looked at me and asked, "What's happening? Why aren't you going?" Before I could answer her, I saw the Beetle come to a screeching halt. A tall, slender man wearing a T-shirt, jeans, and no socks or shoes jumped out of his car, ran to my side, his fist banging on the window. "GET OUT OF THE CAR!"

I was stunned. I wasn't sure what to do. I froze.

He banged on the window again. "GET OUT OF THE FUCKING CAR!"

I looked at my mom for guidance. She too was stunned and asked, "I don't know. What's happening? What does he want?"

Now banging on the window nonstop with his left hand, he reached behind him with his right hand and pulled out a gun. "POLICE! GET OUT OF THE FUCKING CAR!"

He wasn't mincing words. I undid my seat belt, opened the door, and got out. Before I could take two steps, he grabbed my arm, cranked it behind my back, and plowed my head into the window of the car. It was blistering. My head was throbbing. He was strong and incredibly angry. As he patted me down, searching me, I said, "Officer, what did I do?" Before he could answer, my mother jumped out of her side of the car and started yelling, "Arrest me. It's my fault. He didn't do anything. Just arrest me."

I really appreciated my mom taking the blame for me—that was a first in our relationship—but I still didn't know what I'd done wrong. This cop was not in the mood for a conversation. He snapped at my mother, "Stay right there, lady. Don't move. Just stay right where you are, or I will be arresting both of you."

He then spun me around and started yelling at me in an even louder voice. "YOU DIDN'T EVEN GET OUT TO LOOK! YOU DIDN'T EVEN LOOK. YOU DIDN'T GIVE ONE SHIT IF YOU CAUSED ANY DAMAGE. YOU ARROGANT, SNOT-NOSED SHITHEAD. YOU ARE UNDER ARREST FOR FAILURE TO REMAIN AT THE SCENE OF AN ACCIDENT."

By this age, I was accustomed to people yelling at me. He had put away the gun, so I didn't feel as threatened, but now I was upset. First, I was not arrogant. And I was certainly not snot-nosed. But what was this craziness about "failure to remain"? What accident? There was no accident. There was a nudge. I had studied everything in the driver's manual and hadn't seen anything that looked like what he was talking about. I said to him, "Sorry, Officer, I didn't think I caused any damage. If there's damage to your car, I will pay for it." He didn't care about my apology or my offer to pay. He resumed yelling. "YOU DIDN'T

EVEN GET OUT TO LOOK IF THERE WAS DAMAGE! I'M WRITING YOU UP!"

Again, my mother jumped in. "Give me the ticket. Arrest me. It's not his fault. He doesn't even have his driver's license yet. I was teaching him. I should get the ticket."

At this point, I thought his head was going to completely melt down. He went from a hot, pink-colored complexion to deep red. I could see that the vein in the middle of his head was throbbing. "WHAT?!!!" he yelled. "HE DOESN'T EVEN HAVE A DRIVER'S LICENSE!"

He then stepped away and started pacing back and forth. It was springtime, and it had rained. All I could focus on was his bare feet, and I kept thinking how cold they must be.

He walked back over to me, pointed his finger in my face, and said, "Your mother is going to drive you home. You get out of here and never come back here again. I'm not going to arrest you, but I still might give you a ticket. I need to think about it. Right now, just get out of my face."

I nodded and said, "Yes, sir. Thank you."

He jumped in his little Beetle and sped off down the road. He drove right through a stop sign, but I wasn't about to say anything. I just found it to be very hypocritical of him to treat me like a criminal and then he overtly breaks the law.

My mom got behind the wheel and drove us home. My mother kept reassuring me that everything would be OK. She suggested that maybe he "was just having a bad day." She made me feel a bit better, but I still had my driver's test the next morning at 9 a.m., in his neighborhood. Most kids were just nervous about passing the test. I had the added pressure of not getting arrested while taking my test. It wasn't as if I could ask the test instructor if we could go to another neighborhood. Can you imagine that conversation? "Ummm, excuse me, sir, could we go someplace else for the test? I'm a bit uncomfortable around this neighborhood because last night I hit a police officer's car and he told me if I ever came back, he would arrest me for hit and run." Not exactly the way to build confidence in the person evaluating your level of safety behind the wheel of a car.

Anyhow, I passed. Parking was fine. All was well, but I had a difficult time getting excited because there was still the possibility of me getting charged for "failure to remain at the scene of an accident." What made this particular charge terrible was the fact that if convicted, it was a charge of seven points against your license. As a beginner on probation for the first year, I was only given six points. If I was convicted, I would instantly lose my license for a year. Not exactly the place you want to be on your first day of having your driver's license.

Two days later, there it was, in the mailbox. An envelope from the Ontario Provincial Police (equivalent of a state trooper). Inside was a ticket in my name for "failure to remain." Brutal.

My dad fixed many cars for police officers. He made a few phone calls to see if there was any compromise that could be made. There was no damage to his car, and no one had been injured. Surely, there had to be a better solution. All his friends were city cops. This particular police officer worked for the province—he had different jurisdiction and didn't answer to them. A few of them had heard of him. He had a reputation for being a lunatic, and there was no reasoning with him. Great. Lucky me. I'd found the one cop who couldn't be smoothed over with my mom's cookies or a free oil change from my dad.

My parents genuinely felt bad for me so they allowed me to drive until my court date. It was set a couple months out. In the meantime, I tried to make the most of my freedom driving a car. My mother made me spend most of my youth cleaning, so I liked to see things cleaned and polished, including my parents' car.

Any spare moment I had, I cleaned the car. I had several boxes filled with different cleaning and polishing agents. One day, I decided that I wanted even more shine to my car, and the usual products like Windex and Armor All just weren't enough. I needed something with more glisten. How I finally decided on using baby oil, I'm not sure. It was in the house, and it made skin shine, so I thought, "Why not try it on the car?" I used half a bottle of baby oil on the interior of the car. No spot was left untouched—including the steering wheel. Once the entire car was cleaned and polished, it was time for a drive.

I picked up my cousin Dino, and we were just going out for a short ride and a bite to eat. Along our way, we came across a road that was nicknamed Snake Lane. It zigged and zagged for about half a mile in a shape that resembled a snake. As a new driver, I thought this would be a fun road to drive. And as a 16-year-old, I thought it would be even more fun to drive it very fast. I thought it might be like a go-kart track. I had driven those; how different could this stretch of road be?

My parents' car on its surface was an unassuming car. It was a 1977 Cutlass Supreme. My father always liked cars with big engines because he felt acceleration power was important when passing cars, particularly on highways. As a licensed mechanic, he felt it was a safety feature. So, in this car, the engine was a 350 V8 with a four-barrel carburetor, also known as the "350 Rocket."

Up until this point, I had never driven the car at a high speed. My parents were very conservative drivers. I never saw them speed, but on this day on Snake Lane, I wanted to see exactly how fast this "Rocket" engine could go.

As soon as I turned on the road, I pressed down on the gas pedal hard. The front end of the car appeared to jump up, the back tires squealed as they tried to grip the road, the engine roared, and the car just took off—like a rocket. First turn was to the right. I thought I had it under control, but all the baby oil made my hand lose grip. The wheels hit part of the gravel and slid. I turned to the left and steered too much...still trying to get a handle on this very oily steering wheel. This time I went farther into the gravel. I panicked and pushed the gas pedal to the floor. I thought it would keep me from getting stuck in the grass, and it did—but the wheels were spinning so fast that I crossed the road one more time.

Still panicking, I yanked the steering wheel all the way to the left, and the car twisted and lunged forward like a baseball bat—squarely hitting the back end of a parked car. The parked car moved about 50 feet, hitting another parked car. When we finally stopped moving, we ended up in a field on the other side of the road. I was uninjured, but Dino had hit his head against the windshield and was bleeding down his forehead.

When I got out of the car, I saw that the trunk was practically crushed and removed from the main body. A resident in the neighborhood came running out to see if we were OK. The police came shortly thereafter. Dino was taken to get a few stitches. And I stood there thinking about how dumb I was and how lucky I was that no one was killed.

The officer gave me a ticket for careless driving, which meant an additional six points against my driver's license. Less than a month from receiving my driver's license with six points, I had hit-and-run and careless driving charges against me, equaling 13 points for a total of 19. I knew there was no way I would be driving for years. And, even when I got my driver's license back, the cost of insurance would be sky-high and most likely prohibitive. I couldn't believe it. I had just wanted freedom. I just wanted to be able to drive, go earn money, buy my own clothing, eat French fries, and take pretty girls on dates. In less than one month, I had crushed all my dreams of any freedom. I would be relegated to buses and bicycles for years.

The next day, I phoned the lawyer my dad had hired to represent me on the "failure to remain" ticket. I told him what had happened, and he said, "No problem. We'll schedule it to be heard on the same day as the first ticket." I was horrified. "What? Why? The judge is going to hate me. Why the same day?" Very coolly he responded, "Don't worry, Domenic. It's going to be OK. Let me take care of it." I shrugged but went along with it. I didn't know what else to do.

Four weeks later, it was time to appear in court. At nine in the morning, my mother and I met our attorney on the court steps. He instructed us not to say a word unless he gave us permission to speak. We entered the mostly empty courtroom. In the second row from the back, I saw the lunatic Provincial Police officer, but this time he was in full uniform. He saw me walk in and just gave a dead-eyed stare. We followed my attorney to the front of the courtroom. We sat in the front row, and he took a seat at a desk closer to the judge's bench.

Opposite my attorney was the Crown attorney (equivalent to a district attorney). The judge asked the Crown to begin. The Crown stated, "Your Honor, we are here to present the case against

Domenic Aversa, Ticket Number 48739, Failure to Remain at the Scene of an Accident. The Crown calls Officer Jones as the first witness."

There was a long pause, and no one moved. The Crown repeated, "Officer Jones. The Crown calls Officer Jones." And, just at that moment, the police officer who had given me the ticket for careless driving, when I demolished my parents' car, came into the courtroom. He raised his finger, nodded in agreement, and walked toward the Crown. He approached the desk and then took a seat on the witness stand. I turned to my mom and whispered, "That's not the right police officer." She nodded and pointed toward my lawyer. I got up and walked toward him. He leaned toward me, and I said, "That's the wrong cop. He's for the other ticket." My lawyer didn't blink. "Sit down and don't say another word."

I had no idea what was happening. I just knew somehow people would get mad and it would make things worse for me.

The Crown began his questioning of the police officer. "Officer Jones, can you tell the court at approximately what time you witnessed Mr. Aversa flee from the scene of the accident?"

Officer Jones looked confused. He stared at the Crown attorney and then turned to the judge. The judge looked at him and said, "Officer Jones, is there a problem? Please answer the Crown."

Officer Jones replied, "Well, yes, Your Honor, there is a problem. Mr. Aversa did not flee from the scene of the accident. He couldn't flee. His car was critically damaged and could not move."

At this point, the Crown attorney was shaking his head and frantically sorting through the mountain of papers on his desk. Over and over, under and to the side. To the right and then to the left. He was sifting through paper as quickly as he could. A long minute in silence passed. The judge then asked the Crown attorney, "Does the Crown have any further questions for Officer Jones?"

The Crown attorney pushed all his papers into one pile and lifted his head. Clearly flustered and now angry, he said, "NO! No additional questions for Officer Jones. BUT I do have one comment for the court record. THOSE PEOPLE. Those PEOPLE in administration better get their ACT TOGETHER. I'm tired of THIS!"

The judge nodded and said, "Fair enough. OK, is there a Mr. Domenic Aversa in the court?" My lawyer turned to me and instructed me to stand. I thought, "OK, here it comes. The judge is going to make everything clear and then sentence me. Say goodbye to freedom." I got up from my seat and the judge said, "Mr. Aversa, seems like there was some confusion today, but the law is the law. Since the testimony reads that you did not leave the scene of the accident, and the Provincial Police cannot give testimony that you were driving carelessly at your other accident, both charges are dismissed. Have a good day. Please drive safely."

I could not believe what had just happened.

Nothing? No punishment?

My lawyer quickly packed up his briefcase and ushered me and my mom out of the courtroom. As we left, I looked at the Provincial Police officer at the back of the room. He was fuming. I smiled and shrugged as I passed him. When we got outside, my mother let out a sigh of relief as she shook my lawyer's hand. I was still dumbfounded. I asked him what had happened. He too shrugged and said, "They screwed up. Don't worry about it. It's good to be lucky sometimes."

Thank Goliath

I don't know if it was angels, Jesus, fate, or just plain good luck, but on that day, things went my way and now my dreams were back in play. I could have exactly what I wanted—freedom.

6

TWO GUNS

The next few years, I worked a lot of hours at the restaurant. Often, I worked 30 to 40 hours a week. Essentially, I was working a full-time job and going to high school full-time. My parents grew concerned that I was working so much that they asked me to cut back my hours. But I couldn't; I liked it too much.

Every night, I felt like I was living in another world, learning about affluence, people, and fine dining. And during the day, being at school was an entirely distinct experience, but I enjoyed it just as much. That part of me loved being a boundless, free teenager. I loved joining others and being part of the Student Council and other school groups. I had a lot of energy, a lot of ambition, and a lot of curiosity. Gone were the days where I felt chained to my neighborhood and mother. My confidence started to grow, and I ran with it. I wasn't about to cut back on anything. I could only see moving forward. However, to ease my parents' concern, I struck a deal with them. I promised them that I would keep my grades up and stay on the Honor Roll. I told them that if my grades dropped, then I would cut back my hours at the restaurant or in school activities.

By 1984, it was not uncommon for me to come home from work around midnight on a weeknight, make a pot a coffee, and then start studying for a test for the next morning. My parents took turns waking up at 2 or 3 a.m., walking into my room, and telling me to go to bed. But they were futile attempts. My ears were closed, and my mind was open. I no longer had to dream about escaping. I went wherever I wanted or could imagine. Whether it was night or day, all the hours were the same to me. My life in full motion felt perfectly normal to me. My parents were concerned but they had a difficult time complaining; I was working, and I was maintaining an "A" average.

In the mid-'80s everything was big: movies, hair, clothes. It's as if everything was expanding and trying to be larger than life. I was no different. I was skinny, nearly six feet tall, and my hair grew an inch longer in every direction with each passing year. I evolved from a nice, clean-cut, Catholic schoolboy to eventually looking like a giant puffed-up poodle walking on two legs. Better still, you could smell me from 10 feet away. It was as if I had fallen into a barrel of Polo cologne. I was a teenager and had no sense of subtlety or grace. It was silly time, but I was having fun. I had money, good grades, a lot of friends, and plenty of freedom. I was rarely at home, and I barely saw my parents.

This type of life should have made any teenager happy. And for the most part I was. I felt lucky. I should have felt grateful, and I should have led a more cautious life after being spared in that courtroom, but I didn't. I believed that no matter how menacing or dangerous a situation was, I could either fight my way out or luck would be on my side. So, I kept venturing further and further into places I shouldn't have been, and I kept taking chances that no person of a sound mind should take.

When work ended, it was late in the evening and my school friends were at home, so I would go out with my colleagues from Milano's. Most of them were streetwise and older than me. They had been knocked around by life, and each had a hardship story worse than the other. As an Honor Roll teenager, I had no business being in this crowd, but the part of me that believed I was trouble felt right at home. I held tightly to that identity because it's what helped me survive. I was resilient, and I wanted to be indestructible. Whatever my friends did, I tried to go further. If they had one drink, I had two. If they stole something, I'd steal everything.

By my senior year, at the age of 18, I had secured my ability to go wherever I wanted at any time of the day. It was vital that I not miss any party or social outing, especially the ones that involved alcohol. With considerable pride and clever manipulation, I managed to obtain four different identification cards and two different driver's licenses. I had one card that showed I was 18, which I used for student events. One that stated I was 19 so I could get into bars in Canada. Another showed I was 19 but under an alias name just in case I lost the other fake card. And another identification showed I was 21 so I could get into bars in America. And of course, I had one driver's license for Ontario and one for Michigan. All of this was illegal, but in my mind, rules were for other people. To me, freedom was paramount. Obeying the law was just something that got in my way, so why bother?

Having complete disregard for rules was amusing, but it wasn't fun unless I could have friends share in some of my freedom. As such, I made backup plans for all my friends who were underage and didn't have fake identification cards. At any one time, I had at least three cases of wine hidden around the city. I still had my climbing and disappearing skills from my childhood, so I hid the wine in bushes and trees. I didn't know where else to put them. Apparently, it was a good choice because I never lost one bottle.

And then there was my driving. A person of reasonable sanity would have walked away from that car accident on Snake Lane and that courtroom thinking they should drive at a legal speed and enjoy the benefits of not having to walk or take a public bus for travel. Not me. I treated the car and roads as if I had never had a ticket in my life. I loved to go fast. I loved to smoke the tires. Mostly, I loved to race other cars. This was Windsor, Ontario, right across the bridge (over the Detroit River) from Detroit, Michigan. Detroit was the Motor City, and Windsor was the automotive capital of Canada. Everyone loved cars and racing. We were surrounded by muscle cars. At that time, no one cared about gas mileage or emissions; it was all about horsepower.

In the summer, late into the evenings, kids would gather at several different parts of the city, on straight stretches of the highway. They'd line up to drag race. I never lined up in those races because my car wasn't fast enough for that crowd. But I would watch alongside the road with others. One by one, they would light up their tires and take off down the road. It never took long for the police to show up. Half the fun was speeding away and not getting caught by the police.

Most of the time, I would just pick some random car on a city road, usually at night, and we'd race. Often, guys would just pull up next to my car and nod their head and I would nod back and off we'd go.

One evening, on my way home from work, two guys pulled up next to me in a car at a traffic light. I was tired but they gave me the nod and I thought, *Why not?* We took off from the light, and quickly their car cut me off and moved from their lane into mine. This was a stupid thing to do and something that wasn't done...even in these illegal races. Clearly, they were crazy—but in that moment I decided to be crazier. I wasn't mad, I just had no sense of limitations. I wanted to win. In an instance, I braced myself and turned the steering wheel as I crossed the double lines, into oncoming traffic. I passed them, and then crossed back into their lane, landing right in front of them. In my very teenage and reckless mind, I didn't for one minute think that something could go wrong.

At this point, most of these informal, little bursts of street racing would be over. However, I had upset these two gentlemen because I outsmarted them. Therefore, rather than driving off into the evening, they decided to follow me home.

I knew that if they caught up to me, bad things were going to happen. If they were that defiant, then it was possible they had a gun with them or, at a minimum would beat me to a bloody mess. I knew that there was no way I could have them follow me to my parents' home. Even if my father would have come out of the house with his rifle, they'd still know where I lived and were certain to come back and torment us. With my mind racing faster than the car was moving, I did what I thought was best—I turned off all the lights in my car and floored it!

I drove toward the subdivision where I lived. There were no streetlights, and we were surrounded by farm fields. In the evenings it would get very dark. I figured if I turned off my lights and didn't use my brakes, I could eventually lose them. I knew the roads better than them so I was positive that I could time my turns without lights and speed off into the darkness—at least that was my plan.

I raced through this tranquil neighborhood like a bat out of Hell. I'm not sure how fast I was going because I couldn't see the speedometer. I was solely focused on not hitting a human, a tree, or a house. With each turn, my back wheels went farther on the shoulder and lawn. The farther they went, the more grip the car lost. I could drive fast, but I wasn't a professional. I needed to slow down because at this speed, it was just a matter of time before I lost complete control and ended up on some neighbor's front porch.

I made a final turn, pulled into someone's car park, and turned the engine off. I just sat there listening to my heart pound. Twenty minutes passed, and I didn't see or hear a peep. I gathered myself, drove home, went inside, started on my schoolwork at 1 a.m., just like nothing had happened. Somehow, I had the ability to treat it as if it were something that I created in my imagination. It was thrilling and even frightening, but now it was time to move on to the next thing.

Nothing deterred me. For as kind and respectful as I could be, I was also a lunatic that should have been put in jail. Every week, I pushed further down a dumber and more dangerous path. I wasn't just looking for trouble; I was inviting it to be my favorite companion.

One night, at a bar, some guy was shooting off his mouth. He kept bragging about how much money his parents had, how many things he had and the things he did with all that money. He was the best at this, had the best of that, and no one could have what he had. And on and on. I didn't know him. I should have just walked away. But I kept listening to him. The more he talked the more he bothered me. I could have just told him he was a materialistic idiot, but that would have been too easy and too plain. Instead, I decided to steal his car.

I saw his coat on a chair, stuck my hands in it, grabbed his car keys, and then walked outside of the bar and looked for the newest and most expensive car. He bragged so much that I figured that the best one must have been his. Bingo. Brand new Camaro Z28.

I had another friend follow me with his car so I could come back later to the bar to get my car.

I didn't want his car. I wasn't sure what I was going to do with it. I was spiteful, maybe even jealous because life appeared to be so easy for him. My life had been a grind and I worked hard to get anything I had. So, in the most cowardly way, I thought that I would teach him a lesson—I would make his life difficult for one day.

I drove his car several miles away, pulled up to the front doors of a high school, and parked it within inches of the doors. I locked it up and then, just like the ugly knit hats from my childhood, I threw the keys onto the roof of the school.

I got into my friend's car, and we went back to the bar. No one had even noticed that we were gone. We had a drink and went home. I don't know what ever happened to him or his car.

I thought that I understood what I was doing. I was older, but I was still acting like a battered child. I didn't want to hurt anyone, but I did want to see how far I could push things before they broke. I thought it would make me stronger and more street savvy. I figured the more I knew how to protect myself, the less I could be hurt. Then one day, when I wasn't actually looking for trouble, I found myself in a situation where nothing I had learned on the street could help me.

My uncle had recently just opened up an Italian restaurant. One evening, I stopped by to say "hello." He was busy, and his pizza delivery guys were behind schedule. He asked me if I could help by making a delivery. I said "sure." He tossed me his keys, told me to take his car. I grabbed the pizza and off I went.

I drove a couple of miles, got to the home, pulled into the driveway, and opened my car door. As I started to exit the car, a man ran up and pushed me back in. The car was a big, brown Buick with bench seats. He shoved me into the middle, jumped into the driver's seat, and at the same time another man opened the passenger door and jumped in. I didn't say a word. My head turned from side to side. Before I could say anything, the man to my right pulled out a handgun and put it up against my ribs. The keys were still in the ignition. The man in the driver's seat started the car and backed out of the driveway. I had no idea who they were or what was happening.

They didn't say a word, and I didn't dare ask any questions. They were young, perhaps in their 20s, and appeared tense, but they didn't seem like rookies. My heart raced, but I kept the expression on my face neutral. I sat still and tried not to twitch or move any part of my body.

They drove for about 15 minutes, and then they pulled up to the parking lot of a high school and drove behind the school. It was late winter, it was dark, and there was no one around. They stopped the car in the middle of the schoolyard. The man to the right of me exited the car and walked behind the car. The man in the driver's side looked at me and said, "Get out." I exited on the passenger side. When I was out, the man standing behind the car raised his gun and pointed it directly at my head.

I didn't know what to do. My options: If I ran, he'd shoot me. If I screamed, he'd shoot me. There was no place to hide. Every muscle in my body tightened. This was far different than anything I had ever faced. I had no idea what death was like, but I was certain I was about to find out. All thoughts left me. I just closed my eyes.

There was silence for what seemed like an eternity.

Then, the man with the gun said, "Go."

I opened my eyes and stared at him. He repeated, "Go."

This time I didn't hesitate. I turned and ran away from them as fast as I could. I thought that he was going to shoot me in the back, but I couldn't stop to see what he was doing. When I reached a tree line, I ran behind the trees and jumped over a fence. I was so afraid that they might chase me that I just ran as fast as I could. My only thought was to get back to my uncle's restaurant. I ran the entire distance on the shoulder of the main roads. I even ran by a police car, not thinking for a minute that they could help. In total, I ran about four miles. I got to my uncle's restaurant and yelled, "They took the car." My aunt and uncle came out of the kitchen. As I caught my breath, I told them what had happened.

My aunt called the police to report the stolen vehicle. My uncle sat me down and poured me some whiskey. He saw that I was shaken, but he also understood what it was like to have a gun to your head. A few years earlier, he was the manager of a dinner club, and he too had been mugged, robbed, and held at gunpoint. The only difference was that they had tied him to a chair.

As we waited for the police, my uncle asked me questions but also prepared me for what was to come. He said, "Just keep calm.

They're going to ask lots of questions. And they may even try to insinuate that you stole the car." I looked at him. "What?" He replied, "It's true. They tried to do it to me. They will try to confuse you, but keep calm. They're just doing their job."

A short while later, two balding, middle-aged men in long, gray overcoats, wearing matching navy-blue suits underneath, showed up at the restaurant. Detective Kidd and Detective Jackson asked if we could speak in a private area. We led them to another dining room within the restaurant. They asked me to recount what had happened. It was then that I realized the thieves had taken my winter coat, which had my wallet inside one of the pockets. I was in such shock I hadn't thought about it until one of the officers asked me for my identification.

They then drove me to the police station to review "mug shots" of people who fit the description of what I saw. I turned and scanned every page. I didn't see anyone that I recognized but I did see plenty of scary faces. I thought I was tough, but I wanted nothing to do with these people. The pain on their faces ran deep. There were visible scars, pockmarks, and many ominous tattoos.

At that moment, I came to a startling revelation: The men who had held me at gunpoint had my identification and now knew where I lived. I looked up at Detective Kidd. "Do you think they may come rob our house?" Without hesitation he said. "It's possible but it's rare."

The word "possible" was enough for me. Now, as I scanned each page, I thought about these men coming to our home. Detective Jackson then asked me, "Son, have you been drinking tonight?" I quickly responded, "No." He then leaned over my shoulder and asked again, "Have you been drinking tonight?" Why was he asking me this? I wondered if this was the part where they start to turn the tables and blame me. I answered again, "No."

I continued leafing through the pages, and Detective Jackson walked in front of my table and said, "Are you sure about the events that you told us?" I then remembered that my uncle had poured me a shot of whiskey when I ran into the restaurant, and now in close quarters they were smelling it on my breath. I looked at him and said, "Sorry, I forgot, I did have a drink tonight. My uncle poured me a shot to help calm my nerves when I first got to his place. But, yes, I'm very clear about what happened tonight." I went through the entire gallery of career criminals, got to the end of the book, but none were a match.

Detectives Kidd and Jackson drove me home. Realizing that these armed and dangerous men could come to our home, my father pulled out his shotgun and kept it by his bedside. I didn't have a gun, but I had several big hunting knives. I figured that even if I couldn't shoot an intruder, I could still try to slow them down. Nonetheless, it didn't matter. From that point forward, I would sleep even less than I had typically slept. I was too nervous and too worried that they would break into our home. I spent the entire night looking out my window toward the driveway and road in front of our house. I would do this for many months to follow. I thought that I was a rebel, and the rules didn't apply to me. I believed that I was unstoppable and could push the limits wherever I went. But now, reality settled in. This wasn't drag racing or fake IDs. These two men had shown me the face of actual experienced hardcore criminals—and I looked like a child next to them.

My uncle's car was eventually recovered, but the two suspects were never found. Even though luck was on my side again, I was more solemn about it. I did manage to get out of another dangerous situation, but my spirit had been violated. I no longer felt entirely safe anywhere I went, particularly at home. I worried and wondered when would be the next time I was going to be jumped and have a gun put to my head.

Rarely was I present. My mind was always somewhere else, usually scanning the doors of a room, the corners of a bar, the sidewalks, and alleys ahead of me. My eyes were always on the perimeter of where I was. Every time I got into my car, I walked around it first, and even when I went to turn the key to enter, I looked over my shoulder. As soon as I was inside, the doors were locked. The freedom I so desperately enjoyed was now gone. I could still go anywhere, but I felt like someone was eventually going to get me. Someone would bring me to death's door.

And someone did—my mom.

As I spent my days on the lookout for criminals, she spent all her energy just trying to get through the day. Over the previous year, she had grown more tired of performing everyday tasks. She was nimble and started her days early with chores around the home, followed by baking, canning, or cooking. If all those things were complete, she would volunteer her time with a nonprofit, a friend, or her church. In the previous 20 years, she rarely had a quiet moment, but now she found herself laying on the sofa with a low-grade fever every couple of days.

She had met with our family doctor, Dr. Maletto, several times, but on each occasion, he would summarily dismiss her concerns without running any formal diagnostics or bloodwork. Being a consummately arrogant man, he instead asked her questions about her marriage and family life. The first couple of appointments, he concluded that she was just aging, and these changes were normal within women. She was confused with his conclusions. My mother had put on a little weight but otherwise, outwardly, little had changed. She was 39 and soon approaching the age of 40. She gave it further thought and thought perhaps he was right, she was just aging.

During her third appointment with the same over-stuffed and condescending doctor, she expressed greater frustration because she had put on more weight and could not understand why. She had always been petite and disciplined in her approach to food. Why was she now putting on weight in her midsection?

Dr. Maletto was equally frustrated with my mother. He viewed himself as a scholar and learned man. His patients were primarily first-generation Italian immigrants. They went to him because he spoke Italian. Even though they shared the same heritage, he viewed himself to be far superior to his patients. He knew the ways of the new land much better than them. He had gone to college and medical school, and they were just peasants and laborers. However, the reality was that the only thing different between him and his patients was that his family had arrived in Canada 50 years earlier. In those 50 years, people in his family had time to learn the language, become educated and financially stable. The rest of us would eventually get to where he was. Nonetheless, for the present moment, Dr. Maletto kept his nose high in the air and now concluded that my mother must be suffering from psychological problems. In his diagnosis, he stated that she didn't agree with his conclusion that the persistent low-grade fever, weight gain, and fatigue were attributable to "women" issues and aging so therefore she must see a psychiatrist.

After nine months of struggling with these issues and the doctor always coming to the same conclusion, she now wondered out loud whether she was just imagining these problems. She came home that day from the doctor's office and at dinner asked all of us what we thought. Solemnly, she asked my dad, my sister, and me, "Should I go see a psychiatrist?"

In my younger years, there were days I wished my mom would be swept away in a tornado like Dorothy in *The Wizard of Oz*, but those days were long behind us. I now knew my mom to be intelligent, caring, and genuinely happy. She had barely aged. Her skin glowed, and her hair was as thick and shoulder long as it was in her teenage years. However, gone was the insecure, lonely young girl who was seeking outward approval. Also gone were any emotional outbursts toward me. Now she was calm and always consoling. She had matured and come into her own. She returned to things she enjoyed like reading every night before bed.

Other women sought her out as a confidante. They would call or visit daily, looking for a comforting voice in my mom. She listened more than she spoke and rarely judged. She would offer quiet reassurance with simple expressions like "It's OK" or "Just try again." And after years of being nervous and stressed, she resumed laughing, always finding a way to work it into every conversation. She was at her best when she helped others understand that dark days didn't last long. When not engaged with friends, she was a vibrant presence within the community and church, always offering assistance with every spare moment she had. At that time, none of us really knew what a psychiatrist did, but we knew that the problem wasn't in her head. This pain and discomfort were real.

What did we conclude as a family?

"Wait a little longer. Maybe you'll start to feel better."

Even though he was a supreme jerk, my mother and father trusted Dr. Maletto. He was a doctor, and they weren't. They felt that even if he was wrong this time, he would soon figure out what was happening so there was no need to consult with someone else.

My mother waited another three months. She put on more weight, fevers increased in frequency, and she was more tired than ever. This time she went back to the doctor's office, and she demanded that he run some formal diagnostics because she was feeling pain on her left side and back. The doctor got off his high horse, ran blood tests, and sent her for an ultrasound.

While having the ultrasound performed, the first words out of the technician's mouth were: "Mrs. Aversa, is it possible that you are pregnant?" My mother was curiously surprised and quickly said, "I don't know. I don't think so. Why?"

It was then that they discovered a 10-pound cyst attached to my mother's pancreatic duct.

Ten pounds.

Ten pounds of fluid that had begun a path to impeding the proper functioning of several of her critical organs, including her liver and digestive system.

The bloodwork and a biopsy revealed that the cyst was not cancerous. That was a blessing. However, the positioning of the cyst made it virtually impossible to remove. It was situated on the pancreatic duct, near the liver. An ill-placed attempt to remove it could instantly kill her.

Without the ability to remove the massive cyst, the doctor was left scrambling for a solution. Unable to produce a definitive cure, Dr. Maletto had a new prognosis for my mother. "We can try to drain the cyst and maybe cut parts of it, but it will most likely continue to grow and eventually surround and overtake the other organs, which will affect their ability to function properly. We're not sure, but you may only have a few years to live. For now, go home and rest."

It didn't matter what he said because the only thing we heard when she relayed the message to us was, "You may only have a few years to live."

Just like a mugging, without warning, pain hit.

Now, a gun had been put to both of our heads, but my mother had the trigger pulled on hers.

She didn't cry.

She didn't scream.

She didn't want to sue Dr. Maletto.

She just came home, went to bed, and told my father, my sister, and me, "You're going to have to figure out how to do things without me."

My father looked at my sister—she was 14—and said, "Let's go to the kitchen. We should make dinner. I need you to show me where everything is." He then looked at me and asked, "Maybe we should clean a little bit. Do you know where the vacuum is?"

My dad was 44. Up until then, he did few he did a few things but it wasn't his primary role. It was a division of labor. He went to work at a garage every day, and my mom took care of everything inside of the home. Neither was viewed as dominant or superior; they treated each other and their responsibilities with mutual respect. In that moment, my father did not hesitate or debate the circumstances. He accepted that life would be different now and he would have to take on new responsibilities. My sister and I looked at him and followed his lead. The dynamics in our family would never be the same again.

I didn't know what to say to my mother, so I said nothing. When I was younger, she was ever present. It was almost impossible to hide from her. She was always wherever I was, either in person or in my head. I didn't think she'd ever be gone, but now my reality had changed. The prospect of her dying was real. She could be gone from my life forever. Yet, it was a picture I still couldn't conceive in my mind. I just couldn't imagine my life and our family without her—so, I didn't. From that point forward, I did not allow myself to believe that my mother would ever die. I did, however, accept the fact that I needed to change. I realized that I needed to be a better person. I now had seen the face of actual criminals and death, and I knew that I wanted no part of either. I decided to stop the ridiculous and reckless behavior. My mother had enough to worry about; I didn't need to add to her concerns. I stopped racing, stopped stealing, stopped experimenting and exploring dark paths. I decided to instead put my head down and work more hours and focus on getting into a great university.

For the next seven months, I worked three different jobs. I worked as a waiter at my uncle's restaurant, a doorman at a bar, and part-time on the automotive production line, welding, at Chrysler. I knew that the more I worked, the less time I had to slip back into my old ways.

By the time August came, I had all my clothes, books, and radio packed and ready to move on. I was accepted at the University of Waterloo, which was located about three hours north of Windsor. My mother was ill, but she had put on a brave face and believed an answer to her problems would be found. Watching her be resolute and positive helped me be excited to start a new life.

Before my parents got into the car for our trip, my mother pulled me aside and said, "I have something for you." I thought that she may have knit me another sweater or toilet paper cover hat or socks. I sarcastically answered her, "What is it?" She replied, "Be nice or I won't give it to you." She then reached inside the pocket of her coat and pulled out a bank book and handed it to me. "This is for you." I didn't understand what she was giving me. She smiled. "Do you remember all your paychecks from the restaurant? I put each one of them into a bank account for you. I put aside the money because I knew one day you would need it for school...so, here you go. It's yours."

Even in her weakened condition, she was still one step ahead of me.

For many years, there were times I viewed her as the enemy. She had hurt me and could be a colossal annoyance, but I came to realize that she spent far more time genuinely looking out for the best for me.

I opened the bank book. There was $11,480 in it. In 1986, for me, this was a fortune. I could have never imagined that $1.85 per hour would amount to something that significant. I was stunned. I now felt a huge sense of relief. I would have a little breathing room when it came to spending money. It was amazing to me how quickly your path could change with one event both good and bad.

In the shortest amount of time, our fates had changed dramatically. I started high school with a fake kidnapping and ended it with a real kidnapping. I also started high school with a healthy mom, and now it was ending with her life hanging in jeopardy.

This new level of adversity was a wake-up call for both of us. Each one of us started to realize exactly how fragile life was and that most of the distractions we had worried about or engaged in were just that—distractions from what really mattered in life. In an instant, with the slightest change in circumstances, both of us could have died. I could have taken a bullet and she could have been diagnosed with pancreatic cancer—a condition at that time that had zero chance of cure.

I now focused on the future and building a better and safer life. However, my mom focused elsewhere. She stopped worrying about the future and instead paid attention to what was in front of her each day. Death had already found her, so she no longer had to worry about it. Instead of being fearful, she became happier and even more grateful. She had always participated in nonprofit organizations, helping the poor and challenged, but now she decided to take on the role of president of the Catholic Women's League. In this position, she would be able to lead the efforts in fundraising for a wider group of people within the city as well as other countries. She had no plans of letting this ailment stop or even slow her down.

7

WHO IS RESPONSIBLE?

It was 11 in the morning on January 2nd.

I had returned to campus early and was walking through the heavy snow, toward our dormitory. I ran into an acquaintance on her way out of the dorm. "Hi, Lisa." She did a double-take and then said, "Oh, hi, Dom. I'm surprised you're here." Casually, I responded, "I know, it's early." She smiled and said, "It is. But I'm surprised you're here this semester. I was sure that you would be a Christmas graduate. Oh well, glad you're here. Good luck," and she disappeared into the snowfall.

What did she mean, "Christmas graduate"?

I had just completed my first semester of university.

It took me a minute, but then I realized she thought that I would have flunked out. She figured that because she'd seen me out and socializing all the time that I would have failed and been asked to leave school.

It was true, I did go out a lot, and I did organize a lot of parties. That money my mother had saved over four years disappeared into a lot of drinks for a lot of strangers. I liked to share. I had fun when I bought for everyone in the bar. I didn't want to admit it, but I was having a difficult time keeping promises that I'd made to myself. I thought it was harmless fun. I wasn't reckless and lawless. I thought compared to how I used to live that I was doing pretty good. I was simply happy to be in a new world, but clearly, if I kept along that path, I wasn't going to get to where I wanted to be.

She didn't realize it, but Lisa had given me a gift when she punched me in my pride. I didn't like being thought of us as dumb. I could be called many things, but "dumb" really bothered me. I knew what I had to do. I concluded that I needed to be more like my mom and keep myself busy, being grateful for each day. It was an easy fix. I just needed to spend more time at school rather than at the dorm or in a bar.

From that day forward I would go to classes during the day, volunteer time at the Community Legal Aid office in the afternoon, work out with weights in the early evening, then go to the library and stay there until it closed. I stayed there until 11:30 p.m., five or six nights a week. If I had nothing to do, I would sleep on my books. I figured if I was there, I couldn't be doing something stupid. I also didn't have a car, so I walked everywhere I went. Combine that with one to two hours of workouts in the gym, and by the time I got home, I was too tired to go anywhere else.

I stuck to this routine, and my grades rose dramatically. Then, through another student, I discovered a program that seemed compelling. It would allow me to get a degree in arts but also get two years of professional work experience by the time I graduated. The "Applied Arts" program would help me pay for my schooling and would give me a more impressive resume upon graduation. It was a small program that was difficult to get into, but I thought I would try.

I met with the dean, and he explained to me that enrollment was closed, and even if I were allowed in, I was a year behind. I needed to apply to this program out of high school. I understood what he was telling me, but I was determined to get in. I concluded that I would just shadow the program: I would take the exact same courses as they took, and then, every other semester, I would try to get a job in a professional setting, write a report on the job experience, and submit it to the dean for grading.

That first summer, I was able to get a job with the Children's Aid Society in an assessment center. This was a home where children were brought to be assessed for the courts when they were removed from their parents' home or found on the streets. It was a place for troubled and abused kids. I thought that this was something I understood and could offer help and hope.

The Brian Hyslop Home had sleeping arrangements for about a dozen children, ranging in ages from 7 to 17. In this home, there were a couple certified child-care workers who were responsible for final evaluations and reporting to the court. The other half-dozen employees, including myself, were assigned to supervising and providing care for the children through the normal course of a day. Our work shifts varied depending on the day of the week and need of the children, but in general they were long. They ranged from nine to 15 hours per day.

Like most homes, we would wake the kids and help them get washed, dressed, and fed. However, the similarities ended there. Most of these children had suffered terrible mental, physical, and sexual abuse. Many were burdened with weak immune systems, poor digestive health, and psychological disturbances. For example, it was not uncommon to see an 8-year-old suffering from anxiety who had a shaven bald head—an extreme measure taken to prevent the child from continuing to pull out his or her own hair. Cigarette burns, broken bones, and scars from knife cuts were ever-present. Not far behind were issues with attention deficit, anxiety, anger, and depression. The most difficult to comprehend were adolescent children who had STDs or were pregnant.

In one instance, an 11-year-old girl suffered from a multitude of problems, the worst being outbursts of rage. Her mother had been a beauty pageant queen who had killed herself by jumping off the side of a cliff, into an ocean. At the age of 5, this girl was left only with her father, who was addicted to heroin. After his wife's suicide, the father lived in anger and continually raped his daughter. He was eventually taken to prison, and then this child was sent to live with an aunt. There too, the pretty, innocent girl would be raped by her uncle. The extensive trauma and pain never left her. She cycled through a couple foster care homes before ending up here.

Her story was terrible, but it was just one of many. Each week, as I read the histories of the children, my heart sank. I knew what it was like to feel pain at an early age. When that innocence is taken from you, you become an open wound. You want to believe otherwise, but you can't help to see the entire world as a possible threat to you. You also begin to believe that you are helpless. That no matter what you do, you won't get anywhere in life.

Despite what I had experienced in my youth, I still felt loved and cared for. I also was fortunate to be a good student and athlete. Because I had those gifts, I realized that if I applied myself, I could be successful at anything and that I wasn't helpless.

However, these children were abandoned souls. Most of them couldn't even imagine the word *hope*. Most of them struggled with the simplest of tasks. They couldn't conceive of anything that was close to confidence. They were rattled and close to being broken. None of this was acceptable to me. I wanted to change their beliefs. I wanted to show them that there were people who loved them and would protect them. Above all, I wanted them to learn to believe in themselves and know that they could be powerful. I knew if their confidence grew, their courage would also grow. With those two elements, they could leave their past behind and build new lives for themselves, just as I had.

During my first few days working at the Hyslop Home, I was taught that ordinary household items could be used as a weapon and therefore needed to be kept under lock and key. Anything that had some weight to it, had sharp edges, or could be ingested was locked up. As such, most rooms on the three floors of the home were empty except for sofas, pillows, books, videotapes, and a television.

The court as well as the Children's Aid Society had many rules and parameters for these homes. I understood them. They meant well. They were trying to protect these very vulnerable children at a pivotal time in their lives. These children were burdened with so many problems that they were not allowed to go and explore beyond a certain distance of a supervising adult. Taking the group on a road trip with the public was possible but required the dexterity and diligence of the Secret Service guarding the president of the United States. Even on the best days, it was not common to go more than 30 minutes without having at least one child burst into a scream or engage in a fight. Trying to follow all the rules and keep the entire home corralled was exhausting, so most of the assistant child-care workers and employees had the children watch movies all day and all night long. It was the only time that most of them were quiet and calm.

I was new, and I was young. I followed orders, and I also followed the crowd. I watched movie after movie and then would write a report on each child at the end of each shift. Their individual stories were heartbreaking, but this sedentary and sedated pace of life didn't seem right to me. They were protected, but it felt like they were being further debilitated by not being more active and constructive so, at the risk of losing my job, I decided to take a different approach.

One Saturday morning, when no child-care workers or senior staff were around, I decided to get the kids more engaged in real-world activities. I was working with a colleague. At the beginning of the shift, I asked him if it was okay to try something different with the kids. He was easygoing and didn't have any issue with breaking up the typical routine.

I knew that they had previously suffered and struggled, but that was no excuse not to learn basic survival skills. I woke them up, helped them make their beds, and then announced to them that they were going to learn to cook and clean throughout the morning and afternoon. No movies today.

It took at least 20 minutes for the screaming, crying, and protesting to stop. What a mess. Some were kicking doors. Others were stretched out on their bed, sobbing. But most just stood in front of me yelling, "Why? Why? We're supposed to watch MOVIES!" And, one went even further, proclaiming "It's against the law to make us clean the house."

Thank Goliath

There was no turning back. I was committed. I didn't have my own children, but I knew if I gave into them now, they would never listen to me again.

We began in the kitchen. I unlocked the cabinets, bringing out knives, pans, and other possibly dangerous items. I showed them how to set a table, make eggs, cut bread, and even spread peanut butter. Eventually their mouths were full of food, but they continued to protest. "We're not doing anything else!"

Moving right past their complaints, we washed dishes and then it was time to do the laundry, iron clothes, and clean the windows.

This was a bridge too far for all of them. "LAUNDRY!" "WINDOWS! "WE'RE NOT ALLOWED TO USE THE IRON!"

Yup, today, all the rules were getting broken.

I divided them into groups, gave each one a task, showed them how to do it, and just kept coaching and encouraging them until everything was complete. In my mind, at a minimum, these children were going to learn how to take care of themselves. And, I knew, as they accomplished something new, their confidence would grow. As their confidence grew, so would their self-esteem. I knew that they couldn't control their outside world, but all these things were well within their reach.

Little by little, each task was completed, and all protesting had subsided. When we finished on the inside of the home, we went outside. I taught them how to trim bushes, pull weeds, and rake leaves. It was basic and simple, but it was getting their blood and minds moving. It was bringing a new life force into each one of them.

When I returned to work the next day, a handful of kids were already awake and out of bed. They ran toward me and competed for chores. "Can I make the toast today?" "Can I put the clothes in the washing machine?" Within one day of completing something on their own, they started to feel better about life. It wasn't a complete fix, but it was something positive that they could always return to and something that they could build upon.

The following Monday, the director of the home found out what I had done over the course of the weekend. At first, she was upset. Kids were asking for knives, window cleaners, and ironing boards. She saw danger and lawsuits in everything I had done. But, as the day progressed, she also saw that the children were calmer and happier than when she had last seen them.

I was fortunate that she was understanding. I was reprimanded, but she didn't fire me, and she allowed me to continue teaching the children in my own manner for the rest of the summer.

At the end of this first job with the Children's Aid Society, it was time to change gears and return to school mode. I was still desperate to get into the Applied Arts program. I knew that program would help me get better jobs in the future. Over the course of a few weeks, I wrote a report on what I had learned and brought it to the dean of the program. He wanted no part of me. Nor was he the least bit amused. He looked at me and said, "You're not in the program." I smiled and said, "Not yet. Please read my report and tell me what you think." He then added, "I can't let you in." Again, I smiled and said, "Not yet. Please just give me a chance." He shook his head and I said "I know you're busy. I'll come back when you have more time. Have a nice day."

I knew that I came across as crazy, but it was worth trying.

I was now in my second year of university. I had moved out of the campus dormitory and moved into a community of brand-new townhouses owned by the university. It was within walking distance of campus, and there were 100 free-standing townhouses.

It was 1987, three weeks into the new semester, on a cool, clear, September night. It was 1 in the morning, and I was by myself standing on a long, wooden plank, urinating into what was supposed to be my backyard.

I really was trying to be a gentleman.

I had visited two of my neighbors, hoping to use their bathroom, but they were in the same predicament as me—their toilets weren't working. So, instead of playing catch or football on a freshly mowed lawn, we were turning our collective backyards into a cesspool.

It wasn't just the toilet; it was a long list of broken or missing things. No hot water, no phone service, no mail service, kitchen cupboard doors falling off, missing furniture, missing doors, no sidewalks, locks not working. It wasn't supposed to be this way. These were built brand new; we were the first residents. We had signed the lease and had given four months of rent to the university the previous June. Worse still, we never saw anyone working or attempting to finish the work. Why wasn't everything finished?

Still stewing in my twilight toilet frustrations, I decided to write a letter to the editor of the school paper outlining what was happening here at Columbia Lake Townhouses. In the letter, I held the university solely responsible for the delays and suggested that they give back some of our money because we hadn't received what we'd paid for.

The next morning, I slipped my typed letter through the mail opening in the door of the school newspaper. I didn't give it another thought. I didn't think anything would happen. It just made me feel better to get it off my chest.

Three days later, they published the letter. My friends and I had a few laughs at my choice wording and just left the conversation there.

The next morning, I learned exactly how powerful a pen and piece of paper could be.

There was a knock on my door at the townhouse. I answered the door. In front of me was a man shouldering a camera and a woman holding a microphone. The woman said, "Are you Domenic Aversa? May we talk with you about your letter and your actions toward the university?" I smiled. "Sure. But I just wrote a letter. I'm not sure about what actions you are referring to." She continued, "I'm Linda Jones with WKABC. It's my understanding that you are going to petition the university for a refund and a protest rally is being organized. Is this accurate?"

I was too young and too naive to understand the implications of my words. I just wanted my toilet fixed so I didn't have to pee outside in the middle of the night. Clearly, I had learned nothing from the ransom note that I had written to my mother many years earlier. I should have known that carefully or recklessly placed words could make some people very, very mad. But I hadn't learned my lesson yet.

There I was, a teenager hamming it up in front of a video camera for a local television news station. "Yes, ma'am, we're asking the university to give back all our rent until the day they have everything complete. We shouldn't have to pay for something we haven't received. We have a contract with the university, and they haven't honored the contract. In fact, they should pay us lost interest on that money because they've had it since June, and they should pay us damages for all the stress we've had to endure. We can't cook, can't use our phones, can't use the bathroom, and we walk through the mud every day. How would the dean of housing like it if he had to walk through mud every day?"

Clearly, my time volunteering at the Legal Aid office had taught me a few things about law, but it absolutely did not prepare me for what was coming next.

That simple interview with a local television news outlet was relayed to their regional news office, which then ran the segment in the city of Toronto—the largest city in Canada. Once the Toronto news office ran the story, other news outlets throughout the province of Ontario ran the story. Newspapers and radio stations picked up the story and ran it as well.

Within a couple days, there were more reporters at my door. Protest rallies were being organized, parents of students were calling their lawyers, and those lawyers were calling the college. At the same time, the bondholders that had put up the money for these 100 new homes were calling their lawyers, and those lawyers were calling the college. Bankers and insurance policy holders for the college were calling their lawyers, and they, too, called the college. The college called the building contractors, and the contractors called their unions. The unions then called their lawyers.

Lawyers and lawyers and more lawyers. Threats of lawsuits swirled about. Jobs and careers were on the line. A lot of money could be lost. People were incredibly angry.

All this because I just wanted to pee in a civilized manner. Wow.

This had gone way beyond what I could have ever imagined, and now all I could hear was my mother's voice in my head: "Why do these things always happen to you? Why are you always in the middle of trouble?" I realized that I needed to try to help cool things down, but I wasn't sure how.

On my way to class that morning, I walked by the dean of housing's office. It was the same path that I walked every day. As I approached the building, I saw a big pile of dirt and mud in front of the office door. Someone had taken to heart my comments about walking through mud. They had gone through a lot of effort to dig up a pile of soil and turn it into mud so the dean and everyone else had to walk through it. I thought it was over the line, but then I looked down and saw my muddy boots—they had been that way every day for three weeks. I knew it was rude, but I also knew the university staff would survive and care a bit more about students.

Following this swarm of lawyers and flurry of protests, a small army of construction workers magically showed up in our subdivision within a couple days. Plumbers, electricians, carpenters, and landscapers all moved like busy worker bees.

Within two weeks, all the work was complete. All the rallies had ended. Threats of lawsuits subsided. Life went on as if nothing had happened.

But something did happen. A lot of stress and anguish got put into the air, and it still lingered.

Just as the work completed, the dean of housing had a stroke.

He recovered, but he had nearly died. The stress of what swirled around him had been too much. I'm not sure if I was to blame, but I still felt a sense of responsibility for my actions and words. I learned then that even when being honest and with good intentions, if your words and actions aren't carefully measured, a lot of people can get hurt. In this case, hundreds of people were helped by getting their housing problems resolved. However, at least one person was tipped over the edge. Some felt that he had it coming. I'm not sure that I agree with that sentiment. I was too young to know who actually was responsible for all the mess and delays. I just know that I shined a big light on all the issues and helped ignite the firestorm that ensued.

The best I could do with my life at this point was to continue disappearing into the library and work as hard as I could. I continued shadowing the Applied Arts program, and after a year of hounding the dean of the program, showing him my grades and giving him employment reports, he looked at me and said, "You are a pain in the ass. I didn't think you would stick with it, but you did. You're in." I worked so hard for so long and heard "no" every time I asked, so I wasn't sure what I was hearing. I replied, "In where?" He smiled and laughed. "You're in the program. Congratulations. You earned it. You're easily near the top of the class with your grades, and your reports are excellent. You deserve to be part of the program." I walked across the room and shook his hand, "Thank you, sir."

Three years had passed since I left Windsor. I still found myself stumbling or attracted to complex and troubling situations, but I was maturing. I was learning how our behavior can change any outcome. I now understood that we are our actions. What we do is who we are. Our words and conversations fill time and space, but actions create our life.

I also learned that persistence pays off. When the world keeps telling you "No," you have to find a way to keep pursuing your goals and dreams. My mother's actions helped manifest this behavior. She kept me busy. I was either working at some task around the house, at a job, or reading. By the time I got to university, I knew the path to success: Just keep working and learning—eventually you'll get there.

8

THINGS AT NIGHT

"A little bit of oil."
"Mom, I got the brochure for West Point."
"Don't put too much."
"The campus looks great."
"Is it warm?"
"Almost."
"When it's warm, put the garlic."
"Did you ever drive by West Point when you went upstate New York?"
"Why do you have to make your life more difficult? Put in the garlic."
"Mom, I want to try."
"Don't burn the garlic or it will be bitter. Put in the tomatoes."
"How much?"
"Enough."

"What's enough?"
"How much do you want to eat?"
"Should I put the whole jar?"
"If you want to put the whole jar, put the whole jar."
"Mom, I want to try. The cut-off for admissions is 22. I have a year before it's too late."
"Put some salt."
"How much?"
"Not too much."
"A tablespoon?"
"Less."
"Mom, Dad won't agree unless you agree."
"You can kill yourself when I'm dead."
"I'm not going to die. I'm going to get an education."
"Make sure it simmers. Don't boil it."
"How long?"
"Thirty minutes. Maybe 40. Sometimes a little more. Can even be 90 minutes."
"Your brother, your father, and half of dad's family were in the military."
"Just don't burn it."
"MOM."
"They had no choice."
"Mom, I'm applying."

And then, *click*. She'd hung up.

Once a week, I would call my mother while I was at school and ask for help learning her recipes. I missed her cooking. I knew I had to learn to do it on my own if I wanted to eat well when I wasn't with her. She was an excellent cook, but it took me so long to learn from her because she was terrible at communicating recipes. She rarely gave exact measurements, and she always forgot something.

On this evening, she was teaching me how to make a simple sauce with tomatoes she had picked and canned for me. We were also having probably the fifth conversation about me wanting to join the military. Men on both sides of my family had been in the military and had served on battlefields across Europe, Africa, Russia, and Vietnam. I wanted to share in that experience. I knew that I could survive in the streets, but I wanted to see how I would measure up to other strong, cunning, and brave men. I saw these men as men of courage and honor. They had bullets pass by their heads. They watched people die, sometimes up close and in their own hands. They left their homes and families to fight for a cause bigger than themselves.

The more I had learned about my family and their experiences in the military, the more I wanted to become a soldier. I desperately wanted to know what it felt like to climb that mountain. However, my mother had other thoughts. She refused to entertain the idea and forbid my father from giving me even the slightest bit of encouragement toward enlisting. So, I figured I could convince her by getting an education from a prestigious military academy like West Point. But she wanted none of it.

I had been very rebellious at times during my youth, but I was past that type of behavior. My mom was dealing with significant health problems. As a family, we still were unsure how long she had to live. There was always this looming uncertainty that hung over us. I concluded that she and my father didn't need more stress in their lives. I honored their wishes but kept hoping she'd change her mind.

Two hours after my mom hung up on me, my phone rang.

"How was it?"

"It didn't smell right."

"Did you burn it?"

"I didn't burn it."

"Maybe you needed more basil."

"Basil?"

"You didn't tell me to put basil."

"You have to put basil, especially at the end. It gives a nice aroma."

"You didn't tell me to put basil."

"I know. I'm sorry. It's okay. Remember for next time."

"Mom. I'm serious. I'm applying."

Click.

She'd hung up, again.

It was now the fourth month of the semester, and I hadn't secured my next job yet, but I had an interview that I was really looking forward to. I was excited for the chance to talk with them. I couldn't enlist in the military or enroll in one of their colleges, but I had discovered another way that might help me get some of what I wanted to experience.

I was the last interview of the day.

In front of me sat two career military officers: Col. Jim Brock and Lt. Col. Dave Harley. They were polished, clean-shaven, and sitting straight up in their chairs.

Col. Brock looked down at my resume and then back up at me. "You have absolutely no qualifications for this position. Why do you want this job?"

I was 21. I had been on other job interviews, but this employer was entirely unfamiliar to me. I wasn't sure how to dress for the interview, but I knew that I wanted to look "Canadian." At that time, my wardrobe looked very Italian. It was shiny and silky. It was perfect for weddings, funerals, and first communions but not job interviews with a private military academy.

I bought a navy blue, double-breasted blazer, taupe-colored pants, and oxblood shoes with a matching belt. I had my hair cut short, and I prepared a perfect Windsor knot with my royal blue tie. For good measure, I also went and bought a black Samsonite briefcase. I wasn't sure what to put in it, but I thought it was important to have.

I uncrossed my legs, looked back at Col. Brock, and said, "Sir, I've just always wanted to be part of the military." Lt. Col. Harley jumped into the conversation. "Well, why then haven't you enlisted?" I leaned back into my chair, dropped my shoulders, and sheepishly said, "My mom told me she'd kill me before any enemy bullet ever reached my head if I enlisted." He smiled and said, "God bless our moms."

Col. Brock continued, "Son, that doesn't change the fact that you don't have any experience for this position. The job requires a minimum of junior officer military experience. In addition to your teaching requirements, you will be overseeing a company of approximately 65 out of 130 students. We are a private military academy, but other than that we follow every aspect of military code and life. What makes you think you can do this job?"

"Sir, I'm looking for a challenge. I grew up around men that started out on the losing side of World War II. It wasn't fun to be a soldier in the Italian Army. Four brothers went to war. One in North Africa, one on the Russian front, one taken as a prisoner of war to England, and the last fighting through losing battles around Italy. All these men survived. My grandfather and his brothers were incredibly courageous and formidable. I'm certain they would have preferred to have never gone to war, but I feel…I feel like I missed out on something important. I think this job will give me a small entry into a life in the military that I might want to explore more seriously. Everything I learned, I learned from those brave men."

They nodded in unison. They looked at each other briefly and then turned back to me. Col. Brock said, "OK, you're hired."

I was stunned at how quickly they'd made their decision. I stood up, then walked over to them to shake their hands. Before I made it to the table, Lt. Col. Harley pulled out a three-inch-thick binder from his large messenger bag and handed it to me. "Here you go. This is our Academy code and book of rules. You need to learn everything in there as if you've lived it for 10 years. You will have the title of lieutenant. Do not tell anyone that you have zero military training; they will eat you alive."

This book was big and heavy. There were hundreds of extremely specific details. Now I started to worry.

Col. Brock continued, "Son, do you know how to spit shine?"

I paused. I had no idea what he was talking about.

He looked at Lt. Col. Harley as he shook his head. "He doesn't know how to spit shine."

Lieutenant Colonel Harley smiled and shrugged his shoulders. "You have three weeks to learn."

I stared at him. "Sir?"

He outstretched his arm and shook my hand. "Son, new semester starts in three weeks. You better look like a seasoned officer by then, or you will be unemployed on your second day. We're giving you the title, but the *respect* you have to earn on your own. Oh, and don't cut your hair so short. That's for non-commissioned officers—you're a lieutenant."

Col. Brock walked over to me and shook my hand. "Good luck."

Before he let go of my hand I asked him, "Sir, why did you give me this interview if you knew I didn't have any experience whatsoever?"

He smiled wide and said, "Because we wanted to see what kind of lunatic would do such a dumb thing. You'll fit in just fine."

And they walked out the door.

I didn't have a place to live outside of the academy, so I stayed with my parents during the holidays.

I spent the next three weeks doing little circles on my boots with shoe polish and a damp cloth, trying to perfect a spit shine. At the same time, I kept steaming and folding my beret, trying to make it look "seasoned" and full of "pride." The sharper the fold, the more pride you are believed to have.

I had to learn how to march on parade, work a sword, salute, train, and communicate in military terms. I just read and reread until I believed that I had learned everything.

The entire time, my mother just shook her head and asked, "Are you sure you know what you are doing?" I would nod and then resume my training. She wasn't against what I was doing because I was not officially enlisting but she kept a careful and close eye on me. I think she was emotionally preparing for that phone call where I would say, "I'm in. I'm shipping out tomorrow."

On January 2, 1989, I drove to Robert Land Academy. It was about four hours from my parents' home. It was about 30 minutes outside of Niagara Falls and was situated on 168 acres of farmland.

It was several degrees below freezing and snowing heavily. As evening came, one by one, the students returned. I was overseeing Alpha Company, which consisted of approximately 65 boys. Each one entered through the front door and stared at me, up and down, as they walked past. I knew better than to smile or make small talk with them. I kept my mouth shut and held a stern look on my face as I paced slowly up and down the halls.

Robert Land Academy followed strict military structure, but only a couple dozen students were affiliated with the Militia (Canadian Reserves) or would go on to join the actual Canadian Military. Most of the academy was filled with boys who came from wealthy families or from the streets and detention centers. They ranged from ages 15 to 21. Many were there under court appointment. They were criminals: crafty, strong, struggling, and looking for any opportunity to break the rules.

When I accepted this job, I initially thought I would be experiencing more of the high-flying, intense elements of military life. I thought I would be parachuting out of planes, firing machine guns, and running combat training missions. That would eventually happen, but first I had to live through the rigor of teaching and shaping young, defiant men, all day and all night. These boys were as resilient and delinquent as I had ever been. I wanted a challenge—here it was.

Lights were turned off at 10 p.m. It was 9:15 p.m., and there had been no drama. In 45 minutes, I could go in my room and lock the door, crossing the first night off my checklist. Before I could think another thought, a student ran by me at full speed, wearing only a T-shirt, pants, and socks, screaming as if his hair was on fire—as he jumped through an open window. There were no screens on the windows, so he just sailed through the open space as if he were diving into a pool. I ran to the window, and by the time I got there, all I saw was the faint outline of a boy running in the heavy snowfall. He continued screaming at the top of his lungs until I could no longer hear or see him. He just disappeared into the fields.

About 20 students looked at me as if to say, "What are you going to do about it?" But they said nothing. I stood there saying nothing as well. My brain was trying to process: *There's 168 acres of frozen farmland, the nearest town is 30 minutes by car, he's not wearing shoes and doesn't have a coat or hat—there's no way he's going to get far. For sure, he'll come back when he gets cold enough.* And that's where I left it. I looked at the students, shrugged, and said, "Lights out in 30 minutes." I then walked out of the room.

I'm not sure if that was the right protocol, but whether it was or not, the students sensed something was off. I think for that brief moment I looked like a deer in headlights and not an officer. And that's all it took for them to decide that they should test me.

"Lights out!"

I went into my room, shut the door, and waited.

In less than 30 seconds, the commotion started.

"Shit!"

Officer or not, I knew math. The math in this situation was 65 guys to one. You can be as tough as you want, but when you're outnumbered like this, you either better run and hide or come up with a really good plan.

I knew I couldn't just turn on the lights and tell everyone, "Shut up and go to bed." This was the wrong crowd for that song and dance. They would have laughed at me, and I'd be out of a job by midnight.

With each passing moment, they got louder.

It took me a minute, but I came up with a plan. Not sure if it was a good one, but I had to do something.

I took a deep breath. I opened my door. They heard it open and quieted down a bit. I left the lights off. I walked across the room and stood eye level with the top bunk bed of one of the biggest guys in the barracks. He was easily four inches taller than me and outweighed me by 30 pounds. He giggled as he stared at me. Without saying a word, I grabbed his mattress and pulled it toward me as hard as I could. With one big tug, the mattress and this dope came crashing down to the ground. He was still on top of his mattress. Before he could say a word, I grabbed his neck with my left hand and punched him in the head with my clenched right fist. I'm not sure if I hurt him. He had a skull the size of a boulder. I think I hurt my hand more than his head. Either way, I now put both of my hands around his throat to hold him down. He was clearly stunned and didn't move. The room was dead silent.

All the lights went on.

I looked around the room at what seemed to be a bunch of jackals. No one said a word. They just stared at me with narrowing eyes.

I stood up, brushed off my pants, and said, "Lights out."

I walked to my room, turned off the lights, and locked my door.

There was a 50-50 chance I would make it to the morning. I didn't sleep a minute. This night would set the tone for the next four months.

I made it through the evening, and now I had to begin the routine that would take place every morning for the next four months.

Every morning, I was scheduled to greet the company sergeant major at 7 a.m. Every morning, he would inspect the barracks and each student's appearance, bed, and locker. They could be reprimanded and punished for a wide array of infractions including having an unlocked locker or even bad breath—typically a sign that they did not brush their teeth that morning. My principal job in the morning was to wake everyone at 6 a.m. and have them and the facilities be polished perfect by 7 a.m.

It was now 6:20 a.m., and there was what appeared to be a naked, dead 16-year-old boy on the tiled floor of the showers, with water spraying on top of him.

Before I could take another step, another student jumped in. "Sir, he's not dead. Corporal Maurice likes to put guys in the sleeper hold when they're in the showers."

"Go help him up. Thank you."

I yelled down the hall, "Where is Cpl. Maurice?"

I turned around, and this student was standing a foot away from me and looking directly at my eyes with hardly a blink. I didn't even hear or feel him approaching. "Sir, you're looking for me?" he said without expression. "Are you Cpl. Maurice?" "Yes, sir." And then he moved a bit closer.

This was not a student. This was a soldier. He had a heavy, shadowed beard line and a thin mustache, one worn more typical of men many generations before him. His beret melted into his head as if he had served in the military his entire life. Not an ounce of fat on him. He was so tightly wound that there was no doubt he was just praying for a fight. He wasn't going to get one from me.

I looked at him with as little emotion as possible and said, "Don't choke guys in the shower." He smiled, said "Yes, Sir!" and walked away.

The next two weeks continued in this manner. Every day, there was an event, a challenge, or an escalation. They would challenge my authority more than others because I was the new guy. They would keep testing me until one of us gave up. In these first couple of weeks, I sent three boys to the hospital: two with dislocated shoulders and one with a mild concussion. In each instance, one of them would run at me, throw a punch at me, or try to tackle me. One of them was intoxicated on illegal narcotics that he had smuggled into the academy; the other two were developmentally challenged. They couldn't control their anger or behavior. Back then, we only had so many medications that we used in these circumstances, particularly at the academy. I'm fortunate that my many years of fighting helped me prepare for unannounced attacks.

After the third student returned from the hospital, the environment changed. I don't think they gave up. I think Cpl. Jean Maurice delivered a message to back off me or they'd have to deal with him. He was by far the physically strongest student in the academy. He was initially assigned to the school by the court because he had committed multiple felony crimes. Apparently, he enjoyed blowing up cars and trucks. I believe he had detonated explosives in more than 40 vehicles. He took a liking to me so, we became friends.

Cpl. Maurice was only a year younger than me, so there wasn't much I could teach him, but he did help me learn quite a bit about everyone else. He wasn't just a master with explosives and a brilliant observer; he was also a prolific thief. There wasn't a lock he couldn't pick. On a regular basis, he would break into the administrative office to read the files of other students and teachers. He knew everything about everyone, including me.

One night, deep into my sleep, I felt something against my neck, then my nightstand light went on. I tried to move but I couldn't. My legs seemed like there was a weight on them and I couldn't lift my head. I felt something cold firmly pressed against my throat. Looking straight up at the ceiling, an upside-down face came into view. It was Cpl. Maurice with a big smile. His head was hovering over mine. He then walked to one side of the bed, and whatever was on my neck was gone. He then held up his right hand to reveal a jackknife with a five-inch blade. I looked down the bed and saw that he had tied up my legs with blue climbing rope.

This was an assassin. He had broken into my room, tied me up, and put a knife to my neck, and I never heard a thing. I had double locks on the door and window. I also used to stack a couple of beer bottles on top of each other, next to the door, so I could hear them if they were knocked over by an intruder. He looked at me and said, "Have a good night, Sir," then walked toward the door and let himself out. He just wanted me to know that he could kill me at any given time.

I knew that I could never outsmart him. The only thing I could do as his teacher and as an officer was try to challenge him to help him grow in a less menacing and deviant manner. I gave him new and different books to read. I taught him about healthier diets and new exercise routines. Everything I presented to him he accepted and enjoyed.

Then one day, I decided to give him a challenge that would teach him that even he had limits in life.

Robert Land Academy was founded by Maj. Robert McPherson. He came from a long line of family members that had served in the military dating back to the early 1800s. He was a distinguished, intelligent, and generous man. I thought to myself, *No way Maurice will mess with him.* So, I dared Maurice to steal Maj. McPherson's watch from his nightstand at his home. Maurice smiled at me and said, "No problem, Sir."

The next morning, I woke up and on my nightstand was Maj. McPherson's watch. I couldn't believe what I was seeing. Not only did he break into his home and steal his watch from his nightstand while he was sleeping, but then Cpl. Maurice broke into my room when I was sleeping and put it on my nightstand! This was not the lesson I was hoping to impart on him.

I made him bring back the watch, even though it required him to break into the home, again.

Cpl. Maurice was interesting, but he was sideline entertainment in an otherwise serious environment. It was the academy's mission to bring structure and discipline into the lives of these young and often very troubled kids. Unlike my time at the Children's Aid Society, I wasn't just responsible for a dozen children at one time. Here at Robert Land, I had 65 teenage boys, some in their early 20s, for whom I was personally responsible. And, another approximately 65 in Bravo Company for whom I had indirect responsibility. These young men were physically trained every day. Most were strong, but many suffered from learning disabilities and psychological issues. I had to constantly be on the lookout for someone harming another student, themselves, or me.

The first of three suicide attempts I witnessed occurred about a month into the job. One of the cadets suffering from learning disabilities and depression broke into the infirmary, stole several different medications, and ingested them. A handful of cadets knocked on my door to tell me what had happened. It was nearing midnight. I found the boy on the floor of a stall in the bathroom. He lay there, eyes shut, wrapped around the toilet, motionless.

I stared at him, unsure at first of what to do. I had received no training on overdosing. The nearest hospital was 30 minutes away by car across many icy and snow-covered roads. I could see that he was still breathing. I told the other cadets to pick him up and bring him to the front of the barracks while I ran to the head office to get the keys for one of the academy's vans.

We loaded him into the back seat of the van, and I drove as fast as I could. I don't know what came over me, but I was angry. I started talking to him as if he was wide awake "Why are you trying to kill yourself? What is this going to accomplish?" I wasn't thinking about death, but at this moment, I became as irrational as my mother had been with me when I did dumb things. "I can't believe you tried to kill yourself. Why would you do this? You have a good life. Do you really want to die? If you want to die, then I'm going to show you how to die. Right after these doctors save you...I'm going to show you the proper way to kill yourself." I was rambling incoherently. Of course, I didn't want him to die, but emotions overtook me, and I couldn't find a way to be stoic and constructive in that moment.

We arrived at the hospital without any delays. They took him in immediately and pumped his stomach. By the morning, he was stable. I sat in the room with him. A long period of time passed before either of us said anything. I could see from his face that he was embarrassed and still carrying a heavy burden. I was only a couple years older than him, but I knew the expression on his face. It was one that I had worn many times. Reprimanding him would only push him further into despair. Now was the time to lift him up and give him something to look forward to experiencing. I asked him, "What can I do to help you?" He looked downward and shook his head. I knew he wasn't going to talk, but I thought he might listen if I kept talking.

"No one can stop you from killing yourself. If you want to do it, you will eventually do it. But no one can stop you from living either. It's your life. You can do whatever you want. I know you don't want to be at the academy. I know you have a hard time learning...but so what? Just get through it. Get out of bed every day and get through the day. Give life a chance. You're still young, and there are a lot of fun things to experience. Go explore. You're free to do whatever you want, but in the meantime, don't kill yourself on my shift. If I find you passed out again, I'm going to take your limp body and feed it to the neighbor's pigs. Do you want that? You want to be pig food? They will snort you up and devour you in less than 10 minutes. Then, when they slaughter the pigs, you're going to end up as somebody's ham sandwich. Is that what you want? It's your choice, but if you really want to be a ham sandwich, just spread mustard all over yourself and let some cute girls eat you up."

I knew I was being ridiculous, but at least now he had lifted his head up and had a smile on his face. Logic or inspiration hadn't worked, but humor got through to him, and that was enough to keep him moving forward.

This cadet did not try to kill himself again. He managed to carry himself through each day. Some days were happier than others. I think the pivotal turning point for him was when he saw me pick up another cadet from the bathroom floor. A boy who tried to overdose just like he had. I think he superimposed his own image in that situation and realized how ugly and unnecessary it was.

Most of the student body followed the rules and did well with the highly structured environment. They didn't like it, but they didn't fight it. However, there were a couple handfuls of cadets who seemed to always be in trouble. They struggled with their studies, disrupted classes, and acted out their frustrations. As a rule, punishment was some form of physical activity. When faced with a troubled student, officers, NCOs, and teachers would have the cadet do pushups or run laps around the parade square. Sometimes, they wouldn't give them a number for the laps; they would just tell them to run until they were ordered to stop.

For most people, this type of physical activity would be a sufficient deterrent. However, for some it was no punishment at all. Some had been punished so many times that they were in great physical condition. Some boys would run for hours in the evening, in the cold and snow, laughing the entire time. The more they laughed, the more laps an instructor would make them run. In the end, the one being punished was the instructor because he had to stay up supervising this one student running in the snow.

I understood many of these boys. I was just like them. They were being repeatedly told that they were "trouble." The more they were told, the more they identified themselves as misfits, rule breakers, and lone wolves. They wore the scorn and labels of delinquency as badges of honor. I knew this mindset, but I differed from this group because I always enjoyed learning and did well with my grades. I was fortunate; those good grades saved me from a permanent life of crime. However, many of these boys struggled in class. As a result, they naturally gravitated to what they were good at—being tough and being troublemakers. Punishing them with additional physical activity was futile and even damaging. These students were only getting in better shape with each punishment, yet at the same time they were falling further behind in their studies—which was the exact opposite of what we were trying to achieve. In my mind, they didn't need more punishment; they needed more challenge. They needed to be shown that they could continue to grow and learn in different and positive environments.

This was 1989. The Ironman Triathlon had begun about 10 years earlier and was gaining a wider audience throughout the world. I had only been at the academy for one month, but I thought this was the perfect incentive and challenge for the most struggling boys in the school. I approached the academy sergeant major and Maj. McPherson with the idea. They were both skeptical, fearing this would be an additional distraction to the cadets' studies. I assured them it would be the exact opposite. As a condition to participating in the first-ever Robert Land Ironman competition, they would have to maintain good grades, which meant they had to behave and not get thrown out of class. With this assurance, the supervisors gave me their blessing.

I opened enrollment for the competition to 20 cadets. I had strict rules for participants. For the next 12 weeks, they would eat, train, and study exactly what I told them. Any deviation would result in immediate expulsion from the competition. Most of the boys in the academy treasured their free time. They wanted no part of additional training and instruction. However, as I expected, the troubled bunch were looking for bragging rights. This was their new mountain to climb. Each one of them wanted to be known as the best and strongest physically conditioned cadet in the academy. All of them wanted that Ironman trophy and the pride that came with it.

The competition I designed consisted of a 15-mile run while wearing combat boots and a vest filled with 35 pounds of sand. Following the street run, they would portage a canoe two miles over countryside and then canoe upstream a river for five miles.

Once out of the water, they would portage the canoe another mile, then complete a full military obstacle course and run an additional three miles back to the academy.

I began the training with 20 students. Within a month I was down to 15. The next month I would be at 10. By the time of race day, I was left with five cadets. Some of the other officers and instructors thought the entire program was a big waste of time and energy. They didn't believe it was worth the effort to run a race with only five participants. I saw it differently. For me, even though 15 students dropped out along the way, I was able to push them to a new level of concentration for studying and thoughtfulness toward health than they had previously achieved. They studied more attentively. They ate a healthier diet because I eliminated sugar and junk food from their routine. And they learned to train with weights. Above all of these accomplishments, the morale across the entire academy also improved. Incidents of erratic or troubled behavior decreased significantly by the end of the semester.

The race was held on a Saturday so family and friends could attend. Five started the race, and five finished the race. As expected, the toughest of the tough, Cpl. Maurice, held the trophy over his head, finishing in first place.

I was proud of each cadet, but the one that left the biggest impression on me was a boy no one ever imagined could run five miles let alone this entire race. He was 16; his family was very wealthy. On holidays, his father would send a limousine and their butler to pick him up. Often, the limousine would drive him directly to the airport, and he would be flown to a professional sporting event, concert, or five-star vacation resort. In his privileged world, this cadet had grown to become a mouthy, pimply faced, overweight, obnoxious spoiled brat who spent most of his days picking candy out of the metal braces in his mouth. He wasn't mean. He wasn't a menace. He was just an annoying dork that came from a family with a lot of money.

He was constantly being disciplined because he was unkempt. His shirt would hang out of his pants, his pants weren't ironed properly, his boots were always scuffed, he was too lazy to bathe or brush his teeth with any effort, he doodled during every class, and he constantly wiped snot and saliva from his face and often re-wiped it on others. To any observer, this kid was just destined for a useless and meaningless future. He didn't care about anything. He didn't have to because his parents constantly bailed him out of trouble. And, if he caused serious trouble, they would just write a bigger check to the academy.

Despite all of these shortcomings, I recognized that he was still just a kid. He knew only the world he had been exposed to. I wanted to give him a chance to experience a different side of himself. So, when I organized the competition, I planted the seed in his head that he could win it. I told him, "You love sports. Why not be an athlete?" He was stunned. He looked at me with an expression on his face that said, "No one has ever called me an athlete." It was an unexpected notion. He wasn't talented enough to compete on team sports, but I thought that perhaps he could muster the energy to run this Ironman. He gave it some thought and then, surprisingly, jumped right into the program. It was awkward for him at first. He was a clumsy, slobbery mess, but he kept at it, getting better, stronger, more coordinated, and more determined with each training session.

He followed everything I told him to do for three months. He cleaned up his entire disposition, lost 30 pounds, and grew more confident, quiet, and polite. He carried himself in a sharper manner, and the other cadets showed him more respect. On race day, he was the second cadet to cross the finish line. His mother and sisters were in tears. They could not believe the transformation he had achieved in a matter of months. He then became a role model for his entire family.

At the end of the semester, Maj. McPherson offered me a full-time job on the academy staff. It was a great honor, but I realized it wasn't exactly the life I wanted to live. I sincerely enjoyed teaching and working with the boys. It was extremely rewarding to see them grow in confidence and self-esteem. However, beyond that, I learned that military life, when not engaged in a battle or war, is very monotonous. It's repeating many different functions every day. And that's by design. That structure helps prepare soldiers for the unpredictability of combat.

I respectfully declined the offer. I didn't get the exact challenge I had been looking for, but I did learn more about the power to inspire, teach, and change...even with the most unlikely of people.

Unfortunately, at the very same time that I was growing and maturing, my mother's health was again deteriorating.

Dr. Maletto eventually realized the scope of my mom's issues with her cyst were far beyond his skills, so he recommended an interventional radiologist. This radiologist had not seen many cases like this; therefore, the best he and his team could do was hypothesize an approach to helping my mother. Two years earlier, they had drained the liquid from the cyst. That procedure removed a significant amount of pressure on the internal organs. However, the cyst grew back and spread in several directions.

Facing a more complicated situation, my mother sought the help of another surgeon. Upon his review, he concluded that the best solution was to go in and cut out as much of the cyst as possible. At some point following the procedure, the extent of work and pain was just too much for her body. She slipped in and out of consciousness. The doctors struggled to keep her blood pressure up and her heart beating regularly. Her spirit would disappear right in front of us, and then it would come back. It was as if she was debating whether she should stay on Earth or slip away to someplace more welcoming and less painful.

One early evening, I walked into her hospital room and my mother was singing, "Fa la ninna. Fa la nanna," the same lullaby she sang to me as a child. Her arms and head gently swayed to the left and right. I stood back and watched for a few minutes and then in a soft voice, said, "Hi, Mom." Without opening her eyes my mother said, "Come in. Come closer. I'm here with Nonna Teresa and Nonna Giovanna. We're singing."

Apparently, both of my grandmothers had decided to visit my mom and keep her company. Seems like they were there in spirit, because they lived in different cities and in different countries—they certainly were not there physically. I didn't see or feel their presence, but I certainly thought it could be possible. For as much as I didn't like attending Sunday mass as a child, I did pay attention to some elements that were taught. I knew that we were spiritual souls before we were in human skin and that we were on Earth to help one another. My mother was in need, so the two mothers she had came to comfort her.

From that point forward, I learned that help could present itself in many forms, often in an unexpected manner. My mom always kept an open mind and was willing to be healed by anyone and anything that would come to help her.

Soon thereafter, my mom stabilized and was able to return home within several weeks. Now, with most of the cyst removed, she hoped that life would return somewhere close to normal. Unfortunately, her time in the "normal" world was short-lived. Her discomfort grew. She began to experience constant nausea, vomiting, shooting pains, high fevers, and infections. Over the next year, more specialists were visited. One of the best pancreatic specialists in the country proposed a surgery to remove as much of the obstruction as possible and then reconstruct the bile duct. The surgery was successful, but the surgeon didn't see that there was now a tumor growing on the head of the pancreas.

He stitched her back up, and she resumed living in extreme discomfort, exhibiting signs of severe pancreatitis. They had not seen the tumor, so none of the doctors could pinpoint what was happening to her.

Having no answers for her ill health, my mom decided to live with the pain and tried to make the best of each day. When it was too uncomfortable for her to be on her feet cooking or baking, she would sit and knit. Knitting helped fill her days and distract her mind from any negative thoughts. She knit so much that at one stretch of time, she decided to knit every nephew and niece a sweater. In total, she knit 25 sweaters for them, all with a label on the back collar that read "Handmade by Benedetta Aversa." She then moved on to knitting for friends, neighbors, and charitable groups.

Once everyone within her reach had a sweater, she moved on to scarves and socks. Once the feet were covered, she began knitting blankets for newborns and children. Across many cities and countries, everyone knew that Betty was thinking about them. She would knit for hours on end. As my father read the newspaper and watched television, she would sit a few feet away from him, propped up by a pillow for her back, the *clickety-click* of the knitting needles rattling nonstop. Many nights, she would knit until midnight. If she made one mistake, she would undo the entire piece and start over. In her mind, she didn't see the point in giving a gift that was anything but the best she could give.

While my mother was busy with one thing, I was busy with another. Neither of us had idle hands.

For the next year, I put my head down squarely into my books while at university. When I was on a work semester, I took extra courses by correspondence and studied for the Law School Admission Test. I now was certain that I wanted to go to law school, but I knew it wasn't an easy path. There were only 16 law schools in Canada. Getting admitted to one of the better schools was difficult.

However, by 1990, my schedule of alternating going to school for four months and working four months in the Applied Arts program helped me accumulate approximately two full years of work experience, which gave me a competitive resume. I felt better about my chances of acceptance, but it was still a great unknown, and thousands of people were competing for a small number of spots. I had one semester to complete for my Applied Arts degree, but I had taken the LSAT and scored reasonably well, so I decided to send out applications to half a dozen law schools. It was a long shot because I didn't have a completed degree, but I thought I would try anyhow.

In the meantime, I had accepted a position for the next semester with a multinational insurance company in Toronto. The job was in finance. I had absolutely no knowledge of finance, but I knew that I should learn about it so, again, I found someone who was willing to hire me based on pure enthusiasm and no experience.

As I packed up my apartment on my last day in Waterloo, my mother called me.

"Dom."

"Mom."

"It's your mother."

"Yes, Mom, I know it's you."

"I know but just in case."

"Just in case I forget that you're my mother?"

"You never know. It could happen."

"Why are you calling? Are you OK?"

"I just wanted to tell you something."

"OK, tell me."

"Something came for you in the mail."

"What is it?"

"It's from the University of Windsor, Faculty of Law."

"Really? So soon? I wasn't expecting it for at least another month."

"Do you want me to open it?"

"I don't know. If it's coming this soon it can't be good news. I don't even have the results from this semester's exams."

"Well, I already opened it."

"You opened my mail?"

"I'm your mother—I can open your mail. Anyway, you don't have to worry."

"Worry about what?"

"You don't have to worry about getting accepted. They accepted you."

"Really?"

"Congratulations."

"I wouldn't have studied so hard if I knew they were going to let me in this soon."

"You keep studying. You did a good job. Your father and I are very proud of you."

"You already told Dad?"

"Of course, he's your father. Anyway, can I tell other people?"

"Why do you need to tell other people?"

"Just a few people. Just because it's a nice thing."

"OK, sure. I have to go. I will call you later."

In the next couple of hours my mother phoned family and friends in three different countries. If she could have put up billboards and taken out television commercials, she would have. She finally felt a sense of relief. She managed to get her son all the way to law school. Her son, the very kid who many had believed would be dead or in jail long before he entered law school. Countless sleepless nights she had endured, worrying whether I would make it home or not.

But now things were different. She felt like she had succeeded as a mother. I was the first person on both sides of the family to go to law school. She could hold her head high and brag to her friends about her scholarly and mature son. She had waited a long time for this moment. I knew that everywhere she went, when she would meet up with all those hawkish homemakers that had scorned me and friends of hers that had boasted about their wonderfully behaved and perfect sons, she would be serene and nod her head thinking, *See, my son's not a troublemaker. He's a good boy who listened to his mother.*

My mother was also happy for another reason. She knew that I would be moving back to Windsor. It wasn't that she necessarily wanted me in the same city as her, but she did want me to be living closer to my new girlfriend. My mother was celebrating my law school admission, but I knew her. She was already on to her next mission: getting me married and getting her grandchildren.

At this point, Amy and I had been dating about eight months. She lived in Windsor and was attending business school at the university. My parents liked Amy. My entire extended family liked Amy. It was difficult to find someone who didn't like her. She was a beautiful woman with a classic hourglass shape; straight, light brown hair in a soft bob cut; flawless ivory skin; and crystal blue eyes. She was athletic and intelligent. She had an easy and agreeable demeanor. She paid attention to others. She kept a calendar of everyone's birthday and wedding anniversary. Always ready with a card, special note, and a gift for family and friends. Outwardly, she was perfect in most regards. However, like many of us, she had her own private struggle.

Amy and I knew each other from high school. She was a year younger than me. We briefly dated when I was 17, during my hellacious days. She broke up with me, offering little explanation. I was certain it had something to do with the way I drove and how I obeyed very few laws. However, I later learned it had little to do with me and more with her own health.

The world didn't understand much about anorexia and bulimia in 1984. I certainly knew little of eating disorders. I just knew that Amy had been hospitalized for a brief period when she was 16 and had sought help from a therapist. Now, six years later, she seemed fine. She said it was in her past. Like me, she had a rough patch as a teenager, but today was a new day and we were as happy as could be.

9

SACRIFICE

"Hello?"

"It's your mother."

"Mom, why are you phoning my office?"

"Because you won't answer your door."

"I'm not answering my door because I told you when it's locked, it means I'm busy."

"I just need one minute of your time."

"Mom, I have a lot to do."

"I'm your mother."

"What do you need?"

"Can you help me with this algebra problem?"

"No."

"It's just one problem."

"Ask Dad. He's good at math."

"I already asked him. He said to ask you."

"I have a stack of books in front of me. I have another 400 pages of reading to do tonight."

"I know, but it's just one problem."

"Sorry, Charlie, you have figure it out yourself."

"You're not nice."

"I think you should bake some cookies for your teacher."

"I tried that. He's not too friendly. He doesn't care about the cookies."

"Make him a lasagna."

"I tried that too."

"Looks like you have a real problem."

It was 1990, the fall of my first semester of law school. In the previous year, I made a deal with my mother that if I got accepted into law school, she would have to go back to high school. My mother loved learning, but when she met my father, she knew she would need money to get married, so she dropped out of high school. She still needed two years of schooling to graduate. I knew this could take longer than two years, but I also knew this was important to her. She loved learning. Every so often, over the previous years, she would lament not having finished high school. I knew she wanted to do it and all she needed was a nudge to take the first step.

Of course, there were some friends and family who wondered why she would go through so much trouble at her age and with all her health issues.

Some people looked at her and only saw illness. They focused on her medical history and worried how long she would live. In their eyes, the problem grew as time passed. But my mother chose a different perspective. She tended to shrink obstacles. For her, the health issues were just things that were annoying, not much different than flies and mosquitos in the kitchen. So, with this mindset, she held true to her word. Twenty-five years after she dropped out of high school, she took on the challenge, enrolled in the Adult Learning Center, and quickly began her first semester with three courses.

When I decided to move back to Windsor, my sister got accepted to university in another city. With her away, I knew there would be two empty bedrooms in my parents' home. I thought I could move back in with them. After four years of living on my own, I knew that it might be a dramatic change, but I thought, *How bad could it be?* I could save money, be comfortable in my old bed, and not worry about anything else other than studying. I just needed to make a few adjustments, and all would be well.

My parents had a lot of friends, a big family, and were very active in the community. There were always a lot of things in motion in their home. The phone started ringing at 7:30 a.m. and didn't stop until 9 p.m. People visited all day long. There was a knock on either the front door or back door by 8 a.m. and the knocking continued through the entire day until 8 p.m. Every day was the same. Ringing, knocking, ringing, knocking. It was like living somewhere between a bus stop and a customer service desk. I knew all of this in advance. I knew it was not a quiet place. For my move to work, I would need my own space and a soundproof room; otherwise, I would never be able to study. So, the month before classes started, I converted our childhood playroom in the basement into an office.

My father and I put up the walls and door. To keep the sound out, we double insulated every inch of the framing. Then, as we put in the new ceiling, my father looked carefully around the room and asked, "Are you sure that you don't want a window?" "No,

Dad. I'll be fine. I don't want any distractions." He shook his head in disbelief. "But you need oxygen." I smiled because compared to the insect-infected, smelly, noisy, tiny dumps I had studied in for four years, this room was paradise. "Dad, I'll be fine." He was still unsure. "At least let me put in a fan for you to ventilate the air outside. It will get the air moving so you're not completely suffocating." I thought it was a good idea. "Sure. But let's make sure it's a really loud fan. This way it will help soundproof the room."

To make me feel like I had more of my own space in their home, we installed a separate phone line into the office. I then filled every square inch of this 8-by-12-foot office. Filing cabinets, fax machine, stereo, stationary bike, weight bench, punching bag, and a big map of the world. I installed a brown carpet and painted the walls dark green. I wanted to feel like I was in a forest and every day was going to be an exploration. I didn't need a window; I had my imagination. I was now ready to climb ladders and go succeed. At what? I wasn't entirely sure. I just knew that I wanted to be great. However, the bigger challenge now was my mother. She couldn't stop being a mother.

My mother meant well, but she could not leave me alone. She was constantly knocking on my door or calling me. Ringing, knocking, ringing, knocking.

If I didn't answer the door or phone, she'd wait until I'd go to the bathroom...and then she'd knock on the bathroom door. I could turn on the bathroom fan and the shower and flush the toilet, and she would *still* try to talk over them through the locked door.

"I JUST HAVE A QUESTION."

"MOM, I CAN'T HEAR YOU."

"A QUESTION. JUST ONE QUESTION FOR YOU."

Thank Goliath

"I'M IN THE BATHROOM. CAN I JUST GO TO THE BATHROOM IN PEACE?"

Silence.

Finally, she was gone.

Ten minutes later, I would open the door and sure enough, she was waiting.

"You're so impatient."

"What's your question?"

"Your father's friend invited us for dinner tomorrow night. Do you want to come with us?"

"That's your burning question?"

"They have to know how many to cook for. It's just a simple question."

She was right—it was a simple question. But it was never about the complexity of the questions. It's that most of the questions always revolved around the same subject—food.

Every day, there was a knock on my door or a call on my phone with a question about food:

"Are you hungry?"

"Did you eat?"

"When do you think you will be hungry?"

"When do you want to eat?"

"What did you eat?"

"What do you want to eat?"

"Should I make something for you?"

"Do you want to eat with us?"

"Do you mind if I invite other people to eat with us?"

"Do you want to try what I made?"

Every day, I was surrounded by questions, discussions, and the smell of food. I couldn't escape it. Our house, while small, was like that of many immigrant Italians—it had two kitchens: one upstairs and one downstairs. My new office was less than 20 feet from the downstairs kitchen. When my mother wasn't asking me about food, she was making it. She liked to share, so she cooked in big quantities. Most days, in between classes at the Adult Learning Center, both ovens were running for hours. Even with all her ailments and frequent nausea, fevers, aches, and pains, somehow, she managed to pull herself out of bed and find something new to cook or bake.

Making things more indulgent, a couple feet in the other direction from my office was our cellar. The cellar that contained all the homemade wine, prosciutto, capocollo, and sausages. Between the cellar and the kitchen, I was surrounded by the smell of wine, cured meats, pasta sauce, pastries, and cakes—every day, all day. All of it was tempting, but all of it was also distracting. My brain was in a constant battle between logic and food. It had to make decisions of either reading about hundred-year-old property laws or eating fresh manicotti and roasted peppers with a glass of Barolo.

Other than my mother asking for help with her homework and hounding me with food, I had nothing to complain about. It was good to be home. Living with them, time passed quickly; however, at the end of my first year of law school, I had grown disillusioned with the notion of practicing law. I enjoyed studying law. I was fascinated how laws came to be, how they evolved and how societies were built around them. However, I wasn't convinced about the life of a lawyer, much of which was spent at a desk, arguing over words and sentences while billing as many clients as possible.

It just didn't seem fulfilling to me. So, I went looking for something new.

I came across a flyer on a bulletin board advertising a program studying the implications of having a common European Market (the EU), which would go into effect in 1992. It was a joint program between the University of Manchester, England, and the Moscow Institute of International Affairs, Soviet Union. I knew nothing about any of these places or about any common business market, but I figured that it was far away and that it was different than law, and it was just a summer program, so I would try it.

Without much planning, in July of 1991, I found myself in Moscow, USSR. The Soviet Union was fascinating. It was big and sprawling. Rows and rows of buildings. The city was bigger and more imposing than anything I had seen prior. However, there was an element to it that was unsettling. No matter where I turned, the city felt distant and closed off. Prior to this trip, I knew next to nothing about Russians or communism. What I did know came from the evening news or movies like *Top Gun* or *Rocky IV*.

I'm not sure what I expected to see when I arrived in Moscow, but I should have had a clue while I was in Manchester. Before we left England, the Russian students filled multiple suitcases with toiletries such as toothpaste, soap, shampoo, lotions, and creams; ordinary and basic items that we can find at any pharmacy or grocery store in the United States. I found it a bit odd, but I thought they just wanted things they couldn't find in their country. However, now that I was in Moscow, I realized that they couldn't find *any* products. None. The few stores that I did come across were barren. It wasn't only the stores; the entire city seemed like a ghost town. There were people and many buildings, but everyone and everything seemed to be shadows of themselves. There was only a whiff of spirit and soul. There was little color and no advertising or neon signs. In every direction were endless rows of large, cement buildings.

As I walked around, I noticed that the city was spotless. Then it dawned on me that it was so clean because there was nothing to throw away. There were no bags, paper cups, or candy bar wrappers. I walked past an open plaza. I saw 30 people lined up in front of a vending machine. As I got closer, I stopped to watch a very unusual process. When people reached the vending machine, they put in a coin and pressed a button, and water would come down into a five-ounce glass. They would swirl the water around and then throw it out. They'd place the glass back down and press another button, and the glass would be filled with Pepsi. They drank their soda and left the glass for the next person. They were so poor that there was a shortage on materials like tin and glass. I just stared and wondered, "This is a superpower? We were afraid of these guys?" Later I would come to understand that there was good reason to fear them; they spent 35 percent of their GDP on military expenditures as compared to the United States, which spent about 5 percent of their GDP.

Meanwhile, the citizens walked around with "just in case" bags. There were so few products in the stores that they bartered for anything they needed. To accommodate a possible purchase, they always carried a bag "just in case" they found something to buy or trade.

My school program was being offered by one of Moscow's top academic institutions. MGIMO, as it was known, was reserved for the best and brightest of high-ranking Soviet Party members. As such, we were treated very well. Each night, we were offered their absolute best in dining and entertainment. Their music showed signs of life from their rich and dramatic history. Unfortunately, however, their food options couldn't hide the ugly reality of the poverty running through the country. Each meal consisted of butter, pumpernickel bread, and a small piece of fatty, over-cooked beef. That was their best, so I was grateful. Fortunately, there seemed to be no shortage of caviar and vodka. I had never tried caviar prior to this trip, so I wouldn't know how to distinguish good from bad. I only knew that it was some semblance of food and that there were three-pound tins on every table. I'm not sure if I was hungry or legitimately interested but I enjoyed it. In a short while, eating it became second nature to me.

Our accommodations were as drab and desolate as the rest of the city. My room had the added benefit of being absolutely infested with cockroaches. There were so many roaches that they were pouring out of the sink and bathtub drains. I could not turn on the water without having dozens of cockroaches come pouring out. It was a disgusting stream of black, shiny, creepy-crawly things racing to save their lives. It was intolerable. In a desperate attempt to have some semblance of peace when I slept, I bought several bottles of vodka to use as a disinfectant. The vodka smelled and tasted like pure rubbing alcohol. I would periodically wipe down all the walls and floors just to keep them off me and my clothes.

Most nights, to avoid going back to my room, I would stay at the restaurant. One night, after having drunk a little too much, I found myself on the subway with a couple of my classmates. They were from South Carolina, and they loved Jimmy Buffett. Being young and happy, we were having a fun time singing "Margaritaville" on the train ride back to our dormitory. I hadn't noticed those standing around me or others seated, but they were paying attention to us. Unannounced, an old man in a ragged gray coat rose from his seat and lunged at me with a long knife. I didn't see him until he was a couple of inches from my chest. Fortunately for me, one of my new friends was an ex-Marine. He saw the old man and pulled me out of the way at the last minute.

The old man sat back down, grumbling something in Russian. I looked at him and said, "I'm sorry." He had tried to stab me in the chest with a five-inch knife, but somehow, I felt like I had it coming to me. I felt bad for him. I could sense that there was some greatness that had once existed in Russia, but now it was gone and now there were talks about another revolution and taking down all remnants of the Soviet Empire. A cultural, political, and economic change was coming, and it seemed very promising to many people but not to all.

For some, like this older gentleman, it meant erasing everything he had ever known. He and others like him thought, *You told us we were the greatest, then why do we have to change?* Now, in front of him, instead of a quiet ride home on a subway, he had to listen to young idiots singing songs he didn't know and didn't want to know.

The program ended, and I left Moscow not really knowing what to make of it. A few weeks later, a first coup attempt was launched against the government. Boris Yeltsin sent tanks into Red Square. By the end of the year, the Soviet Union was dissolved, and it was replaced with a democratic and capitalistic model of government under the name Commonwealth of Independent States (CIS).

Soon thereafter, I was back in Canada when I received a telephone call from one of my Russian classmates. He asked me if I would help him start a business. He really didn't know what type of business to start; he just knew that he wanted to be a "capitalist."

He presented me with a wide range of options: aluminum, oil, cars, furs, and bee pollen. It was exciting because it didn't seem like there was a limit to the possibilities. However, what was clear was that the country needed many things. They needed every consumer item for the home, but they also needed to rebuild their infrastructure. They needed electricity, roads, garbage removal, and gas stations. After a long and positive conversation, I ended by telling him, "This is all great. I just need to think about a few things."

As much as I didn't like the idea of practicing law, in my mind, it was guaranteed employment, and financial freedom was what I had been chasing for a long time. I was determined at a minimum to finish law school. Though this opportunity with the Russians sounded interesting, I didn't know where it would lead. It could be a big waste of time.

I spent the next two months thinking and looking for answers. I received advice from several senior attorneys and academics who helped me reach a decision. Each of them believed that this was a once-in-a-lifetime opportunity. That I would be participating in a pivotal moment in history when the Soviet Union collapsed, and new and free democracies would emerge. All of that sounded monumental, but I would be starting at the bottom again. I had worked my way up the academic mountain, and now I would have to start at the bottom of the business world—a world that was completely unknown to me. I was taking a huge risk walking away from a career in law, but at the same time I had almost nothing else to lose. I had about a thousand dollars in my bank account and a couple of department store credit cards with a $500 limit.

In addition to having little money or credit, I also didn't understand the place where I would be starting my business. I didn't speak Russian, and I knew almost nothing of communism or Russian history. Similarly, my potential partner and his friends knew nothing about capitalism.

Further complicating the situation, the Russian currency, the ruble, was not convertible on the open market; it could only be used in their country. Any money we made there would have to stay in the country, or we would have to buy goods with it and sell them in another country to generate cash that could be used globally.

However, by far, the biggest obstacle I faced was that I knew nothing about starting or running a business—any business. I had no formal or practical business education other than a couple courses in economics. I had not even taken accounting or finance courses. My father owned a small garage, but I didn't know much beyond fixing cars and pumping gas. He had an accountant handle all of the bookkeeping. Despite all of this, I still decided to give it a chance. If this was truly a once-in-a-lifetime opportunity, then I couldn't let my lack of experience or knowledge get in the way of my dreams for a better life.

While still attending law school full-time and working part-time at the Children's Aid Society, I spent the next couple of months trying to figure out how to start a business and how to get paid. I spent countless hours in libraries combing over textbooks and phone books. I researched everything I could and called anyone that might be able to help me start an international business. I knew that I needed money, so I visited a lot of bankers. I told them that I wanted to start a company and asked if I could borrow money to do so. They asked me about my collateral. I wasn't sure what "collateral" meant because the only thing that I owned were milk crates full of books and a duffle bag of clothing. I had been in university for five and half years at that point, and I had just enough money to get by. Many of the bankers laughed at me and my prospects of succeeding, but a few had sympathy. I asked them for advice, and they'd say, "Do what you know." I was 24, and the only thing I knew from being a student was pizza and beer.

After exploring countless options, I took what seemed to be the easiest path—I listened to the bankers. I decided to export beer, meat, and cheese from North America to Russia. It was 1992. It was a period of time in Russia when there were long lines for bread and any kind of food. People were starving, so it seemed like a good place to start.

The next challenge came in trying to figure out how we would buy this product. My contacts in Russia only had access to rubles, and that currency was only valid within their country. We explored various kinds of barter scenarios, but no one was interested. American beer companies didn't want to be paid in bee pollen—they wanted U.S. funds.

Months had passed, and we still couldn't figure out how to buy any product with rubles and bartering—it was just too complicated and was taking too long. It felt like we weren't getting anywhere. I was young, I had a lot of energy and could work long hours but now it felt like we were at the end of the road. I was ready to walk away from this experiment. Finally, I said to my counterparts in Moscow, "If you want to do business here, you need to get me American dollars. I don't care how you do it, but that's the only way." I hung up thinking that was the end of my entrepreneurial adventure. However, two weeks later, I received a fax from my partners in Russia that stated, "Check your bank account. Please tell us the amount of the wire that you received." I went to the bank, and I was stunned. In my account was a deposit of $200,000. It was incredible. That account had never seen more than a couple of thousand dollars in all my years as a student.

Money in hand, I was now ready to move quickly. I thought it would be fun to spend $200,000, but it turned out to be a huge pain. I struggled to get anyone to sell anything to me. I called company after company. As soon as they heard my name and "Russia" they would hang up. By this time in the economic cycle, there was a mad rush of companies trying to ship products to the former Soviet Union. Many were trying, but many would fail, principally because of rampant theft and fraud. In the eyes of older businessmen, I was just a kid. They assumed there was no way I could be legitimate; I was either a con or I would *be* conned.

I decided to try another approach. It was time to be bold. I put on a suit and tie, grabbed my briefcase, and drove to a food distributors' office in Detroit. It was located in a very rough part of town, and all of the crime associated with the crack cocaine epidemic was at its peak. This warehouse was surrounded by barbed wire, guard dogs, and security men. It was common that employees holstered guns to protect themselves. Getting mugged was a regular occurrence in this part of the city. If I showed the least bit of indecisiveness, they wouldn't give me the time of day.

The receptionist was seated in a bulletproof glass case. Through the vent in the glass, I asked to speak to the head of sales, Michael. She asked if I had an appointment with him. I knew if I said "no," I would be asked to leave…so, I lied. "Yes, I have an appointment. My name is Domenic Aversa." She looked up and down her appointment schedule and didn't see my name. I said, "It must be a mix-up." She put her head down and continued to look for my name. I took a deep breath and thought, *I'm going for it.* I looked down the hallway at the security guard standing in the corner. He was holstering a very big gun and an even bigger nightstick. I looked at him, nodded my head as some sort of expression of agreement, and walked straight toward him. The receptionist raised her head and said something, but the bulletproof glass muffled the sound. It didn't matter; I was moving fast. I was in dress shoes, and my only thought at this point was that I wouldn't be able to outrun the security guard chasing me with that big, black nightstick. I reached the security guard, gave him a stern look, and said "hey" and then went through the next door. I just figured that I would keep walking until someone threw me out.

At each corner, with authority, I would ask, "Where's Michael's office?" Someone always diligently pointed toward a spot farther down another hallway. After three turns, I walked into a very large room with approximately 30 desks, all facing forward. Salesmen were seated at each desk and were on the phone trying to hustle and sell meat. Every kind of meat possible; chicken, pork, beef, and every other creature that walked or flew. The back wall had a big white sign on it with a picture of a stout but cute pink pig. The caption on the sign read "We sell everything but the squeal." These were seriously aggressive salesmen and I liked them. They were making money.

There was a rapid, frenetic, and angry din to the entire room. Phones and desk drawers were constantly being slammed. Profanity rang through every conversation. I stopped at the first desk and asked the salesman where I could find Michael. Without saying a word, he pointed to the front of the room.

Standing behind a big oak desk, there was a slender, middle-aged, average-height guy talking into one phone with another phone slung over his other shoulder. He spoke in a low tone in short and fast bursts. All I heard was, "No." "Is that it?" "Just do what I'm telling you." "I don't care if you don't want to be my customer. That's the price."

He looked miserable and mean. It's as if he was just waiting for an excuse to take your head off. As I approached his desk, I saw that he was holstering a gun on his belt on his left hip. I slowed my pace, stopped directly in front of him, and just stared at him. Still on the phone, he looked at me, up and down. We were both dressed in blue, only he in jeans and me in a suit. His expression then turned to somewhere between contempt and disgust. Without further examination or delay, he cupped his hand over the receiver and asked, "Can I help you?" I replied, "Yes. I would like to buy some meat from you." He gave me a scowl, then looked away and returned to his phone. I shook my head in disbelief. How hard could it be to spend money?

I pushed aside the papers he was looking at on his desk with my hand, put my briefcase down, opened it, pulled out a cashier's check for $50,000, handed it to him, and asked, "Is this enough?" He put down both phones and just continued to stare at the check. He was dumbfounded. I said, "It's real." And he said, "Oh, I know. I just don't know who you are. What kind of lunatic walks around this neighborhood with a $50,000 cashier's check?" I then told him who I was, and he responded with, "Oh, the Russia kid. Where did you get the money? Are you a gangster?" I smiled and said, "My grandmother left it for me. What do you care where I got the money? Do you want to sell me meat or should I go to your competitor?" Without missing a beat, he said, "Have a seat, kid. I will sell you whatever you want."

And this is how my life went for the next year—fast.

I divided my time between my business and school. Each night, I would call my partners in Moscow generally around 9 or 10 p.m. and we would discuss business matters until 3 a.m. Then, I'd go to bed and get up and go to classes around 8 a.m. It was an intense period of time, but everything came together better than expected.

Within months, our company had grown at a rapid pace. We soon started a finance company and a real estate construction company. Shortly thereafter, we had a license to own and operate a commercial bank. We were selling food across most of the former Soviet Union, and we were developing one of the first subdivisions to be built outside of Moscow.

In a brief period of time, my life grew big, wide, and faster than I could have ever imagined. I was no longer poor and no longer constrained by anyone or anything.

Despite this success with my business, I continued to live with my parents. I now had a formal business office in Michigan and another in Moscow, but I felt most comfortable working in my parents' basement. I was doing business in multiple countries, but I was learning much more about the world from my mother and our family.

My mother had a terrific memory and was in constant conversation with everyone she met. People loved talking with her because she was a good listener. The phone receiver was constantly wedged between her ear and shoulder. She had two extensions—one from the wall to the base of the phone and another from the phone to the receiver. It was such a long extension that she could cook in the upstairs kitchen and downstairs kitchen at the same time and never have to put the phone down. Nothing got in between her and her phone. If she watered the garden, she was on the phone. If she was knitting, she was on the phone. Laundry, sweeping, ironing, and even sometimes vacuuming, she was on the phone.

I listened to her talk throughout the days and evenings. When something intrigued me, I'd ask her about her conversation. She never held anything back. Most times she'd begin her answer to me with "Don't say anything, but..." And, then she'd give me an entire history on whomever she had been speaking with and whatever they were going through at the moment. My mother didn't gossip. She kept secrets and respected privacy, but she did share a lot with me. She and I were now becoming friends, and she was still teaching me about life.

I knew many of the people she spoke with and spoke of, but they had always been two-dimensional people to me. I would exchange "hello" and "goodbye" with them, but I never really took time to learn about their lives. My mother, however, did take the time. As the years passed, she shared with me hundreds of stories, always in detail. To her, each person was unique, and she was careful to describe them as such. However, by the end of every story, she was certain that all humans had at least one thing in common—pain. Over and over, she listened to hours of stories about people who were struggling, confused, and uncertain of which direction to take in their lives. She listened carefully and always offered encouragement, but she knew adversity would eventually find everyone.

Her favorite way of ending many stories would be by looking directly at me. Nodding her head, she'd say, "In life, there's always a sacrifice you're going to have to make. You might have to make it at the beginning of your life or at the end of your life—but one way or another, you're going to sacrifice." And then, with a hint of a smile, she'd ask, "Are you hungry?" She was comfortable with serious conversations about strife and loss, but she didn't linger in them. She always kept moving forward.

After three years of stories in my parents' basement, it was time for all of us to graduate. Within the same month, my mother received her high school diploma, my sister received her Bachelor of Arts, and I graduated from law school.

My father was the only one who didn't receive a diploma, but I think it was the happiest I had ever seen him. Never having had a real chance to pursue a more formal education past the eighth grade, he nonetheless educated himself. He read the newspaper cover to cover every night. When he learned something new, he was completely focused on every detail. He knew how long the journey had been for all of us, and now he dreamed of how much further it could go.

By 1994, I was no longer working with the Children's Aid Society, but I was still keenly aware of issues that were plaguing adolescents and teens. I was busy with my companies in Russia, however. Wherever I traveled, there was one issue that kept presenting itself and was a particular threat to teenagers; HIV/AIDS. My mother and father had instilled in me the importance of helping others in need. They didn't have much money, but they had time, skills, and compassion. When they thought they could help someone in need, they did. So, this is how I viewed this situation. I didn't know a great deal about it, but I know I wanted to help in some manner.

In this time of HIV/AIDS, fear, worry, confusion, and accusation rose to the surface in every aspect of our lives. Everyone took a side. Race, religion, and politics all had a home for one or more conspiracy theories. The science was unclear. Doctors, nurses, and healthcare professionals did their best to help mitigate pain and suffering, but the problems persisted.

As years passed and more people died, the worst came out of many. Children were banned from schools, homes were burned down, people were beaten in the streets, neighbors fought with each other, families were torn apart. Politicians threw money at the problem but not nearly enough because it was now considered a disease of "fringe" people—outcasts and misfits.

I had seen enough destruction and hatred that I decided to get more involved in looking for solutions for this mess. I wasn't gay, I wasn't bisexual, I didn't have HIV, I wasn't a scientist or a politician, and, I suppose, I wasn't the most ardent Christian. But I understood enough to know that too many people were dying unnecessarily. I also knew that the constant fear, exaggeration, falsehoods, and hatred could not go on.

It was my estimation that many problems could be solved if we just talked with each other—and, more importantly, listened to each other. Rather than try to prove one point over another, I felt it was more important to just understand where each of us was coming from.

With pen and paper in hand, I wrote down the best and worst of all communications I had witnessed and overheard about HIV/AIDS, STDs, and teen pregnancy. I mapped out all the issues and then decided to write an animated book. I felt that it was important to reach kids in a manner that was approachable so I started with a book that would serve as an "ice-breaker" and teaching tool for adolescents. I was hoping to influence them before they got too set in their views and before they contracted HIV or some other STD.

I called the book *Lemonades*. Together with the help of an illustrator, Marc Ngui, I made each character a colorful, cartoon animal figure. The story begins in a familiar and simple manner: two adolescent girls set up a lemonade stand on the front lawn of their home and decide to give away a free condom with each glass of lemonade. Today this may seem harmless, but in 1994 there were plenty of people who thought I was the Devil's Advocate. These topics were just not discussed in most homes or even schools. There still was a level of shame and embarrassment that was associated with the mere mention of a condom. And any discussion that went past the condom was just terrifying, awkward, and considered sinful for many people. My intent was to take all of that away. To make conversations around STDs, teen pregnancy, and HIV/AIDS normal, casual, and, most importantly, accurate.

Concurrently, I developed a program called "Prophylactic Pals." Pals consisted of pouches that held condoms. Embroidered on each pouch was a different character from *Lemonades*. I was only in my mid-20s, and I had no idea of the world I was getting into, but I threw myself into it. I called, wrote, and visited many people in multiple industries. I spoke with people in publishing, clothing, condom manufacturing, government, health officials, and celebrities, and I even contacted MTV. I thought that maybe the new, modern-age video pop stars might help. I went high and wide hoping to get the attention of as many as I could.

At the time, this was not an easy subject matter to discuss with complete strangers. I grew up in a home and a world where I never even heard the word *sex*. But now, I had to maneuver this conversation through receptionists, assistants, and mid-level managers to get to a decision maker. Call after call, hundreds of them, people would hang up on me as soon as I said, "I have a book and a program that addresses AIDS." I tried different approaches, but they were just as futile. Any manner that I phrased my introduction, as soon as I said "condom," "sex," or "AIDS," the other end of the phone went *click*.

Unimaginably, somehow, *Lemonades* ended up on the CDC (Centers for Disease Control and Prevention) recommended reading list. I have no idea who sent them a copy. At the time, I didn't even know such a list even existed. Nonetheless, with that endorsement, I received requests for the book and Pals from all around the world. Health ministers, doctors, nurses, and social workers from all walks of life called and wrote to me. From the island of Palau to Portugal, Cuba, Native American reservations, and Harlem, New York. Apparently, the entire world was not only fighting the virus, but they were also confronting many ugly stereotypes, fears, and falsehoods.

I spent several years distributing the book and program. I met people from all walks of life each with their own unique interpretation of sex and HIV/AIDS, but my favorite day was when I saw my parents in their garden. They were tying string bean plants on a trellis so that they could grow taller. My mother wore a Prophylactic Pals T-shirt, and my dad wore a Lemonades T-shirt. On the back of the Pals shirt was a very large picture of an animated condom shaking hands with an animated pouch. The caption beneath read, "When in Need, There's a Pal." I smiled and looked at my mother, nice Catholic Woman's League lady who had never even uttered the word "sex" in our house, and said, "Nice shirt."

She turned toward me and replied, "I need a different size—this is too big." "Aren't you worried what your friends are going to say?" She turned her head back to the beans, continued to tie the branches upward. "Maybe a small or even a medium." I knew she didn't want to answer. "They're going to call you a sinner." She focused intently on her task at hand and said, "AND THEY'RE SAINTS?" I laughed out loud. This was great. She no longer cared what others thought about her or her family. It was a step in the right direction, for all of us.

10

ONCE AGAIN

Moscow in the mid-1990s was a very menacing place. The city had become prosperous and colorful but also much more violent. For $500, you could have any man killed. The price of life was cheap, and the level of violence was increasing exponentially.

On this evening, in a dinner club, with the backdrop of classical music being played by a small orchestra on a stage, my business partner's girlfriend Elena was arguing with a very intoxicated, large, older man. At first glance, Elena appeared to be significantly outsized by this man. However, what onlookers didn't know is that she was probably the most lethal person in the room. She had not hesitated to have people who crossed her executed. In most other situations, she would have already pulled out her gun and shot this man. However, on this evening, everyone had to check their guns at the front door, walk through a metal detector, and be given their bullets to hold with a claim ticket. Nonetheless, this drunk man was undeterred.

The first punch to her face was to let her know he was serious.

The second punch was to prove that he could break her nose in a crowded room.

He then spit on her to make his final point.

It happened so fast that no one moved in to help her. Even if they had, no one would have dared question him on his actions. He appeared to have drunk enough alcohol to not even know where he was, but he very much knew exactly *who* he was—a dangerous leftover from the past.

Blood poured down Elena's chin. She walked across the room, grabbed my partner's arm, and screamed into his face, "Kill him. Kill him. You coward, kill him!" As his girlfriend, she expected my partner to do something. But these were complicated matters. We learned not to move hastily no matter how ugly the situation. Hit the wrong man and you may be hitting an entire gang of mobsters.

My partner, Yuri, gave Elena his pocket handkerchief to help her wipe the blood from her face. Tonight, he wasn't in the mood for caution. Yuri was only a few years older than me, but he had served in the military and his father had been a high-ranking member within the Soviet Party. Having been raised as privileged within a desperate world, there was only so much he would tolerate. Without missing a beat, he turned to our security guards and gave them a nod of his head. In an instant the security guards locked arms with the drunken savage and began to drag him toward the bathroom.

I turned to Yuri. "NO."

Yuri was unfazed and expressionless.

Again, I said to him, "Yuri—NO."

Still unbothered, he simply stared at me.

I was furious. "Yuri, you know the deal."

In this very unpredictable and lawless new world, I had two basic rules for my partners: no breaking the laws in America and no killing in Russia.

He looked at me and shook his head. "Why do you care?"

"How long before they start killing us?" I replied. Hoping he'd be pragmatic about the situation.

Yuri shrugged. "Precisely."

Like many former Soviets, the decades of communism had stripped away any sense of redemption and notion of an afterlife in Yuri. He was a nihilist. He believed whether we were capitalists or communists, Jewish or Catholic, human or animal, we were all going to die...so, who cared how it happened.

I nodded. "Fine. Get yourself another partner. I'm closing up all operations in America."

Yuri smiled. "Dom, you're a child."

I couldn't appeal to his sense of morality, but I could punch him in the wallet. He didn't believe in God, but he did love all the good things money could buy him. In his eyes I was naive, but I controlled all the bank accounts in the U.S. Without me, his life of champagne and strawberries would be difficult to come by.

Yuri turned his head toward the security guards, put his lips together, and whistled. Just like well-trained police dogs, they stopped. Yuri shook his head. Without any words, they understood the message. They then dragged the old, drunken man to the bathroom.

I looked at Yuri, nodded again, and left the restaurant.

The old man who had violated Elena was going to receive a thorough beating for hitting her. He would be taken to within a minute of the end of his life—but he would still be alive. Had I not intervened, they would have killed him, left him on a toilet seat with his pants down around his ankles, and then beheaded him. All of this for what? An argument over a chair at a table.

Several years had passed since starting my companies in Russia. Despite being surrounded by crime and unchecked violence, we had done very well. Our timing had been perfect. Money continued to pour into Russia, but only in the hands of a small group. The standard of living for some was noticeably improving, but most were still poor.

Among the burgeoning businesses, competition grew quickly, and it was ferocious. In the first few years, we were concerned about being robbed and the possibility of being caught up in a political coup attempt, but now our primary focus was on staying alive.

For me, Russia officially became the Wild East the day a couple of gentlemen showed up at our office with a bag filled with explosives, threatening to blow up our building and kill all our employees. They wanted us out of the finance business and were willing to stop at nothing to make it happen. They told us we could keep our importing and construction companies, but they absolutely would not allow us to continue in banking. The mafia in Russia had grown tired of shaking down businesses one at a time so they just decided to take over all the banks in the country. They liked being efficient. Owning all the banks would make it much easier to skim and launder money for all their other criminal activities. They had a grand plan, and we were not part of it.

Personally, I was more than happy to oblige the gangsters with explosives. I was quite comfortable running just the other businesses. However, my Russian partners didn't want to give up anything. I had seen enough fights in my life that I knew there were only two options in front of us: kill or be killed. I didn't like either. We certainly had a big enough security team with military experience that was ready to do as we instructed, but this wasn't who I was. I had worked hard to make a life for myself, but I wasn't prepared to become a gangster just to stay in business. I knew that once I ordered to have someone killed, or I pulled the trigger myself, I was crossing a line that I could never come back from.

Despite my pleadings, my partners dug in their heels. They refused to back down.

Within a day, our new adversaries held true to their word and delivered their first assault.

One of my partner's homes was completely shredded by machine gun fire, and he and his family had disappeared. We weren't certain if he had escaped or whether he had been kidnapped or killed. We decided to send all of our employees home. My other partner, Yuri, went into hiding, and I buried myself in my office in the States.

I didn't have any books that prepared me for being hunted. This was a far cry from being chased by my mother. I didn't know what to do. I was angry, scared, and terrified that my family and friends would be killed. I was an idiot for playing with fire. I thought all would be well because the "trouble" was "over there." In a land, far away from my family. I thought that "over there" was a playground to make money and my home was something different. Some place safe. I also believed that I if I was honest and held to my own standards that I could tiptoe around the violence and lawlessness. That somehow, the stink of moral and legal corruption wouldn't get on me. I was very wrong. I was wrong, and now I had dragged others into my naive and arrogant view of the world. This was a beast I didn't know how to answer. I just sat at my desk and waited for the smoke to clear. It would all pass, or I would soon be killed.

Within a couple of days, just as I had expected, two men showed up outside of my home. They sat in their car each night, all night, and stared at the windows on my home. I was convinced that I was a dead man. I couldn't call the police because even if they arrested these men, others would follow them. I couldn't leave the house because they would certainly shoot me. I put my head on my desk and searched for a miracle.

On the third day, a plan came to me. I sent messages to Moscow and to all of our employees that we were closing up all of our businesses, including the food and real estate divisions. I immediately wired out any outstanding monies that we owed or had borrowed. I cleaned out our accounts, paying everyone that I could.

Yuri was very upset with me, and we argued about staying in business. We didn't need the bank to be in business; we had a food import company and a real estate development company that were doing very well. We had worked hard to get to this point. He didn't see why we had to dismantle all of it, and he was right; we didn't. But I knew that if I stayed, I would be facing this decision again—kill or be killed—and that wasn't what I wanted. I considered myself lucky to be alive, so now it was time to leave.

Within a short while of emptying our accounts, the men in the car outside of my home left. Despite my partner's pleas, I don't think that I would have made it to the end of the sidewalk if I had decided to stay in any business. I think we were marked and now perceived as weak. This time it was about banking; next time it would be about something else they wanted. It was just best to end everything.

I unplugged my phones, threw away all my mail, and avoided people for weeks. I eventually pulled myself together. Once again, I vowed to try to be better and to avoid trouble. I knew that this had been the dumbest and most dangerous mistake I had ever made, but I felt that I could do better. That I had finally learned my lesson. I just needed to stay on a straight and narrow path, and all would be well. With this in mind, I focused on the positive. I was fortunate to still be alive and to have put aside some money. More importantly, I was very fortunate to have escaped with my family unharmed.

It was now the summer of 1997. I had cleared my head about Russia and now focused on my future with Amy.

My mother, Amy, and I sat in front of the manager of the same Italian club that I had set on fire as an adolescent. We were reviewing the menu for our wedding that was fast approaching. Amy and I had initially planned for a small, intimate gathering, but that proved impossible when we factored in all my parents' friends and family. They had been invited to a lot of weddings, so culturally, it was now important to show the same respect to all those people. In total, 550 invitations were sent out. Amy prepared giant spreadsheets to keep track of the responses, families, seating assignments, and gifts. While she was doing that, I spent the year working with my grandfather, making the wine that would be served on the day of the wedding. An event of this size was a big undertaking, but all moved along smoothly. The last item on the checklist was finalizing the menu. My mother wanted to attend the meeting. She was very excited for our wedding, and she was also paying for all of her and my father's guests, so she liked to participate in the planning. However, on this day, she promised to honor our wishes for the menu. She said that we "could do whatever we wanted." She gave me her word that she would stay quiet the entire time.

The manager looked at his list.

"You're going to start with prosciutto and melon."

I responded, "Yes."

"Followed by fettuccine with tomato sauce."

"No soup?" my mother interjected.

"Mom, no soup."

"It's a wedding. You need soup."

"Mom, no soup."

She shook her head. "It's not a wedding then."

The manager continued, "Risotto with mushrooms will be served at the same time as the fettucine."

"No penne?" my mom asked.

"Mom, no penne."

"Not too many people like rice."

"Mom, Amy likes rice. It's her wedding."

"Oh, OK. I'm sorry. OK, we'll serve risotto. Hopefully, they'll eat it."

The manager continued, "Next course will be veal medallions, followed by a mixed seafood platter."

"Yes. And the veal will be sauteed with a lemon piccata sauce?" I asked.

The manager nodded in agreement. "And next will be string beans sauteed with garlic and olive oil, followed by a mixed green salad."

"What about chicken?" my mother asked.

"Mom, no chicken."

"But everyone loves chicken and potatoes."

"Mom. I know. They serve it at every Italian wedding."

"Yes, because people love it."

Amy looked at me and laughed. I shook my head. "No." I wasn't giving in.

"You have to have roasted chicken and potatoes."

"Mom, there's veal and seafood. That's enough."

"I'll pay for it."

"Mom, it's not about the money. It's too much food."

"It's a wedding. It's not too much."

"Mom. You promised. Just let us do what we want."

"OK. Fine. Do what you want. Don't blame me when people start asking for chicken and potatoes."

The manager stared at us, patiently waiting for our debate to end. "And then the cake will be served with ice cream."

"What flavor?" my mother again interjected.

"Mom!"

"I'm just asking a question."

"Vanilla."

"No chocolate?"

"The cake is chocolate."

"People like chocolate ice cream. The kids. They're going to love it."

I looked at Amy, and again she laughed. Nothing my mother said ever bothered her. I bit my tongue, turned to the manager, and said, "Perfect. I think we're done. We'll have a final count for you two weeks before the day." We shook hands and walked out the door. I knew I had to end the conversation because my mother was tenacious, and she would have us there for hours.

As we exited, my mother continued her plea. "It really wouldn't kill you to have chocolate ice cream." I looked at her. "Mom, keep it up and I'm not going to allow you to attend the wedding." She knew that I could be just as stubborn as she was. "You wouldn't do that to your mother?" I smiled and said, "We'll see."

The summer passed quietly. All went as planned, with 375 guests in attendance for the lovely and fun-filled day. And, of course, magically, roasted chicken and potatoes were served right after the veal and seafood. My mother called the club manager and paid him separately for that course and tipped him to keep quiet. Always one step ahead of me.

Shortly before we married, Amy received a job offer from an investment banking firm in Cleveland, Ohio. It was a terrific opportunity for her, one that was not available in a small city like Windsor. I loved my hometown. I had grown closer with my family and friends, and I didn't want to leave, but Amy had been patient and very supportive of my entrepreneurial pursuits in Russia. She had been there once. She liked the Russian people. They were enamored with her beauty. They believed she had the perfect face to be a Russian princess. Everywhere we went, people stared at her adoringly. On one occasion, a wealthy man offered to buy her from me. It took a bit of time to explain that she wasn't my property, nor was she for sale.

All of this was amusing to her, but beyond the amber jewelry and random infatuation from strangers, she didn't pay much attention to my business dealings. A few times she did help me with financial projections, but I never shared more than that with her. She knew who I was and what I was capable of getting myself into, but she didn't want to know about the ugly and dangerous aspects of my work. She knew it existed and was quietly excited about it; however, it was a world she could only imagine through me.

For all the things we shared, up until that point, we had lived vastly different lives. She had a reputation for being a picture-perfect woman who never broke the law. I don't think she ever received as much as a parking ticket. Real or imagined, she was perfect to me. I loved being with her. For most of my life, I was either a whipping boy or a bulldozer, but with her I was different. She helped me open my heart and be free. Whether we were eating ice cream or dancing, she never judged me. She took me as I was. Amy had supported me without question or worry. Now I wanted to offer her the same in return for her career and her happiness.

After years of running my own companies, I knew that I still did not have the technical skills I required to be a good manager and business leader. I could sell and motivate, and I had a good sense for money, but I still did not know the specifics of things like finance, accounting, industrial engineering, information technology, manufacturing, and distribution. So, when I moved to Cleveland, I took a job with a consulting firm as a business analyst. The job required that I travel five days a week. Each week, I would be in two, sometimes three different cities, analyzing small companies and looking for ways to improve their financial performance. It was grueling work, but I was learning a tremendous amount in brief period of time.

I didn't enjoy being away from Amy five days a week. At this point, we had been together almost eight years. We had a strong and loving relationship that we felt could endure the absence for any period of time. Amy was also busy. She worked no less than 60, sometimes 70 hours a week. She had lost a fair amount of weight, but when I spoke to her about it, she reassured me that it just had been the stress of the wedding and the new job.

Nine months into my new job, I had zigzagged across a good portion of America. I was growing tired of being on the road five days a week, but I was more concerned about Amy's well-being. On two separate occasions, I found her passed out on the floor: once in the bathroom and once in our closet. Each time, I picked her up and carried her to the bed. She'd wake up, fortunately without any concussion or cuts. And, both times, she reassured me that it was just low blood sugar. Not understanding low or high blood sugar or much about health, I believed her. I worried, but I didn't think she would lie to me.

We were in the kitchen. It was 7 p.m. on a Saturday. I was next to the refrigerator. Amy stood across from me, leaning against the counter.

I asked her, "What would you like for dinner?"

She responded, "I don't know."

"Pasta?"

"I don't know."

"Pizza?"

"I don't know."

"I can barbeque?"

"I'm not sure."

"We can make a big salad."

"I don't know."

"Pick anything. I will eat whatever you want."

"I can't."

This discussion went on for another 30 minutes. The pauses between my suggestions became longer. She could not decide. The thoughts in her mind raced. She was once again living in a prison. The mental aspects of anorexia and bulimia had taken over her. She stood there and began to cry uncontrollably. Over the years she helped me understand more about these issues, but her relationship with food was still confusing to me. From what she had explained to me, it was not about food but about the ability to control something.

She told me that she often felt frightened and fearful of the world spinning around her. To calm herself, she would control the ingesting and purging of food. Intellectually, I understood some of this concept, but it was still difficult to reconcile at times because food had been paramount to my upbringing. We grew it, curated it, cooked it, and viewed it as something sacred and to be celebrated. But with Amy, food was a servant and the enemy. Regardless of what I had known to be true in my life, none of it mattered now. I didn't want her to suffer any longer. I didn't want her to die. I just wanted to see her happy for the rest of my life. I wiped her tears, pulled her close, and held her tight.

I wasn't certain where to turn, but I was confident that if I went looking for answers, I would find them. I knew I needed to help Amy in whatever way I could. To do that, I needed to find a different job and stop traveling as much. I had to be close to her. She needed me by her side. I promised her that we would get through this together. I knew that she didn't discuss these issues with her family and friends. It was just too uncomfortable for all of them. I made a decision early on to protect her dignity and privacy, so I didn't discuss any of her health issues with my family or friends. It was a challenge, but it was just the two of us looking for answers.

As I explored options, I came across a type of work that I had never heard about. It was called corporate restructuring and sometimes referred to as crisis management. Companies that were failing or on the verge of filing for bankruptcy would hire this special skill of consultants to try to help turn them around from financial insolvency. For me, it seemed like a natural fit. After working in Russia, I was comfortable working in chaos and dire situations. I knew it would be very intense because in most circumstances people were losing their companies, jobs, homes, and even identity. And, often in failing companies there is fraud, corruption, and a tremendous abuse of power. I had already experienced this. It was not fun, but I still felt that this was the perfect environment for me to learn the best and worst practices of all aspects of business.

I met the owner of a three-person turnaround firm. He had written a couple of books on the subject matter, and he seemed knowledgeable on all the things I wanted to learn. He had been consulting for almost 10 years but was unable to grow his firm to any significant size. Based on my experience in building multiple businesses in Russia, he thought I would be the perfect person to help him finally grow his business. He figured that if I could dramatically grow a company in a foreign country, I could certainly do the same in America.

We met three times. Each time, I grew more impressed with the depth and range of knowledge he had on many different technical aspects of running a business. They were precisely the skills I wanted to learn. I did have some concerns. I saw that he had an odd personality. He sometimes made comments that had nothing to do with the current conversation. We might be speaking about the stock market and out of the blue he would ask, "Are you familiar with timeshares in South Africa?" And he was always sweaty and fidgety, despite being in an air-conditioned office. He had trouble making and keeping eye contact, even in the briefest exchange, such as a "hello" or "goodbye." These characteristics were a bit off-putting, but I concluded that he was just probably more of an introvert and didn't warm up easily to people. Nonetheless, each of us had the skills that the other one wanted. So, we struck a deal: I would help him grow his firm, and he would teach me technical skills. I got the job that I wanted, and I would be able to spend more time at home with Amy.

During the following year, she appeared to be a bit more stable. I urged her to take time off work and check in to a long-term therapy facility, but she resisted the notion, fearing it would hurt her career. I then found therapists and doctors who could treat her from a myriad of perspectives. I recommended that she see everyone from a psychiatrist to an acupuncturist and even a Native American shaman. I also encouraged her to attend personal improvement conferences and listen to motivational and spiritual audiobooks.

For some this may have seemed excessive, but to me it was urgent problem-solving. She was an acute bulimic. By her own admission, at her worst, she would purge 15-20 times a day. The years of purging caused the enamel on her teeth to wear away. It also caused a heart murmur and stress on her other vital organs. I began to worry that one morning, I would wake up and I would not be able to revive her. Every night, I quietly panicked. I worried incessantly that her heart would stop while I was sleeping. I worried that she would collapse in the middle of an intersection and get hit by a car. I begged her to stop running, but she was adamant. She ran three miles every morning at dawn, regardless of the weather. She ran every day throughout winter. I would ask her where she was running so I knew where to find her in case she didn't return. I didn't know what to do, but I knew that the threat of death was real, and I was willing to do anything to keep her alive.

While we treated the bulimia, we also tried to focus on a positive future and the prospects of building our family. We discussed having children, though as we did this, we had to confront another significant medical issue. One side of her family had a history of schizophrenia. Some doctors believed that may have contributed to Amy's eating disorders, but they were uncertain. Either way, I was OK with it. To me, none of us are perfect. I believed that working together, we could overcome anything. We would take the issues one by one as they presented themselves. At this moment it seemed like we were making progress, so that's where I focused.

My mother, however, wasn't as fortunate during this same period of time. She continued as president of the Catholic Women's League at her church. She kept busy organizing fundraisers for many different causes; however, she had to spend additional time taking care of herself. In a period of seven years, she had more than 20 different surgical procedures performed by several different doctors. The most important of the procedures involved having an external drain for bile duct created and inserted near her liver. The insertion of this drain was complicated by its location and the ever-growing cyst, but it was essential because her bile duct was obstructed. The drain tube was attached internally, but it exited through her skin and rested on the outside underneath the right side of her ribcage. Bile drained into a bag, and then the bile would be re-inserted into her body each day through another tube. Registered nurses visited her home every day to change the bandage dressing around these open holes in her skin, but most of the work was done by my father, every day.

By this time, my father had scaled back his working hours in the garage and replaced them with taking care of my mother. He knew her health issues were sensitive and complex and often placed her in a state of constant pain and nausea. At times, she could barely eat, and when she did eat, it didn't stay down long. She spent years plagued by infections that were being created by this bile duct drain. The infections forced her to be on antibiotics, which caused her immune system to weaken further.

My parents' bedroom began to resemble a hospital room and pharmacy. One half of their credenza was filled with medicine, for digestion, pain, hormones, and bacteria. The other half was filled with bandages, gauze, swabs, and tubing. In the center was an 8-by-10, white, lined notebook. In that book, my father wrote down everything he did, everything that was performed by others, what medicine my mom took and what time of day it was taken. She now needed round-the-clock care, and he was the one doing most of it. He slept little. He was often exhausted, so he didn't want to leave things to memory. His solution was to write them down in a book that could be used to advise nurses and doctors.

In 2001, my parents spent the entire summer going back and forth to the hospital in London, Ontario, two hours north of their home. The cyst kept growing and had now wrapped itself around my mother's portal vein. The portal vein is the main channel of blood to the liver, enabling it to function properly. In medicine, the liver is often referred to as the workhorse of the body because it has so many responsibilities and functions to perform. Once the liver goes, it's impossible to live.

A new doctor was consulted. This doctor was so exceptional that he had been given a medal by the prime minister of the country. He had been awarded the "Order of Canada" for his excellence in medical surgery. This was promising. We were now in the hands of a miracle worker. This could only be good news for my mother.

However, quickly and unexpectedly, our promising miracle worker turned out to be nightmare.

It was the first week of September 2001. Dr. Morgan was scheduled to come to the hospital and use his masterful and highly decorated hands to surgically remove parts of the cyst from the portal vein so my mom could resume a better and healthier life. However, now that Dr. Morgan was taking a closer look at my mother's charts and meeting with her in person, he had become tentative. Days passed and her pain intensified, but no surgery was scheduled.

By Friday of Labor Day weekend, Dr. Morgan met with my parents and informed them that he believed that the cyst was cancerous and that there was nothing that could be done to change its course. He had not performed any biopsies on the cyst, but a man of his experience certainly knew cancer when he saw it on a CT scan.

He then informed my parents that my mother only had weeks to live. That she would experience liver failure. The best that he could do for her was offer additional pain medicine for her journey toward death.

He had received the highest award in the country for surgical excellence, yet he spent little time with my mother and chose to not even attempt a surgery on her. I can only imagine how many other people he had done this to. It appeared to us that he was a successful surgeon because he only took on the easy cases.

Nonetheless, we had no additional time to waste with Dr. Morgan.

My mother did not believe what she was hearing. She was jaundiced, dehydrated, nauseous, and in extreme pain, but she had absolutely no faith in the words that were coming from this doctor. She looked at him with complete disdain and said, "Give me my charts. My son will know what to do."

I, of course, was aware of none of what was happening. I was five hours away from where they were. I was living in Cleveland, Ohio.

My parents got in their car, drove two hours south, and returned home. They informed the rest of the family what the doctor had told them, and most were left in shock. At the same time, my father called me to bring me up to date. I was furious at the doctor, but I had no time to be upset. We had to find another doctor. We had exhausted all the best Canada had to offer, so it was now time to look in the United States. Dr. Morgan said she had weeks to live, and it was now Labor Day weekend. It would not be easy to find another doctor, but we had to try. However, before I started searching for a solution, I had one call to make. I needed to speak with Dr. Morgan.

I hung up with my father and made the next call to the doctor.

Me: "Hello, Dr. Morgan. This is Domenic Aversa, Benedetta's son."

Morgan: "Yes. OK. Hello. How can I help you?"

Me: "My parents have informed me of your diagnosis. Is it possible that I can get a copy of that diagnosis in writing from you?"

A long, uncomfortable pause.

Me: "Hello. Dr. Morgan. Are you still there?"

Morgan: "Yes, I am. Can I ask, why do you want a copy of my diagnosis?"

Me: "I would like to know exactly what you concluded. I'm just trying to understand what is happening to her."

Morgan: "Certainly, Domenic. Give me your fax number, and I will send it to you shortly."

I wasn't entirely sure why I wanted that piece of paper, but something in my legal training and my fighting experience told me that I may need it. By this point in my life, I had dealt with so many liars and criminals that I didn't want this doctor to be able to go back on his conclusions. I wanted what he had stated to my parents, in writing.

True to his word, I received that document within the hour. In the meantime, I called everyone I knew in my network to find a specialist who could address my mother's pressing health concerns.

I called for hours, and many others in our family did the same. Everyone chipped in and helped as they could. This was a good time to have a big family and a lot of friends.

And then, there it was—hope. It arrived just in time.

Around 9 p.m., I spoke with a doctor who had been a neighbor to my cousin Pete's wife. She had contacted his mother to see if he could help. We made calls all around the United States only to come full circle and find the exact specialist we needed right next door to our family in Windsor.

Dr. George Vasili worked at Toledo General Hospital. Toledo, Ohio, was approximately 45 minutes from Windsor. He was an interventional radiologist. By reputation, he was a brilliant doctor. He had been offered Chief of Radiology at the Cedars-Sinai Medical Center in Los Angeles but turned it down because he wanted a quieter, more balanced life. He was deeply spiritual and enjoyed spending more time with his family. This is what I knew of him, but over the last 15 years we had heard of several different brilliant doctors who all ended up being disappointing. Only time would tell what he had to offer.

When I spoke with him, I asked him what time he wanted to see us at his hospital. He quickly responded, "No, no. I'll come to you. She's the patient. She's ill. I'll drive to your parents' home. I'll be there about 10 a.m.—is that OK?"

OK? It was better than OK. This was a first. A doctor that came to us. "Sure, Dr. Vasili. That's very thoughtful of you. We'll see you at 10 a.m."

I drove to Windsor from Cleveland that evening. My mother did not look well, but she now felt anger more than anything else. She then told me what she had told Dr. Morgan, "My son will know what to do."

I didn't ask her why she'd said it; it just made me smile. For decades, my mother always wondered why it was *me* in the middle of trouble—and now she was asking me to get in the middle of this crisis. I'm not sure what my mother was thinking when she said that, but I'm sure by now she knew that I was tenacious, and I would fight for her. There was no way I was just going to let her whither on a vine, taking pain medication, watching her die. That was not an option for me.

Dr. Vasili arrived the next morning at my parents' house. He was not big in stature, standing five-foot-seven, average build, but in possession of crystal blue eyes. I've met many doctors and noteworthy people. People of great accomplishment. They have a presence about them. There's an energy that attracts others to them. Dr. Vasili was different. His presence warmed and calmed the room. His eyes and his spirit came to you and reassured you. He greeted my parents, sat at the kitchen table, and immediately reviewed her CT scans. He spent a few minutes holding them toward the ceiling light. He muttered to himself, "OK, OK. Yes, there it is. OK."

He put down the scans, looked at my mother, and said, "Benedetta, there are five serious issues that need to be addressed in your body. I can guarantee you that I can fix four of the five of them."

Before she could respond, I jumped in. "What percentage rate of success do you think you'll have with these four procedures?"

Soberly, he looked at me. "One hundred percent. I guarantee you that they will be resolved 100 percent and there will be no issue."

I continued. "What about the fifth issue?"

Nodding, he said, "We'll cross that bridge when we get there."

I looked at my mom and asked what she thought. She shrugged and said, "I suppose it's OK."

I knew she was uncertain because in less than 24 hours, one doctor had told her that she had weeks to live and now a stranger was telling her that he could guarantee her recovery with almost every issue. She wanted to trust but had been down the road with enough doctors who were wrong. My father was in the same place as her. This was a significant risk. How do you trust a stranger who walked into your kitchen on a Saturday morning, looked at a scan, and within minutes told you that you would be fine? In their eyes, I saw that they were worried. I knew they wanted other opinions, but I didn't.

I looked at them and said, "One hundred percent guarantee on four out of five—that's good enough for me. Let's do it."

I then turned to Dr. Vasili. "When can we start?"

He took a moment to gather his thoughts. "Well, I suppose, first we have to get approval from insurance. You will have to contact OHIP, get their sign-off and the parameters of the procedures that they will cover, and then we can begin scheduling your mom's procedures."

OHIP stands for Ontario Health Insurance Plan. OHIP is the government. Canada has a socialized medical system that is administered through a government agency. To have medical work done in the United States, at Toledo General Hospital, where Dr. Vasili worked, we would need their approval in advance, or we would have to pay for everything ourselves.

I shook my head. "Dr. Vasili, I appreciate where you are coming from, but I'm not going to sit around waiting for government approval while my mother gets weaker by the day. There's no way I'm going to let her die while I wait for the proper paperwork. You start working on her as soon as you can, and I'll take care of everything else. There won't be an issue with the paperwork."

He smiled and said, "Seems like you are a good man to know."

I nodded. "When can we start?"

He looked toward my parents and said they could come the next day, and he would schedule to have the first procedure performed the following day, Monday.

I asked my parents if they were OK with this, and now they seemed much more reassured. My father asked me if I was certain that OHIP would pay for all this work. I nodded and told him not to worry about it and to just focus on taking care of Mom.

The reality is that I didn't know what OHIP would do. I had never dealt with them. Nor had we ever had an issue like this. I just knew that we were in a crisis. And, in a crisis, you take on one issue at a time. Fix one problem, then move on to the next. Right now, we were fixing four out of five problems. We would address the insurance and money issues later.

The next day, my father and I drove my mother to Toledo. By the time we arrived at the hospital, she was so weak, she could barely walk. Her skin had turned a darker, brownish yellow from the previous day. There was no doubt that her liver was failing at an accelerated rate. We quickly put her into a wheelchair and arrived at the front desk. They had a room waiting. We brought her upstairs, and they immediately began with diagnostics.

Dr. Vasili arrived several hours later. By the time he met with us, he was visibly upset.

He approached my father. "Benedetta is severely malnourished and dehydrated. Has she not been eating? Did they not connect her to a feed line? Didn't they give her electrolytes?"

My father tried to process what Dr. Vasili was saying, but he just shook his head. "No. They didn't give her any of those things. She's tried to eat but hasn't been able to keep the food down. She doesn't like drinking water, so she doesn't have much of it. But she's also been vomiting quite a bit, for a long time. We told all the doctors in London. They knew."

Dr. Vasili became angrier. "She was going to die of malnourishment before anything else!"

Malnourishment? How could she be dying of malnourishment? I was confused. No one was starving her. How did this happen? Why didn't anyone notice?

Dr. Vasili then explained to us that the cyst had grown so large that it not only wrapped itself around the portal vein, but it had effectively crowded out and closed part of her duodenum so little food and water could get to her digestive system. This obstruction was the principal reason that she continued to vomit so frequently. All the doctors and my parents were so focused on the threat to the liver that no one paid attention to her nourishment.

My mother didn't like to complain. She didn't bathe in self-pity. If there was a problem, she just wanted it fixed. However, she also came from a background and place that believed "whatever the doctor says, then that's what it must be." If no one told her that she had a hydration and nourishment problem, she didn't think about it or question it. When she defied Dr. Morgan, it was a rare and bold act for her. In general, she listened to whatever doctors told her. I suppose she was willing to listen to everything they had to say except for the fact that she would die. She wanted to be the one who determined her exit from earth.

At this point, my father and I started to realize how much pain she must have really been in. She had pleaded for pain medication every day. In those moments, we would tell her, "Just a little while longer. We have to stay on schedule because it will be too much for your liver." Every day, for weeks, she stared at the clock in whatever room she was in. She'd stare and count the minutes until she would get her next pill for pain. And why? Because Dr. Morgan was too busy polishing his medal of honor. She grinned and bore an extraordinary amount of pain that was completely unnecessary and that had brought her to the brink of starvation.

Dr. Vasili and his team would not be so careless and negligent. They employed every resource they had and applied immense thoughtfulness and thoroughness to my mother's care. She was now getting what she needed and resting comfortably. Dr. Vasili waited a few days to allow her to regain nourishment and hydration before he would begin working on the cyst.

The day of the first procedure, I visited my mother in the surgery prep room. She looked healthier and was in good spirits. To pass the time, I brought a copy of *People* magazine. The cover story featured women who had overcome great obstacles. I thought this would give my mom an extra boost of encouragement. I showed her a picture of one of the women and read her story. This woman had suffered from depression. She struggled so badly that one day she poured gasoline over her head and set herself on fire. She managed to live, but she had significant burns all over her body. From that horrible low point in her life, she was able to get help and the right medication, and she eventually put herself through law school. She now had a successful law practice and two healthy children.

My mother listened intently, then looked at the photo of the woman with visible burn scars. "You see. I don't have problems. This poor woman had problems. I'm fine. You know why? Because I still have my mind. Everything else isn't so great...but my mind, thank God, is still there."

I was fascinated by her view of the situation. She still found a way to be optimistic. Five days earlier she was dehydrated, malnourished, experiencing liver failure, and told she had weeks to live, yet she believed that she really didn't have any problems.

Once she had nourishment and the proper amount of pain medication, she believed all was fine and everything would be taken care of.

I stayed in Toledo for about a week during those first procedures. When I saw that things were proceeding well, I returned home to Cleveland. It was the evening of September 10, 2001.

I was exhausted but relieved that we had avoided losing my mother to this never-ending illness. I just needed some quiet time to rest, and I needed to get back to work.

At this time, our firm had grown considerably. We now had 22 employees, and our revenue had improved almost 500 percent. I had learned a lot, and my network expanded significantly.

I was now traveling to New York City approximately once a month. I met with lawyers and bankers, always trying to secure restructuring work for my firm. A handful of bankers whom I met with regularly were located in the financial district, specifically in the Twin Towers. I was last there the second week of August. I had planned on returning there in early September but dropped all plans to help take care of my mother's emergency.

On the morning of September 11, as I was getting ready to go to my office, I sipped on coffee and watched the news.

And then it happened.

The first plane. Then the second plane. Before the shock set in, I picked up the phone and began dialing people whom I knew worked in the Twin Towers. No phone line would go through. I then called a cousin who worked in the area. He was in the building adjacent to the second tower. Still no phone line connection. I then dialed my aunt, his mother, who lived on Long Island. That call didn't go through. All phone lines were down.

As I watched the buildings burn, an emergency notice was given by officials in Cleveland. The air traffic controllers were in contact with a plane that had been hijacked but lost tracking of this plane. They then played a tape of the exchange. Most of what could be heard was yelling and what sounded like scuffling between men. Officials then announced that they were concerned about an attack on the city of Cleveland because the tallest buildings between New York City and Chicago were in Cleveland.

Realizing that Amy worked in the tallest building in the city, I immediately called her and told her, "GET OUT NOW." She was so dedicated to her work that she hesitated, but I just yelled into the phone, "GET OUT OF THERE—FAST."

My heart raced, and I flipped through the television channels hoping to get better information. At the same time, I dialed my office and told our office manager to clear out. She told me that it was only her and two others. I said, "Drop everything and get out of there." Our office was in a tall building about three blocks from the tallest building in the city.

I then sat and watched the television for hours wondering, like everyone else in the country, "Are we at war?"

Thankfully war never came. The worst was behind us and now, like the rest of the country, I needed to return to some type of normal routine.

With my mother stable, my father by her side and safely healing in Toledo, I felt comfortable returning to a full work schedule.

Mid-way through October, I was hired for a new project. My client was a bank based in New York. The city and people were still shaken and cleaning their way out of the rubble. It was a small project. The banker needed help collecting the accounts receivables for a small business in Pittsburgh. The problem was that the owner of that business had committed fraud, his accounting ledgers were complete works of fiction, and no one could make sense of what was real or not. The bank feared they would never be paid back on their loan. I assured the banker I was the right person for the job. It was essentially a debt collector job, and most consultants didn't like this type of work. They felt it was beneath them or just too rough and dirty. However, I was willing to do whatever it took to be successful. I had never done this type of work, but I didn't think it would be too complicated. I just had to find where things were hidden.

The next morning, at 8 a.m., I arrived at this big warehouse on the outskirts of the city. The parking lot was empty but for one car. I walked inside this abandoned building looking for any sign of life. As I called out "Hello" for the third time, I was greeted by a portly, bald man wearing a collared shirt and tie and carrying a pot of coffee. He looked at me and said, "Oh, good, you're here. Come on in," and he pointed to a door. I walked through the door, into a sizable meeting room. There was a table large enough to accommodate at least a dozen people. I took a seat in the middle of the side closest to the door. The portly man, Sam Napor, the owner, turned to me and asked, "Would you like some coffee?" I replied, "Sure. Thank you." Sam then pointed to a silver tray in the center of the table that was filled with two dozen donuts. "Help yourself," he added.

He poured my coffee and then took a seat at the head of the table. Before I could take my first sip of coffee, he started what appeared to be a rehearsed speech. "Thank you for coming, but the bank is really wasting your time and my time, and quite frankly, my money and their money. I don't know why you are here. There's nothing that you can do and nothing that I can do. The bank knows this. I've explained everything to them. So, I think you should just go."

I found this amusing. I knew he was a thief, and he was clearly just going to try and dance around until I got frustrated and left, but Sam didn't know anything about me. I knew a few things about criminals. I smiled and said, "Sure, Sam. I understand. I don't want to waste your time or money. I just need the inventory list and then I can go."

His tone and demeanor changed quickly. He was no longer the jovial host with donuts. I thought we would do this verbal sparring for a while, but his fuse was short. "Boy, you really are some kind of idiot. I thought the bank was sending someone smart, but you're an absolute moron. I'm going to call them and tell them not to pay you. You're just an idiot. There is no list. I told you; the entire system is down and there's no way to get it until it's fixed. Now, will you just get out of here?"

I smiled again and said, "Sam, I just need the list. I know there's an inventory list somewhere. I'll even take an old one. I'm certain it hasn't changed much. I don't need a system or a disc. I just need a paper copy."

He stared at me with his dark pupils as sweat appeared on his forehead. He turned around and moved his suit jacket off the back of his chair. I saw a gun in a holster hanging on the chair. He pulled out the gun, pointed it at me, and said, "I told you to go. So go."

I knew he was desperate and clearly crazy. I also knew that there was no one else around to even hear a gunshot. I stood up slowly and said, "No problem, Sam. I'm going. Sorry to bother you. Thanks for the coffee."

I walked out hoping I wouldn't be shot in the back. But by the time I got into my car and got to the end of the parking lot, I was angry.

I called the banker in New York and explained what had just happened. He was shaken by what I told him, but I wasn't. I told him to call Sam and his lawyer and that we would meet them the following morning. In the meantime, I hired the most menacing

Thank Goliath

off-duty police officer I could find. I was courageous but I wasn't dumb. I wasn't going back into that building without a skilled marksman next to me. My instructions to the officer were simple: "If he pulls a gun out, put a bullet in his head."

We entered the same room that I had been in the previous day. Again, there was a silver tray with two dozen donuts in the center of the table. And, again, Sam politely asked us if we wanted coffee. It was as if yesterday never happened.

But, just like the previous day, Sam became heated and lost his temper with each question I asked. He would alternate uttering profanities and storming out of the room in a rage. My hired cop never left my side nor lost sight of Sam. This temper tantrum charade would continue for a couple of hours. I was patient. I wasn't leaving until I had what I needed. Eventually, in a whirlwind of anger, Sam tripped himself up and stated that he had an inventory list, leaving himself with no choice but to give it to me.

Over the next couple of months, my colleagues and I were able to collect everything that was owed to the bank. We found just about everything Sam was hiding. The banker became a good friend, and Sam ended up where he belonged, in jail.

It would have been easy to leave the job when the gun was pointed at me. No one would have faulted me for not returning, but I had been here before. I had grown tired of bullies and criminals. Like many, I felt powerless at the sight of those buildings falling on 9/11. The image constantly replayed in my mind like a nightmare I couldn't shake. It surprised me. It stunned me. Now, weeks later, I wanted to do something about it. I couldn't fight terrorists, but I could certainly fight this criminal. I knew it wouldn't change the world, but it was a positive step forward.

While I wrestled the sweaty man with donuts, Dr. Vasili was engaged in more complex matters. During this time, he completed four of the procedures he initially addressed. And, just as he had promised, they were 100 percent successful.

My mother needed one last procedure. This involved reconstruction of her biliary drain. For this, my parents returned to Canada. Dr. Vasili found a surgeon in Hamilton, Ontario who would take on this challenge. The procedure ended up being more complex than anticipated, and several errors were made in the process, so my mother remained in the Hamilton hospital for three additional months.

Around this time, all the bills for the work at Toledo General Hospital had come in. A two-foot pile of invoices sat on a desk at my parents' home. The total for all services was approximately $500,000 in U.S. funds (approximately $750,000 in Canadian funds, in 2002). My parents did not have anywhere near that money, nor had we made any progress with OHIP. Their intent was to have us pay all of it. I had retained a lawyer to help us with the process. OHIP's argument was that we had voluntarily left Canada and sought out medical care without their approval. They cited sections of the Health Care Act, and according to our lawyer, they had a persuasive case. He asked me for help in reviewing the legislation to see if I could come up with a viable argument.

To me, the argument was simple. "We didn't voluntarily leave the geographical boundaries of the healthcare coverage—we were forcibly pushed out." The day the alleged best surgeon in Canada declared "There's nothing that we can do. You will experience liver failure. You only have weeks to live" was the day the country and OHIP gave us no choice but to seek a solution outside of the country. The only other alternative was to let my mother die, which really didn't seem like a choice.

Our attorney prepared the legal briefing and went forward with this argument. OHIP received it but dug in their heels. They knew they were wrong, and they didn't care. They were the government; they had endless dollars for in-house lawyers, but they had a strict budget for actual citizens' healthcare. In their mind, it would have been so much more cost-effective if my mother had just listened to the Canadian doctor and gone home and died. But for now, they had no intention of paying that bill.

Of course, there was always the option of suing Dr. Morgan for malpractice. We would use the same argument: "You were very wrong; she's clearly alive." However, suing a doctor in Canada that works for the Canadian government is even more difficult and cumbersome than suing OHIP. These doctors are members of the Canadian Medical Protective Association (CMPA). The doctors practically had unlimited funds to defend themselves. At that time, the CMPA had a $3 billion "war chest" for legal defense attorneys. Additionally, the federal government had put limits on negligence claims. For example, the maximum payout for "pain and suffering" was $100,000. Between the onerous federal restrictions and the unlimited funds for legal defense, the outcomes of medical litigation if you are a patient that has been wronged in Canada are abysmal. Less than one percent of all malpractice cases brought against Canadian doctors win in court. Approximately 35% of the cases, after extended periods of time, settle out of court and in general for amounts that are woefully insufficient. On average, during this period of time, a wrongful death claim took about seven years to reach a conclusion, and the average payout was approximately $112,000.

Knowing the odds were against us and that it would take countless years to resolve, I knew this approach wasn't going to work for my parents. They didn't want to spend years fighting with lawyers and administrators. Life was already enough of a challenge for them. I had promised my parents I would take care of all of this for them. Without thinking about the consequences, I took a leap of faith and told them, "Don't worry." But now, I was worried. I felt like I had messed up. I could have handled the financial and legal matters in a more diplomatic manner. In my anger and haste, I completely disregarded OHIP the entire time my mother was in the hospital. I was mad at the system, and I just figured that when the final bill was received, I would deliver it to them and force them to pay. Their doctors had made mistakes, but I still should have shown respect for the money coming from Canadian taxpayers. That money would keep my mother alive and my parents financially solvent. Perhaps I had been courageous in the beginning, but without a doubt I had been immature and spiteful with the rest of the matters. I created this mess, and I was desperate to clean it up.

I went into my files and pulled out the piece of paper that had been faxed to me by Dr. Morgan, the one in which he'd declared her dead in a matter of weeks in the previous year. With that paper in hand, I got into my car and I drove five hours to London, Ontario with the hope of meeting Dr. Morgan in person.

The following day, I approached him in the hallway of the hospital. I explained to him who I was and what had happened in Toledo. I told him about the procedures that Dr. Vasili had performed on my mother and that she was alive and doing well. When I finished, I pulled out the fax and showed him his diagnosis. I looked at him and said, "I just need you to call your bosses and tell them that you were wrong, and they should pay the bill. That's all I need; please just say you were wrong. If she listened to you, she would be dead. She's alive."

He just stood there looking at me without saying a word.

He couldn't admit he was wrong.

He showed no contrition. No emotion. I wanted to threaten him. I wanted to choke him. My blood boiled. But force was not the answer. This was an immensely arrogant man. He needed to feel like he was in control.

"Dr. Morgan, please help us. My family has no intention of suing you. We're just grateful that my mom is alive. Perhaps we can send her files from Toledo to you and you can use them to teach other doctors. Maybe we can all learn from this."

He was unflinching. I didn't understand how he could show no emotion whatsoever.

I took a different approach.

I moved toward him, put my left arm around his shoulder, pulled him close, and said, "Just say you were wrong."

I held him tight. I didn't want to, but I was desperate. I was letting him know that this could be a friendly gesture or a threatening one – it was his choice.

I'm not sure if he was surprised, embarrassed, or frightened but I certainly had his attention. He didn't look toward me, but he nodded. I don't think he was conceding that he was wrong. I think he just wanted to get away from me. Either way, I didn't care. I stepped back, shook his hand, and thanked him.

The next day our attorney called me to tell me that OHIP had settled and agreed to pay all outstanding bills from Toledo General Hospital.

Despite my previous feelings for Dr. Morgan, in this moment, I was grateful for his actions. I don't know if he ever admitted his error, but he helped remove a tremendous burden for me and my family.

11

NOT WHAT I HAD IN MIND

"Mom, how are you?"
"I'm fine."
"Are you sure? You don't sound fine."
"I'm fine. How do you want me to be?"
"I want you to be great."
"Great. OK. I'm great. Everything is great. What are you doing?"
"I'm working."
"Why are you calling me?"
"I wanted to give you good news?"
"What's the good news? Are you having a baby?"
"No, Mom. I'm not having a baby."
"Oh. Well, I just thought that maybe you were. You know it would be good if you had a baby."

"We're trying."

"OK but hurry up."

"Mom, please."

"I'm not getting younger. I'd like to spend time with my grandchildren."

"You have a grandchild. AnnaMaria has a daughter. Spend time with her."

"I know. I do. But, you know, I want more grandchildren."

"Maybe you can adopt some. Or go to Grandmas Are Us...it's a store where they sell grandchildren to people like you."

"You're not funny."

"Guess what?"

"What is it now?"

"Harvard Business School asked me to speak at their school. They invited 12 people and I'm one of them. I'm the youngest of the group."

"That's nice."

"Mom, you understand this is Harvard. It's Harvard Business School. I don't even have a degree in business, but they want me to speak to their students."

"Yes. I understand. It's nice."

"This is one of the best schools in the world, and that's all you have to say. It's nice."

"What do you want me to say?"

"You could say that it's *great*!"

"It would be great if you had a baby."

It was spring of 2002, I had just turned 35, and I felt like our lives were returning to some level of normalcy. My mom's health was relatively stable. Amy and I were trying to have a child, but we were both spending more time working at our careers. I was OK with us working hard because I just thought that was what we were supposed to do. We had spent many years in university, and we were working our way to a greater level of prosperity. It felt good. But then, the very moment I began to feel comfortable that everything would fall into place with work, family, and everyone's health, adversity found me again. And this time, I didn't think I could overcome it. In a matter of nine months, anything that seemed important to me would be taken away.

One day, unexpectedly, without discussion or preamble, Amy handed me an envelope with a letter she entitled "Spill." In this letter, she confided that she had been lying to me about her whereabouts, every day for more than a year. Almost every afternoon, she would call me and tell me she was working late. I would ask, "How late?" "Not sure" was always the answer. I told her it was fine and to take her time. I would make dinner and wait for her. On most nights she would show up at eight, sometimes nine. I was there, dinner table set, waiting patiently. I thought it was great; I admired her work ethic. I, too, worked hard, and she was always supportive, so I returned the respect and encouragement. I thought we were on stable ground. But now, in this letter, I was reading about not just one lie but *hundreds* of lies.

At this point, we had been friends for more than 20 years and in a relationship for 13 years. I had full knowledge of her mental health the entire time. At least I thought I did; clearly, though, I knew only the tip of the iceberg. In the letter, she said that she told me she was at work, but then she would go out to binge. Sometimes she would frequent fast food restaurants and all-you-can-eat buffets; other times she would just load up the car with food from the grocery store. She would sit in her car and eat enough food for 10 people, then purge.

I read all of this and felt horribly sad for her. I thought about the loneliness and desperation she had been experiencing in those moments. It was too painful to envision the grotesque aspect of ingesting and then purging such a large volume of food. I could only handle that image for the briefest moment. I was more concerned about her well-being and her will to live. I couldn't understand how someone with so much talent, kindness, and beauty could destroy herself.

I wanted to understand more just so I could help her.

I asked her where she would go to do this, and she told me she couldn't remember because she would black out or just have a complete disconnection to her actions. Of all the things she had to say in that exchange, it was her last answer that bothered me most.

"You blacked out?" I asked. She nodded.

"You don't know where you were? Were you alone?"

She started to cry and replied, "I don't know."

My heart sank. I was crushed. I folded into myself. All the devotion, love, and support; all the years fighting and cheering for her, and that's where we were at: "I don't know."

As the days passed, I thought about the hundreds of phone calls telling me she'd be late, and I wondered how many "I don't knows" were involved. A few? A hundred? My mind constantly wondered about where she went, what she did, and whether she was alone. I thought that if she had lied to me so convincingly for such a lengthy period of time, what was to stop her from telling more lies in the future?

Despite all these startling revelations, I tried to make peace and forgive her. I couldn't envision being without her. I loved her deeply. I poured my heart out to her. I wrote poems for her. I made her laugh. I knew the smell of her skin. What her lips felt like. There were days, years, I couldn't wait to pull her closer. I did not want to let her go. I tried. I sincerely tried to move past what had happened, but the sheer volume of lies was too much for me to overcome.

Each day, I became less trusting and more resentful. If she told me the sky was blue, I would go check for myself. I had supported her, encouraged her to greater happiness, and stood by her even though she was confronting serious health problems. I could have left a long time ago, but I didn't. I stayed through so many dark days and nights, and now, here I was, feeling like a fool. I knew she was contending with serious mental illness, but I was still human. I was hurting, and I wanted to protect myself. I had been deceived daily. So now, every day, I would look at her and wonder where the next lie was. After a period of time, I knew this was no way for either of us to live. Both of us deserved the right to be free. We needed to be in a loving and open relationship where there wasn't daily scrutiny or fear. After two decades of friendship, we still loved each other, but it was time that we went our separate ways.

Like many who go through a divorce, I was living in a state of disillusionment and melancholy. I was not certain what to feel. I was constantly questioning whether it was the right decision. My parents certainly weren't happy, nor were many other relatives and friends. I had established another "first." I was the first person on both sides of my family to get divorced. It was an achievement I really didn't care to have. My mother kept encouraging me to "try one more time," but I didn't have it in me. After years of trying to climb this mountain, it was now time to walk around it.

The weeks passed as I tried to make peace with my decision, but it was still confusing. Then one day, as my mind wandered, I saw a car racing toward me as I crossed an intersection with my car. I knew my light was green, but I also knew that the car headed straight for me was not slowing down. It's quite an experience to watch 2,000 pounds of steel hit you when the only thing separating you is a window and a door. I remember tensing and leaning into it, instinctively thinking I might stand a chance at stopping it with my shoulder. I quickly discovered that I wasn't a linebacker, and this wasn't pick-up football in the park. The car plowed me directly into a telephone pole.

Smoke billowed and steel crackled as I tried to open my door. I had no luck. I managed to crawl to the passenger seat and open that door. I got out of the car, straightened myself, and looked at the car that hit me. A woman with long, faint blonde hair, in her mid-30s, jumped out of the driver's side of the car and said, "I didn't see the red light." I nodded. She continued, "I have to pick up my son at daycare." Again, I nodded. She then walked away and made a call on her cell phone. A police officer arrived within minutes. He asked me what had happened and then asked me if I needed an ambulance. I shook my head. "No. Maybe just a ride home. I live about a mile away." He suggested that I go to the hospital, but I had so many other things on my mind. I thought I would be fine. I was too young and too dumb to realize that it wasn't a smart decision.

I was lucky to be able to walk away from that accident. I didn't break anything, but I had plenty of pain. I smashed my head into the driver's side window and snapped back and forth with the rest of my body. From my neck to my waistline, my entire spine hurt when I moved in any direction. At times, over the next two months, the pain was so intense that it was difficult to walk, sit, or sleep. I didn't go to the hospital that day, but I spent a great deal of time working with a kinesiologist, acupuncturist, and chiropractor in the following months.

Despite being in pain, I still needed to work. I didn't want to sit and stew in the sadness of the divorce, so I worked longer hours. It was during this time I discovered that the senior partner and principal founder of our turnaround consulting firm was keeping a second set of accounting books.

In our firm, we had a practice of getting a deposit at the beginning of every engagement. Unlike law firms that typically bill weekly against a retainer and then replenish when empty, we held the deposit until the end of the engagement. When the last invoice was billed, we would generally deduct it against the deposit and return the remainder. In a consulting firm that specializes in working with distressed companies, things often slip through the cracks. In a crisis, things get lost or forgotten. The principal founder discovered that clients often forgot about their deposits. He would send them a final invoice, they'd pay it, and he wouldn't remind them about their security deposit. Unless they explicitly asked for it, he wouldn't return it, even though returning the deposit was clearly delineated in our contract.

When I discovered that one of my clients had not received his deposit nearly two months after the end of an engagement, I asked the senior partner about it, and he made no effort to hide his scam. He explained it to me in detail and was proud of this balance sheet enhancement. He gleefully told me he'd been doing this for years. When I asked how much he had put aside, he informed me that it was a few hundred thousand dollars, and he showed me the list. Most of the clients were from before I joined the firm, but a handful were recent. I was upset, but I still tried to find a positive solution for the problem.

I looked at him and said, "You messed up. But that's OK. What you did in the past is the past. But now, we can't do this again. We're going to return all of it, right now."

Rather than being relieved at my forgiveness, he went in the other direction. Instead of showing contrition, he was disgusted and said, "There's no way we are returning it."

He then explained that some of the companies were no longer in existence and wondered who we would send the money to. I suggested we find creditors that had not received full repayment of their loans and offer them the money. If not them, then the employees who got short-changed when the company was closed. If not them, then any suppliers that had lost. In my mind, there was a lengthy list of people that were entitled to this money. Essentially, everyone but us should have the money.

Nonetheless, he dug in his heels and said, "We earned that money."

I asked, "If we earned it, why have you been hiding this information? Why didn't you just invoice for the services delivered?" I received no response.

Since I was getting nowhere with him, I went to the other partners in the firm, but their consensus was to let sleeping dogs be. I explained to them that I would call and tell people that we discovered an accounting error, and this money needed to be returned. The more options I offered, the more resistance I received. The senior partner was defiant, and the others were lazy and cowardly.

They had to think about their reputations and how to explain all of this once it was made public. They knew the odds of anyone else finding this money was slim, so why make a fuss about it? In my mind, this was theft, but they believed it was something else. I'm not sure what they thought it was, but it was accounting. It was black and white. It was a number that went into a box that didn't belong to us.

It was now clear to me that I could no longer be a part of this firm. I couldn't understand any of the behavior. We were very profitable, successful, and trusted at prominent levels, so why take this money from struggling and suffering people? Why not return it? What would they do with the money? Distribute it among the partners? Why the greed? They had enough. How much is enough? None of this made sense, and none of it was in my moral compass. I knew that small problems would become big problems. If they could take this money, what would they take next? If they could sleep easily with this act, it would only give them more resolve for the next one, and I wanted no part of it.

After years of challenging work and great success in helping to build the firm, I decided to walk away. I resigned and gave up my partnership stake. I hated having to leave many of my colleagues. Most were talented and of high ethics. I was upset at the notion of having to start over again, but like Russia, it was a path I wasn't willing to follow. I could not go along with theft, let alone theft from people who were in dire need.

For most people, by this point in the year, it would have seemed like enough—enough suffering, enough surprises, and enough loss. It was too much. In less than seven months, I had lost my wife and my firm and had been plowed into a telephone pole by a speeding car. I thought it couldn't possibly get any worse. But that wasn't the case. It was only August; there were five more months left in this very long year.

My next car accident was as painful as the first, but the circumstances around it bordered on ridiculous.

I sat in my chiropractor's office as he examined me. He went up one side, down the other, moved each arm and then each leg, and then said, "You're in good shape again." He was conducting the final physical examination after my treatments for the first car accident. He said I was "good to go." I walked out the door a healthy man. I felt good; most of the pain was gone. I got into my car, put on my seat belt, and drove out of the parking lot. Seconds later, just outside his office, a car drove into the passenger side of my car. This time, I didn't see the car coming. I just heard the loud smashing of steel and glass as I bounced around the inside of the car like a beat-up rag doll. All the pain came rushing back into me. I'm not sure what nerve got pinched or which disc in my back was out of place, but I lost all my strength to lift my arms.

The police came, they filed a report, my car was towed away, and then I walked back into my chiropractor's office for a brand-new examination and treatment.

In the coming weeks, the lawyers for the two accidents wrung their hands with joy; they knew no doctor or judge could determine exactly which car accident had caused which injury. As such, despite the extensive ligament and soft tissue damage in my neck, back, and hips, I had to settle each case for basic expenses.

Life wasn't finished with me yet. The long year was still to become longer.

In late fall of 2002, without warning, I was diagnosed with acute keratoconus, an eye disease that causes the cornea to weaken and morph. It may have taken time to surface, but the diminished vision happened very quickly. One day I could read the labels in the grocery store, and the next, I couldn't. At first, I thought it was just stress from all the events of the year, but once I sat in the doctor's office, the answer was clear: One day I had 20/20 vision, and the next I had 20/1600, with no prospect of ameliorating it with contact lenses or glasses because the bend in my cornea was very steep.

In the following weeks, I consulted with three separate ophthalmologists hoping for a better diagnosis. At that point, I could see very little out of my left eye. It was very blurry, but light and color came through. My right eye had 20/40 vision, which made the loss of vision in the other eye more complicated. The eyes work in unison with the brain. If one side is clear, the brain believes the other eye should be clear as well, so it keeps sending messages to "clear up." As the brain struggled to adjust to my diminishing eyes, the muscles on the left side of my face became strained and I developed vertigo. Each day, the symptoms became worse. As I walked, my head would spin, and it felt like someone was punching me on one side of my face. The only way to make the pain subside was to wear an eye patch over my left eye or just close my eyes. When I did that, the brain would stop trying to synchronize it with the right eye. As I met with each ophthalmologist, my question was the same: "Will I lose my vision in the right eye, like I did with the left eye, and if so, when?" Each doctor gave me the same answer, "Yes, you will. It could be tomorrow, or it could be in 10 years." So, complete blindness was definitely in my future; I just didn't know when.

In less than a year, before my 36th birthday, the lights had literally been turned off on so many things that mattered to me, and now

I was facing the prospect of imminent and possible permanent darkness.

I went from feeling sadness to confusion to anger.

I lay on the floor in my living room, stared at the ceiling, and cursed out God and anyone I could remember from the Bible.

"FUCK YOU."

"Really. Just go *fuck off!*"

"Are you done? Are you done with me? What do you want from me? What is it? Please. Just go away."

I was in so much pain. My body hurt. My head hurt. My heart hurt even more.

"I CAN'T DO IT ANYMORE."

"I—can't."

"How much abuse do you want me to take in one lifetime?"

"ANSWER ME."

"HOW MUCH?"

"Fuck You and your son. Where is he? And your Holy whatever, your angels and your saints. Where are they when I need them? TELL ME. Where? I'll go there. Just tell me where. I'll go there. I promise."

No response ever came. I'm not sure if God was listening, but no one was answering my questions. I just sank further into despair as tears ran down my face.

"If you want me to die, then kill me. Just kill me."

"HELLO?"

"HELLO?"

"Please just go away. Please. You're hurting me. I can't take anymore. I just can't. Please."

I couldn't make any sense of it. I could typically handle one big problem, even two, and maybe three on a good day, but this was too much. This had reached a level of understanding that was beyond my reach and comprehension.

I eventually picked myself up and went to bed. I was getting nowhere talking to invisible air. I cleared my head and tried to be rational about where I was in life. With this clarity, I realized that there had to be a better way to live, and I knew I needed to do something other than swear at the sky and bathe in self-pity. My mother taught me that when things aren't going your way and you're not sure what to do, just do something. Anything that keeps you moving forward. Eventually you will find an answer, or, at a minimum, you will forget about what was bothering you.

She was right.

It was time to do something.

12

SEARCHING

"Where are you going?"
"Mongolia."
"Why do you want to go there?"
"I want to see how people live."
"You can't run from your problems."
"I'm not running. I'm doing something."
"OK, but can't you do something different?"
"Mom, do you even know where Mongolia is?"
"They live in those things. The jurts."
"Yurts."
"It's cold there now."
"I'll be fine."
"You made money but now you want to go live like you're poor."
"They're not poor."

"Your father didn't have an indoor bathroom until he came to Canada."

"Mom, I just want to go away. Everyone and everything are bothering me."

"Why don't you come here? Put a tent in the backyard. Stay in the cold. And you could use our bathroom whenever you want. Nobody will bother you."

"Mom, you're bothering me."

"I'm your mother. I'm supposed to bother you."

"I'm going to learn how to hunt with eagles."

"Why?"

"Because it's interesting to me."

"Are you bringing food with you?"

"I have some power bars. I can only bring one duffle bag."

"That's not enough. You're going to be hungry."

"They'll have food."

"You can accomplish the same thing in our backyard."

"Is Genghis Khan in your backyard?"

"No one ever said life was supposed to be easy."

"Maybe it can be easier."

"OK, then come here. It's easier. You can stay in the snow as long as you want."

"Do you think dad can run a cable line to the tent so I can watch television?"

"Sure. Why not?"

"Mom, I'll be fine. I'll talk with you in a couple weeks."

My mother knew I was hurting. She wanted to comfort me and keep me safe, but she also knew that I was like her. Once I had made up my mind, no one was going to stop me. She knew I needed to do something to help me heal; she just didn't feel that I needed to go to this extreme.

On December 31, 2002, I boarded a plane in Cleveland, Ohio. My final destination would be somewhere in Outer Mongolia, near the borders of Siberia and Kazakhstan. A year earlier, I had read an article about nomads who lived in the barren lands of the Altai Mountains. One of the customs of these nomads, which dated back a couple thousand years, was a sport called "eagle hunting," The nomads didn't hunt eagles but rather used them to hunt prey such as fox and rabbit. It was like falconry, only with golden eagles. I was fascinated by this phenomenon. I didn't understand how they could corral and train such a powerful creature that could fly away at any moment.

I was also captivated by the day-to-day life of nomads. I was curious why they were living the way they were in the 21st century. Up until that point in my life, I pursued financial freedom in any manner I could. I had grown up poor, and I believed having more and having the latest and greatest in every material possession was the pinnacle of success. Yet, these people appeared to live with the exact opposite intentions. They lived in tents and owned very few worldly goods, and from everything I read, they were very happy. I didn't understand how you could live essentially the same way for thousands of years and not want to experience more or different.

Four planes and three days later, I still had five hours of driving to reach my host in his home. I was with my translator and guide, Anya. I met up with him in the small, modest town of Olgii.

Within minutes of deplaning, I realized my toes were getting cold. It was -25 Celsius. For the trip, I was only permitted one duffle bag, which had to carry a sleeping bag, water, medical supplies, and some food. The clothing I wore would be the only clothing I had. When I prepared for the trip, I did a lot of research trying to find the right clothing and footwear. I needed clothing and boots that allowed me to be nimble because I would be on horseback four to six hours a day. However, I also needed clothing that could protect me from the extreme cold. During storms, the temperature could drop to -80 Celsius very quickly. In extreme situations, if you could not make it back to your shelter, you would have to kill your horse, gut it, and get inside of it until the storm passed.

Knowing all of this in advance, I set out to buy the best of what I could find. I wanted to be prepared for every possible change in climate. And I thought I was. But now, within minutes, I was feeling my toes get cold in my brand-new boots. I thought to myself, "I'm never going to make it." I thought if my toes were cold now, what would they feel like after hours or days in the cold?

I looked at all the people who were in front of me, including the children. I saw that they were all wearing similar boots. I figured if they were warm, then those should work for me. I turned to Anya and asked where everyone bought boots. We got in his car and drove a short distance to a utility truck that was parked at the edge of a park. This 8-by-15-foot truck was filled to the very top with stacks of leather boots. I gave them my foot size, they grabbed a pair, and they fit perfectly. The boots were made of simple leather, wool lining, and a wooden heel and sole. They were so well insulated that I only needed to wear one pair of socks. They cost $20 and were far warmer than my expensive, high-tech boots.

On our last leg of our journey, we traveled in an old Russian military van. It was uncomfortable but seemingly reliable as it meandered through a frozen desert following what appeared to be a path or road. There were the slightest traces of wheels in sand.

Anya was affable and highly informative. He had worked for National Geographic in the past and explained to me that the area we were traveling to had been visited by approximately 40 people from the Western world. Our host, "The Eagle Hunter," had been filmed by National Geographic but otherwise was a private family man. I didn't know his first name because Anya explained to me that it was a sign of respect to only refer to him by his title because it was held by so few others in the world.

At the outset of darkness, we arrived at a mud hut. It was a wooden framed home, covered with simple plaster and cement. The rectangular home was about 20 feet wide and 30 feet long, with a transparent glass, paned window on either side. Smoke billowed from a chimney, goats and sheep milled around in a nearby pen, and a dozen or so horses roamed in the open on the far side of the home. The home was almost pitch black when we entered. There was no electricity and no plumbing, and the only heat came from a small oven in one corner of the kitchen, which was fueled by animal dung. A few candles were lit throughout the home, but other than that, it was dark and cold. The outside temperature was now -34 Celsius. It was warmer inside but still cold. A little pile of burning sheep dung and a thin layer of plaster wasn't enough for me to take off my three layers of clothes.

Anya introduced me to The Eagle Hunter, his wife, mother-in-law, two daughters, his son, and, of course, their eagle. In the far end of the corner of one room was an eagle with a hood over its eyes, sitting quietly on a wooden perch. Just like any other pet, this eagle was adored, comforted, and considered to be part of the family.

The family had been waiting for us. Dinner was already prepared. We sat down at a simple round table, and within minutes, a large stainless-steel platter of steaming meat was placed in the middle.

I turned to Anya. "Looks good. What is it?"

Plainly, he said, "Horse."

"Horse?"

"Yes. Horse."

"But, Mongolians revere horses."

"We also eat them."

"You're celebrated warriors on horseback."

"We also have to eat."

"I understand but...you eat the thing that you treasure?"

"Do cowboys eat cows?"

I stared at Anya and nodded in agreement.

People need to eat. Who was I to judge? It was greasy, chewy, and not the least bit appetizing, but the entire family ate it calmly, quietly. It was peaceful. The food may not have been as tasty as what I was used to, but my hosts were sharing with me something I hadn't experienced in a long time—contentment.

After our meal, we retired early for the evening. Nine of us took refuge on the floor throughout this small home. Several of us were in sleeping bags, and the rest were under several layers of thick wool carpets and blankets. Anya explained to me that it would get much colder later in the evening because the fire in the kitchen was lit only once per evening. Eagle Hunter's mother-in-law controlled the fuel and the fire. She managed the animal dung carefully to ensure they had enough to last through the entire winter.

Each day, on horseback, we would head out into vast expanse of the land. The Eagle Hunter decided where we would stop to watch the hunt. When he found a suitable location, he would release the eagle into the air. The eagle would then circle around above us at varying heights, waiting for us to scurry up prey. We would go up and down smaller mountains and hills, hoping to flush out a fox or rabbit. When one did come out, the eagle would begin its attack. It wasn't as easy an attack as one might imagine—rabbits are fast, and fox fight back.

When the eagle did win an encounter, she wouldn't eat her catch until the Eagle Hunter came by her side and gave her permission. I was fascinated that this eagle wouldn't fly away. She had a wingspan greater than six feet and no ropes tied to her, and she would circle above us sometimes for miles at a time while we rode. She would fly up a thousand feet or more but then come down when the Eagle Hunter called for her. She would then circle on down and land on the Hunter's right arm.

Each day, Eagle Hunter would let me practice receiving the eagle. The eagle would sit at a nearby hill, and I would be anywhere from 100 to 200 yards away, wearing a thick leather glove on my right hand, holding a piece of meat tightly between my fingers. Eagle Hunter would whistle, and the eagle would swoop down in a graceful and majestic manner. She alternated between a slight tip upward and a slight dip downward with each movement of her wings. It was as if she was rowing through waves in a sea. When she was about 10 feet away from me, she would turn her talons up and head toward my arm with her feet first.

As the talons wrapped around my arm, her beak moved downward, and before I could blink, she would snatch the meat from my hands and have it halfway down her throat. As she swallowed the meat, she quizzically stared right into my eyes. I was never sure if she wanted more raw meat or wanted to eat my eyeballs as a snack. When the talons wrapped around your arm, there was no mistaking the ferocious power of the golden eagle.

After a couple days of training, I felt ready to ask the Eagle Hunter how he conquered this great beast of the wild and how it could peacefully live in his home, with his children, without threat of harm.

Through my translator, Anya, I asked him, "How do you get the eagle to be so obedient?"

Eagle Hunter nodded, shrugged, and said in Kazakh, "In the spring, I climb the very tall mountains where the eagles build their nests. I wait for the mother to be away from the nest, and I take one of the baby eagles. I bring it home and I feed it. It grows up thinking that I'm its mother. I am a steady supply of food and shelter, so that's all that matters to the eagle."

I then asked, "But when it's flying high above us, why doesn't it fly away?"

Eagle Hunter smiled. "There are these smaller wings in the middle of her back. Those wings allow eagles to fly at high altitudes. I clip them on a regular basis. She can still fly but never extremely high, which is what keeps her thinking that her food supply is here, so she stays nearby."

And there were my answers to this 2,000-year-old tradition. I was expecting more stoicism and mystery in the response, but instead it was brutal and straightforward. It was another awakening to simple realities in life and in nature that never seem to change. All of us need food, shelter, and companionship, and we'll take it in whatever manner it comes to us.

Despite the stark origins of eagle hunting, the Eagle Hunter and the Kazakhs and Mongols whom I met were exceptionally serene and gentle. They spoke in a hushed tone, a whisper. It was as if they didn't want to disrupt nature around them with their presence. Every day, they sang. They would sing to each other, to the animals, or just alone. They were in a constant state of welcoming life, nature, and others. One evening, a gentleman nomad was en route to sell some wood branches he had cut from trees in the taller mountains. He was on a camel. It was around two in the morning. He knocked on the door, introduced himself, and then asked if they had space for him to rest until the morning. Eagle Hunter and his wife gladly accepted him. They made him tea and gave him space on the floor with a few blankets. I asked Anya if they knew each other and he said, "No." He was just a stranger passing by who needed shelter for a few hours. The small home was already crowded, but they easily made room for another.

Over the coming days, we rode on horseback, hunting with the eagle. When I first arrived, the land appeared vast and barren, but now, even with my limited eyesight, I began to see detail and depth in stones and sand. I started to understand why the people had hundreds of ways to describe the coloring on a horse and why they sang to each other. They were more thoughtful about their observations and communication. They put a great deal of time and care into understanding each other and their surroundings. I may not have found answers for what was troubling me, but I gained wisdom that had been carried through many generations. Now it was time to go home. On the long trip back, I wondered if I had changed and what might come next for me in my world.

When I returned home, my first telephone call was to my parents.

"Mom, do you need a television?"

"Are you tired from your trip?"

"How about a sofa?"

"Ours are brand new."
"Twenty years old is not brand new."
"I had them reupholstered a few years ago."
"Do you want any paintings?"
"What did you eat?"
"I'm bringing you some paintings."
"We don't need anything."
"OK, then I'll give it to someone else."
"You can bring it here."
"Mom, did you ever eat horse?"
"Sure. It's a delicacy."
"Not exactly the word I would use to describe it."
"What's with all of this commotion?"
"I'm making my life easier."
"Are you going to become a nomad now?"
"Do you need a blender?"
"I think you're doing too much."
"Having less furniture is too much?"
"Sitting in a room, by yourself, with nothing, is too much."
"I'll see you next week."
"Why don't you invite some friends over?"
"Mom, I'm fine. I have to go."

And I hung up.

I wasn't fine. I was restless. Whatever sense of peace and harmony I had in Mongolia left me the moment I returned home. I thought I was running toward answers, but perhaps my mother was right; I may have been running from my problems. I had certainly learned new things about how to live and how to be grateful for the simplest of items or gestures, but the memories of my past were exactly where I left them. Maybe both of us were right. I had grown, but I still had important matters to resolve.

It was January 2003. I was back in Cleveland and determined to simplify my life. I started to believe that bad things happened to me because I had too many distractions in my life. I felt that if I had paid more attention, I could have avoided people lying or stealing from me or, even hitting me with their car. I was convinced that it was time to clear away everything that wasn't absolutely essential. I didn't have a lot, but emotionally, I felt that I had more than I needed.

There was also a very practical reason for going through this exercise. I wanted fewer material possessions around me because eventually I would go completely blind. I wanted fewer things to take care of, and bump into.

Once my home was cleared out of anything I deemed unnecessary, my mind went in the opposite direction I had planned. It began to race. I couldn't shut it off. Every night, I went to bed thinking, "Is this the night?" I worried and wondered if this would be the last night that I could see anything with my "good" eye. The doctors told me that I could lose the vision in my right eye as fast as I had in my left. I didn't want to be depressed about it, but I felt a sense of urgency to "see" as many things as I could before everything went dark.

I still had aches and pains from the car accidents. A significant amount of damage had been done to the ligaments around my hips. Some days, it hurt regardless of whether I was sitting, standing, or laying down. But, without question, the pounding headaches from my strained vision were more severe and persistent than anything else. The only way I could function was by wearing an eyepatch. I didn't enjoy wearing it, but it was necessary. At first, I felt like a pirate or a wounded animal. But eventually, I put my ego aside and decided to have fun with it. I bought eyepatches with different prints and logos on them. Everything from camouflage to leopard print and even a crucifix.

As I worked to manage the pain, I filled my days with reading and my evenings with watching movies. I just felt like I had to learn more about the mysteries of life and at the same time, watch movies before the time came when I might not be able to see the television screen.

For the next year, I became a regular at two places in my neighborhood: the video rental store and the used books store. I watched several movies every night and purchased no fewer than 10 used books every week. As I pored through the books, I kept the ones I really enjoyed, and I returned the rest back to the store to be resold.

Somewhere along this time, I learned from a friend about a monastery where visitors go on three- and five-day retreats, and they try to stay in complete silence the entire time. Like the nomads of Outer Mongolia, I was fascinated by the notion of people wanting to live a life in almost complete silence and prayer. I wondered why anyone would do this, and I was curious if I could do it, too.

In the spring of 2004, I made a trip to the Abbey of Gethsemani, in Trappist, Kentucky. The abbey, founded in 1848, sat on approximately 2,000 acres of rolling hills and woods. The monks who were custodians of this abbey belonged to a sect known as the Order of Cistercians of the Strict Observance. Sometimes they are just known simply as Trappist monks.

To stay at the abbey as a guest, you call them, and they print your name in their registry, in pencil, along with the days you want to visit. There are no email, mail, or phone confirmations. You just show up on the days you requested. They also do not charge any money for your stay. They provide you with your own room, bathroom, and several meals throughout the day, but you are not required to pay anything. If you decide to make an offering for what you received, it is completely voluntary and anonymous. You put your donation into an envelope and slide it under a locked door. This is done so those with limited means won't feel ashamed or burdened with payment. Also, those who have unlimited means are prevented from seeking favor or boasting. The primary purpose of the abbey is to provide a place of rest, nourishment, and prayer.

When you arrive at the abbey, you check in, they hand you a key, and then they scribble over your name in their registry book to the point that it's no longer legible. Privacy and anonymity are paramount. You are then instructed not to use your phone, computer, or radio or speak with other guests. The monks themselves do not have a vow of silence, but they instead have a practice of silence. They believe in no unnecessary talking. To communicate with the outside world, they designate one monk to work the receptionist desk, and they also have a monk or priest who is available for private one-on-one, spiritual consultation.

The monks believe their path through this world is best achieved by living a life in fraternal union and in solitude and silence. That the highest expression of God is found through work and prayer and a disciplined life. As such, each day, they rise at approximately 2:30 a.m. The first of seven prayer sessions that are done as a group begins at 3:15 a.m. The prayer sessions consist of singing the book of Psalms. Every two weeks, the entire book of Psalms is completed, and then they start again from the beginning.

Eight o'clock to noon is the principal time for monks to work. Each monk has one or two areas they focus on. For example, there are those who garden and those who cook food. Someone else focuses on sewing and repairing clothing, including shoes. And so forth. The goal of the abbey is to be as self-sufficient as possible, which minimizes their interaction and distraction with the outside world. However, one room has a 5-by-10-foot corkboard hanging on a wall. The corkboard is filled with letters from people who are requesting prayers. Most come from America, but many are from other countries. The prayers are for those who are ill, troubled, or just in need of a little extra guidance. Each monk scans the board, reads the letters, and chooses which people he will pray for throughout the day.

I found this lifestyle and discipline compelling. So much of my private and professional life was immersed in consternation and confusion. Often, I lived at a whirlwind pace. My work was surrounded by struggle, loss, and often deceit. But this was an entirely new world to me. This was a place of certainty and predictability. The monks did the same thing, every day. Over and over. They prayed and they worked and nothing else. I saw this great selflessness in them. They brought people into their home, asked no questions, cooked, and cleaned for them, and offered an expansive place to rest and renew peace within themselves.

In the coming days, I spent time with two monks who alternated duty on the receptionist desk, greeting and registering guests. Both men were in their 60s, but the similarities ended there. Brother Thaddeus was a gentle soul in a big body. He was brought to this monastery as an adolescent. He lived most of his life behind the walls of the abbey. It was the only world that he could remember. The other monk, Father Julian, came to the monastery later in life. He had been a lawyer in his younger years, then went on to join the seminary and eventually ended up at the abbey. Our conversations consisted of me asking them many questions about their way of life.

Brother Thaddeus and I sat on a wrought iron bench near one of the vegetable gardens.

I asked him, "Are you lonely?"

With his cherub face and a gleeful smile, he said, "No Domenic, I'm not lonely. I'm in prayer with the other monks, the world, and God."

"Are you bored?"

"No, Domenic. Every day, I go deeper into the silence to connect more closely with God."

"Do you ever want a change?

"No. No. This is the only world I've really known. I love it. I feel safe here. When I want to meet people, I just volunteer for the front desk position and I get to talk with wonderful souls, like you."

"Have you ever left here?"

"Yes. Several times. I went to visit my mother. I tried to drive myself. It was a terrifying experience. So many cars on the road. So many people driving so fast. It's supposed to take me five hours to drive to my mother's home, but it usually takes me eight or nine hours. I have to stop and pray every 30 minutes because I'm so nervous."

The monks loved the predictability and simplicity of their life. They stripped away most of what an average person would consider typical so they could focus on what mattered to them most—prayer. I was intrigued by the notion of having such a narrow range of focus and life. In one sense, it made them stronger because they felt they could reach the entire universe with their prayer. However, at the same time, they became more vulnerable to the outside world because of their lack of exposure to it.

The days passed and I tried to keep the exact same schedule as the monks, but it was too difficult. I had nothing to do other than think, sleep, and attend mass, but getting to church by 3:15 a.m. every day was a challenge. I would usually slide in just before 6 a.m.

As I sat in the church for hours and hours every day, my mind eventually wandered to thoughts about criminals. I had come across a lot of criminals in my life. It often left me in permanent protective state of being. As such, I developed a habit of thinking through how I or others might be harmed and how I could prepare for it in advance. It was common for me to scan rooms, look for potentially menacing people, and study the best exit from the building.

I stood in front of the reception desk. Father Julian was on duty.

I asked him, "Why don't you lock up the kitchen at night?"

Without lifting his head from the registry book, he answered sternly, "Someone might get hungry."

"Aren't you worried that they will take a lot of food?"

Still with his head down, "If they do, they must be really hungry."

"So, I can eat as much as I want, and no one will say anything to me?"

Nodding, "They may a say a prayer for you and your health. Clearly, you feel the need to eat."

"No, I'm fine. I'm just curious why you're so trusting."

Father Julian raised his head, turned to me, and said, "Our role is to provide a place of shelter, food, and worship if they so desire. It's not up to us to judge a person's path on Earth. It's between them and God."

It sounded virtuous to me, but I still didn't fully comprehend.

"What about hardcore criminals?"

"What about them?"

"This is an excellent place for a serious criminal to hide. You don't ask for identification. You don't ask questions. You erase every name written down. A murderer could come here and stay, free of charge, virtually invisible from the outside world." Father Julian again put his head down, resumed reading the registry. Patiently he answered me, "All of the abbeys of St. Benedict around the world have the same sign over their front door. It reads 'God Alone.' Did you see it when you came in?"

I nodded.

He continued, "It is possible that we could give safe harbor to a criminal. We don't ask for identification. We don't run a police background check. You, in fact, could be a criminal and I wouldn't know. It's not my place. If someone decides to be a criminal, that path is between them and God—alone."

This was a new and powerful concept for me. There was no scrutiny, no judging, no pre-determined path to righteousness and salvation. It was a path that you chose. No one could tell you what was spiritually right or wrong. It was between you and God, alone.

This was a big departure from the Catholic world where I was raised. From birth to death, there were rules and sacraments. The message was drilled into your head by priests: "If you want to get to God, you must go through us. The benevolence of your afterlife will be judged by how well you follow our instructions." All these instructions and rules were off-putting and confusing. Like many fallen Catholics, I went to church twice a year, Christmas and Easter, just to keep up appearances and just in case everything the priests were saying was true. Other than that, I tried to live a life of reasonable integrity and follow most of the 10 commandments. I wasn't sure if God actually commanded those to humanity, but they made sense for those who wanted to live in a civil and respectful society.

But now, learning about the Benedictines, I found something I could completely follow. I believed this philosophy and way of living of the monks was liberating. I thought this could free me from worry and from judging others. I was still upset at people who had wronged me, but I finally thought it was possible to stop the constant analysis and questioning, like "Why did they do that?" I could now just leave it at "It's between them and God." I knew it wouldn't be easy undoing a lifetime of preaching, but I thought I could try.

Over the next 18 months, I made several additional visits to the abbey. Each time, I stayed longer. Once, Father Julian invited me to do my retreat at a cabin farther in the woods. It was a place used by monks when they felt they needed to go even deeper into solitude and prayer. I spent a week at the cabin and enjoyed each day more than the previous. I came to learn from the monks that although they appeared selfless and they donated all their profits to various charities, most of them felt they were leading a selfish life. They believed their lives were much easier than those on the outside world because they never had to worry about bills, jobs, children, family, work, and a boss. They led a simple, sheltered life of prayer, and they felt they were in communion with God every day. To them, this was the best gift they could ever ask for. I was grateful for the silence. It created an environment where I could examine the past without distraction. The quieter it became, the more peaceful I was. In that space, I could reflect and explore without anger or irritation. It gave me greater objectivity, which ultimately made me more hopeful about my future.

By fall of 2005, I had read everything I could about dozens of subjects. Everything from bird watching to astronomy. I also had watched every movie in the video store at least one time. I had been away from turnaround and crisis management for more than two years. My eyesight was not perfect, but I was used to the daily pain and limited vision. My life was quieter and calmer. I should have been happy. I thought that I had made peace with my past.

I hadn't.

There was something under my skin that clawed at me. I wasn't violent. I didn't pick fights. I wasn't angry. But I just wasn't settled.

One evening, I sat on a stool at the bar of a highly regarded restaurant in Cleveland. In my left ear, I listened to a man brag to the bartender about taking advantage of a woman on his second date. In my right ear, I listened to my friend ask me for help because his girlfriend had been raped. I couldn't look in either direction. I looked forward, and as I began to feel like I was shrinking into my stool, my eyes scanned the liquor bottles on the shelves of the bar.

In my left ear, I heard, "She was tight. I did her a favor. I could tell she hadn't had it in a while."

In my right ear, "He did it in the office. There were no witnesses. He's friends with a lot of cops."

I didn't understand why after all I had been through, all the spiritual searching and growing, I still found myself here, in a dark and disturbing place. How was it that again, I was in the middle of ugliness? Why couldn't I be hearing nice stories? Why didn't people come to me wanting to share their joyous moments? Why did they bring their worst to me?

In my left ear, it continued. "I'll go out with her again. She's a little snobby for me, but I'll teach her how to have fun."

My eyes kept scanning the bottles. My anger grew. It bubbled from deep inside. My stomach turned at what I was hearing. Making it worse, the evil around me seemed to grow as the story continued. I watched the male bartender smile and laugh along to this clear admission of rape. No one cared. They just chuckled like ignorant schoolboys.

I continued scanning through the bottles of liquor. I analyzed each one—gin, rum, whiskey, vodka, tequila, brandy. *Brandy. I think brandy will create the most flame.* I remembered the waiters from the restaurant of my youth. They used to make cherries jubilee in front of the customers. They would pour brandy in the pan and light it on fire. A dramatic light gold and blue flame would rise and swirl about for a few seconds of entertainment. *Yes, I think brandy will do it.*

In my right ear, my friend's voice continued, "Dom, I was thinking maybe you could bring over one of your guys from Russia. A security guy. And, you know, take care of this asshole."

I turned to my friend. "Take care of him how?"

He took a sip from his martini and sheepishly said, "You know, kill him. I'll pay whatever it takes. Just have your guy kill him. We have to do something. She was raped, and nothing else can be done about it. So, this is what we need to do."

I turned back to again face forward. I shrank even further into my stool. I was 38 years old, and my life was still this. It felt like a never-ending game of British Bulldog. The left side of my head was trying to figure out which alcohol would burn faster because I wanted to set the arrogant rapist on fire. I wanted him to feel the burn of an unwanted predator attacking him. To feel just as he had made that poor woman feel. At the same time, the right side of my head was trying to understand why my good friend was asking me to participate in a murder. One side of me was planning to commit a crime, and the other side was being repulsed by the suggestion of corporal violence. I felt as if I was on the verge of insanity. That at any moment, I might just lose all sense of reason.

My mind slipped away. It floated above the other tables. I wondered what other people in the restaurant were talking about. I wondered if they too were hearing awful stories and being asked to commit crimes. It didn't seem plausible to me, but what if it was? What if I was just permanently stuck in a world filled with evil?

Somehow, through my sense of dread, I thought, *I have to get out of here. I'm not going to jail. I'm not setting anyone on fire. I'm not going to have someone murdered. I'm not judge and jury for the universe.*

I turned back to my friend. "What comes next?"

Quizzically, he asked, "You mean, like the money? I can get it right away."

I shook my head. "No, not the money. What happens after my guy kills your guy?"

Still with a look of wonder. "He goes back to Russia, and no one knows anything."

I pulled myself up and straightened. "But I know. You know. And he knows. And one day, he's going to come back to you for more money. And he's going to keep coming back to you for money. If you don't pay it, he will kill people close to you. He will keep killing until he has everything you own. You understand? Once you cross this line, you're in another world. If you want to do that, it's up to you…but that's not how I live. If you want my advice, I suggest you go home, eat your pain, and move on with your life."

I got up from my stool and left the restaurant.

The following morning, I went looking for answers as to why I kept finding myself in the middle of trouble. I remembered a book I had read on trauma. It was one of countless books I had read in the previous couple years. It was a book written by a trauma specialist who had treated more than 16,000 patients. It was titled *The Healing Dimensions* by Brent Baum.

In *The Healing Dimensions*, Brent shares his belief of how trauma is dealt with by the soul and the physical body. In his definition, trauma includes physical, emotional, and spiritual trauma. Brent carefully explains through many different patient stories how our soul and mind take the very last second of the impact of a trauma and cause a momentary "short-circuit" in our brain. This "short-circuit" is a mechanism created so we don't feel the most painful part of the moment of the trauma. Rather than having the pain flow through you, it is instead "frozen" in a cell and stored away in our subconscious mind. This phenomenon occurs to protect us from our nervous system being completely overwhelmed and collapsing.

The actual physical pain will be felt in that moment, but most often, the memory of the trauma will be forgotten or just partially remembered. Brent's theory is that we are designed not to remember all the pain of the trauma every day or all at once because we would not be able to function in the present.

Brent believes that when we experience trauma, it stays buried within us, waiting to be released. We don't want to carry around that pain with us forever, so our subconscious mind looks for ways to surface it and release it. Often, the best way to surface this pain is to recreate circumstances that are similar to the ones that caused the initial trauma. In other words, like attracts like. This is one reason why people will find themselves in similar situations, reliving conversations and dynamics that constantly seem to be the same. And this is why sometimes we just look at someone or hear their voice or smell something and it upsets us. We don't know exactly why, but there is *something* about that person, sound, or scent that makes us uncomfortable, worried, or angry. According to Brent, that feeling is tied to an unresolved trauma from the past. Your subconscious mind keeps bringing it back to you so you can deal with it and release it.

To aid and expedite the release of trauma in the gentlest of ways for his patients, Brent spent decades developing a methodology called Holographic Memory Resolution (HMR).

HMR is a process that uses a myriad of images and senses to help people access the very last millisecond in time of the trauma that is stored away in their subconscious memory.

After rereading the entire book, I called Brent's office and scheduled to consult with him in person.

Three weeks later, in Tucson, Arizona, I was in his office, sitting on a plain, black utility chair. Brent was sitting in front of me on a similar chair. He was of modest size, with jet black hair. His skin glowed, and he looked much younger than his actual years. After a brief discussion of why I came to see him, he calmly began asking me questions.

"Is there anywhere in your body at this moment where you feel pain or discomfort?"

As he asked the question, my head started throbbing.

"Yes, the back of my head just started hurting."

"Is there any color, shape, or sound that you feel or see when you focus on that pain?"

"I see a park. I think it's the park across from my grade school."

"What's happening in the park?"

"I'm on my knees and two boys are there. They're bigger than me. One is standing behind me and the other in front of me. The one behind me is holding my coat, and he's punching me in the back of my head."

Now, my head began to hurt more intensely.

"How old are you when this is happening?"

"I'm not sure. About eight or nine."

"Why is the boy punching you?"

"We were playing football. There were a lot of us. The older boys got mad because we were scoring more than them. They just started pushing and punching some of us."

"How do you feel when this happening?"

"I'm hurting. I want to run away, but I can't because he's bigger and he's holding me down."

"OK, we don't want that to happen any longer. If you could go back in time, in this moment, what would you like to see happen?"

"I don't know. I just don't want to hurt."

"To do that, what would have to happen? Would you want to not be in the football game at all? Or be bigger than them? Or would you want to be extremely fast so you could outrun them?"

"I want to be big. Twice their size."

"Terrific, let's imagine you being a giant, so they don't even think of hitting you. Can you picture that?"

"Yes, I can. It's funny. Now, they're scared."

"Great. When you picture you as a nine-year-old giant, is there any color that comes to mind?"

"Yellow...and red."

"Perfect. Let's take the color yellow and red and run them through your entire body, starting from the top of your head to the bottom of your feet. Let's do that a couple times."

I ran the colors through me, and instantly, the pain in the back of my head went away. I had not remembered or thought of that instance in the park, but once this memory surfaced, I thought back to the times we did play in the park. We always played a bit rough, but there were a couple of occasions where big fights did break out. This happened to be one of them.

I spent the next 90 minutes going up and down my body, following aches, pains, twitches, and surfacing memories from all ages. Some were highly emotional moments, like my mother yelling at me; some were surprising, such as a car accident. However, most were some type of physical pain where I was being hit or falling down. The only commonality among all of them was that prior to that session, I had never thought about or remembered any of those moments.

I left Tucson feeling calmer than when I had arrived. The HMR process allows you to remember traumatic moments, but once you have reframed them, those original feelings of anger, fear, anxiety, etc. go away. The process allows you to look back at those instances without being so emotionally charged. You will have emotions, but you will be in a better position to constructively reflect on them.

As I thought about the memories that surfaced, I didn't find anything alarming or peculiar about them. I knew I had a rough and tumble life and that I had been physically disciplined a lot, but prior to that point, I didn't invest too much time in looking back. Brent explained to me that more traumas could surface in the future, but that this is all my soul and body could handle at this particular time. I heard what he said, but I had reframed dozens of moments, so I figured that I was done, and I would now be a better version of myself.

I was wrong.

After a brief period of being calm, my irritability and underlying anger came back.

In the next six months, I met Brent three times. Each time, we did multiple hour-long sessions over the course of two or three days. By the end, I surfaced hundreds of traumatic memories. On one level, emotionally, I was feeling better. However, I was struggling to contend with the sheer volume of pain I had endured over the course of my life, in particular my childhood.

Brett was also surprised at the extent of what I had lived through. However, he was most intrigued by the fact that I was able to carve out a constructive life for myself despite going through all these ugly experiences. He was surprised I hadn't ended up in jail or addicted to narcotics. After lengthy discussions, Brent concluded that at some point in my childhood, the pain was too overbearing, and that part of my soul just detached from my body to protect itself. In that detached soul was someone more gentle, artistic, and giving. I survived by occasionally drawing from that energy while on the exterior, I cultivated and lived with a tough guy persona that was comfortable in troubled and even dangerous environments.

I spent years looking for answers for the world I lived in and the people who surrounded me, and now I had some of them. But I was still unclear as to why my mother had been so enraged and so forceful with me. As adults, we had become friends. We had a great relationship, talking with each other and helping one another. However, I couldn't brush the past under the rug any longer. More than 25 years had passed since she last hit me, but I needed to hear from her why she did this to me.

In the spring of 2006, shortly after my 39th birthday, I was in the basement of my parents' home, helping my mother can and preserve artichokes. All of us loved artichokes, so there was box of about a hundred of them in front of us that needed to be cleaned and cooked. With steak knife in hand, both of us spun and trimmed one artichoke at a time. I thought this would be a good time to talk.

"Don't trim too much."

"Do you realize how many times you hit me?"

"You were a handful."

"What did I really do? What was so bad that I needed to be hit?"

"You're cutting too much."

"Mom."

"There's going to be nothing left. They're expensive."

"Mom."

"It wasn't that much."

"Are we boiling all of these together?"

"I was a good mother."

"Yes, you were but you also beat the daylights out of me."

"That's what people did in those days. We were stupid."

"I don't care about other people."

"I'm sorry."

"Do we boil them all together, yes or no?"

"I was young. I didn't know what to do. I was trying to protect you."

"By hitting me?"

"I'm sorry."

"Together, yes or no?"

"I knew you were special."

"Special? Did you just say special?"

"You were very smart. Very creative."

"I'm 39 years old and this is the first time you tell me this."

"We're going to boil them in four batches."

"Special."

"We do 25 at a time, so they don't overcook when we're putting them in the jars."

"Why didn't you tell me what you really thought when I was a kid?"

"I didn't want your head to get too big."

"What? So, instead you beat me?"

"Sometimes when people are gifted, they get arrogant."

"MOM!"

"It happens."

"There was no other way you could find. None. That was your only solution?"

"I didn't know what I was doing. I'm sorry. If I could change it, I would. I'm sorry."

She put down her knife and started to cry.

Again, she repeated "I'm sorry." Then she walked out of the room.

It's the first time I ever saw my mother cry.

I wasn't comforted by her answers, although it was nice to hear that she thought that I was "special." I knew I wasn't unfortunate in life, but whether it was true or not, it's always uplifting to hear that you're special, at least to someone.

By this age, I knew my mother well enough to know that she was hurting. She was never overly expressive with her emotions, but I could see in her eyes and certainly in her tears that she was genuinely remorseful. Apart from her method of disciplining me, she had been an incredible mother to me and my sister. She put our needs before hers and gave us everything she could give so that we could build our own lives. I couldn't go back in time, but I did know the path forward.

Everything I learned from my time with the monks to my sessions with Brent taught me the importance and power of forgiveness. Jesus forgave. The Dalai Lama forgave. The seminal lines of the central prayer for all Christians are "forgive of us our trespasses, as we forgive those that trespass against us." If these spiritual leaders across different religions and across many centuries could forgive, so could I.

I knew that by forgiving, I was releasing pain, anger, resentment, and frustration. Without that release, the best I could do in life was survive. If I couldn't forgive, I would never have the freedom to truly grow and experience life at a higher, more fulfilling level. I could never genuinely love without having that compassion and courage to forgive. I loved my mother, and I wanted a closer relationship with her, so I chose to make peace with the past. I let all of it drift away. I forgave my mother, but I'm not sure my mother was ready to forgive herself. I believe she had been carrying that pain and regret for decades. I often wondered if all her illness manifested because of it. She had great empathy and acceptance for the mistakes of others, but unfortunately, I never saw her treat herself with the same gentleness and understanding.

13

YOU'RE NOBODY TO ME

By the summer of 2006, my eyesight began to stabilize. I was still legally blind and most of my world appeared as if I was seeing it through a glass of water. However, the vertigo and double, sometimes triple, vision had subsided. I could walk around without an eye patch and not experience a persistent spinning or off-balance feeling. I felt it was time to return to work.

By then, I had been away from crisis management and corporate restructuring for more than three years. I suspected the turnaround world had not changed, but I knew I had. Despite the intensity and complexity of corporate crisis, I felt that I was more mature and wiser. I carried myself in a slower and more humble manner. My pace and words were more caring and measured. I had sincere reverence for life. I wanted the best for everyone, but at the same time, I was profoundly aware of the duality that existed in all of us. That we could be both resilient and weak. Now, it was time for me to see how I would approach helping others and leadership with this new disposition. Was I profoundly different, or was I just older and more experienced?

In the next couple of weeks, I met with several turnaround firms. All were equal in opportunity, but one seemed like it would align more with my interests. It was a firm staffed with only senior executives. I felt that there were a lot of senior and experienced people whom I could learn from and work with. At age 39, if I joined them, I would be the youngest person in the company.

We had a long meeting. We discussed parameters and compensation. All seemed agreeable, so I signed an employment contract on the spot. I shook my new boss's hand, thanked him, and said, "I'll see you in a week." A little surprised, he responded, "I thought you were going to start right away?" I smiled and said, "I'm going on vacation. It might be the last one I take for a few years. Might as well go now while I can." My new boss laughed. He knew there was a lot of truth in that statement. He knew the work could be unrelenting, and when you were in the middle of a crisis, there was no such thing as downtime or vacation. You worked until the bitter end.

The next day I was on a plane to Italy.

It was a vacation, but it was also great timing for a trip to Italy because my parents were already there, visiting family. My mother had a stretch of time when she, too, had her health stabilize, so they decided to visit their hometown of Ceccano, Italy.

"Kwe-stoe?"

My Italian was terrible. I hadn't spoken it in a long time.

"Per rinfresecante."

"Ree-frey-sey-con-tey."

I think that means "refresh." I was fairly certain it meant "refresh."

My mother and I were visiting the Abbey of Casamari. It's about 30 minutes east of Ceccano, closer to the Abruzzo mountains. She had been here in the past but wanted to see it again because of its rich history dating back to the 11th century. The monastery is framed with stunning architecture and filled with beautiful sculptures and paintings. The grounds of the abbey also house a hybrid between a retail store and an apothecary. For many centuries, the monks residing at the abbey grew their own food and made their own medicinal remedies. I was curious to see what they had to offer because I could not shake my jet lag. The six-hour time change was keeping me up all night and making me groggy during the day. I needed something to keep me awake so I could enjoy the time with my parents.

I stood in front of a glass case filled with little bottles of herbal remedies. A very patient, elderly monk, dressed in a plain chestnut brown robe, stood just behind it. No one other than my mother was in the shop. She quietly and curiously looked at items on the shelves as she roamed around the far end of the store, about 30 feet from me.

I pointed to the next bottle and again asked, "And this one?"

"Kwe-stoe?"

"Per stitichezza," the monk replied.

My very tired ears and my poor Italian skills heard "stanchezza."

"Stahhn-ketzza." Perfect. This is for fatigue.

"Mom. They have something for fatigue."

My mother stared at me and in a hushed tone, mindful of the sacredness of the abbey, said, "Stee-dee-ketzza."

"Mom, I know. Stahhn-ketzza."

Again, she repeated, "Stee-dee-ketzza."

"Mom. I know. It's to wake you up."

Now louder, she said, "STEE-DEE-KETZZA."

"What? What are you saying?"

"STEE-DEE-KETZZA."

I knew that my Italian was rusty, but I had no idea what she was saying.

"What?"

She stopped walking and said.

"CONSTIPATION."

I began laughing, thinking my mother had lost her mind. Before I could say anything, she continued.

"IT'S A LAXATIVE."

Oh my. That would definitely keep me awake. I turned to the monk and said, "No Grazie." I nodded my head, thanked him again, and walked away.

As I approached the door to exit, my mom looked at me with a big smile and said, "Where would you be without your mother?" I smiled and said, "After a bottle of that stuff, I'm sure you'd know where to find me."

The rest of the week continued in the same way. Days filled with funny, whimsical moments and, of course, terrific food. My parents had left Italy 50 years earlier, but they had just as many friends as they had in Canada. Despite all the medical issues my mother had been through, now at age 60, her skin still glowed, her hair was dyed but thick, as it always had been, and she moved and walked without worry, as if she had never been ill. She loved being around people. She would visit or be visited by a handful of friends and relatives every day. She remembered all their families and their stories. Always listening intently and expressing genuine care for those in front of her.

It was my fourth trip to Italy since my childhood, and it was the most relaxing and enjoyable time we had spent together in many years. It was great being able to walk through the same fields and mountains and along the same roads my parents and grandparents had walked as children. The stories they shared with me when I was younger were taking on a more complete and richer meaning in me as an adult. I could physically see and feel how far our family had come from the days of the Depression, World War II, and working the land as impoverished citizens. It was a long, hard road that gave me and others an absolutely wonderful life.

When I returned from Italy in the fall of 2006, the corporate restructuring was sleepy. There wasn't much activity in the Troubled Loans departments of banks across the country. The economy was booming and was being led principally by a very fast-growing housing market. Both rich and poor were buying, building, or renovating homes everywhere you looked. I was hoping to put my newfound wisdom to use, but I was spending my time having coffee and dinners with others who were just enjoying the good times of the roaring 2000s.

However, as each month passed, an ominous sign of trouble would bubble to the surface. Private equity firms were buying companies for amounts far more than they were worth. Bankers were making loans without any real and detailed scrutiny. Others in our industry assured me this was the "new normal." That there was more money in America than there were places to invest in. I listened and I watched. I tried to understand, but none of it made sense to me. I felt that you couldn't just keep throwing money around. At some point, the bills have to be paid.

By the early summer of 2007, as the stock market continued to climb to record highs, I was thrown into a burning corporate fire. A complex and complicated situation between multiple banks, private equity firms, and the largest automotive makers in America.

I had just turned 40, and I was appointed chief restructuring officer of a $150 million automotive parts supplier. The company had three separate locations and employed approximately 1,500 people who were not part of a union. It had been in a power struggle with its customers, the automotive makers, for more than two years. They needed price increases to stay solvent, but the automakers refused to give them a penny more. For the automakers, it was part of the automotive supplier industry: You make a certain number of parts for us at a loss, and over time, we will give you profitable business to stay afloat. Unfortunately, for this one supplier, the automakers had personality conflicts with its senior managers. The automakers decided that they no longer wanted to work with them. They stopped giving them new business, so it was losing money every week that passed. Eventually, the company was completely out of cash and credit. There was no choice other than to file for bankruptcy.

In this instance, as chief restructuring officer, my job was to shepherd the company through the bankruptcy process. Typically, in this role, I would attempt to do everything possible to re-organize and re-structure the company to make it profitable. However, in this situation, I was instructed by all the parties involved to just sit at my desk, put numbers into a spreadsheet, and make sure the parts got made on time while they tried to find new owners for the business. Not wanting to make waves, I just went along with the program, figuring it would be best for my professional career, and it would also help as many employees as possible.

As each month passed, the abuse of power grew. I sat and watched as people lied and tried to manipulate each other. The slightest provocation would bring out no fewer than a dozen lawyers to argue the matter. People and institutions fought over nothing. They fought just because they could. With every fight came a ticking clock where consultants and lawyers charged for their time. Everyone was fighting to resolve things that should never have come into existence. Money was wasted on pointless debates rather than being used to repay suppliers that had extended credit to these bigger companies.

In the fifth month of this bankruptcy, we were coming close to finalizing the sale of the company to a new owner. However, there was one unresolved issue. At the beginning of the bankruptcy, the automotive makers agreed to pay for the employees' health insurance and workers' compensation. The one sticking point was claims that were made in the last couple weeks of the bankruptcy. The bills for those claims would not be processed and come in until after the company was sold; therefore, the automotive companies needed to put the money into a fund. That fund would then settle any outstanding claims.

Each month I asked when the money was going to be set aside for this fund. I had to ask because it was not an insignificant amount. The fund required at least $1.5 million. Each month, I was brushed aside and told that it would be taken care of "soon."

I finally realized that they had no intention of paying into any fund for healthcare or workers' compensation claims. They knew this company was not unionized so there wouldn't be a fight. Most of the 1,500 employees were single moms and dads in small towns in Ohio, making $12 an hour. They had no leader, no representative, and no attorney advocating for them. I knew if the funds were not put aside for their claims, each of the employees would get stuck paying their own doctor and hospital bills – even though each week they were paying into an insurance policy. I had sat and played nice for many months, but I needed to do something to help these people. I needed to do something that would wake people up and get their attention.

At each plant, the automotive companies had half a dozen engineers monitoring all production. They were the eyes and ears for the big bosses that ensured things ran smoothly and the parts were shipped on time.

I knew that without these engineers on-site, the automotive companies felt blind and deaf. So, this is where I would start.

I called the plants and had my team escort these engineers to the door. I threw 18 of them to the curb at 3:30 p.m. Some of them were confused, but most of them laughed. They had never been thrown out of a plant, and they giggled at the prospect of watching me be punished by the big bosses. They knew a move like this would guarantee that I would never again work for the automotive companies. An obnoxious move like this would certainly cost me a tremendous amount in lost future revenue.

It took 20 minutes for the lawyer representing the biggest automaker in Detroit to call me.

"Domenic, did you throw all of my client's engineers out of your plant?" he asked.

"Yes."

"Why would you do that? It's illegal. We have an agreement. We will get an injunction."

"That's a good idea. You should go to court. We should all go to court. I want to explain to the judge how you are cheating 1,500 employees out of their healthcare insurance and workers' compensation claims."

"We said that we'd pay those claims. We're going to pay them."

"Great. Pay them today."

"This is not the way to negotiate."

"It's not a negotiation."

I hung up on him before he could respond.

Ten minutes later, my lawyer phoned me. "Domenic, you can't..." I hung up on him before he could finish his sentence. I wasn't in the mood for a lecture.

Ten minutes after that, the bank's lawyer phoned me, and I hung up on him, too.

I had a succession of lawyers calling me over and over. I ignored all of them.

I then called my team at each plant. I told them to buy a disposable camera and go to the bar where these engineers were hanging out. Our plants were in small towns; I knew it would not be difficult to find them, and I knew for certain they were drinking and still laughing at my certain demise. I then instructed my team to take pictures of each one of them. Not in secret. I told them to walk up to them and snap a picture. Most posed and smiled.

Twenty minutes later, Detroit was on the phone again. This time, there were three lawyers on the call. The most senior lawyer began the conversation in a confused and almost hushed tone:

"Domenic, did you take pictures of all of my client's engineers?"

"Yes," I replied. "And I have pictures of you and your legal team, too."

"Why? Why would you do that?"

"I'm going to put all of the pictures on the company bulletin boards."

His voice tightened. "What exactly are you trying to do?"

"Well, in a couple of hours, all the employees are going to find out that they're not going to have health insurance or workers' compensation. They're going to be really mad. They're going to want to kill people. I just want to make sure they kill the right people."

Before he could respond, *I* hung up the phone.

Ten minutes later, they phoned back.

"Domenic, we already agreed to pay this amount, so why are you doing this?"

"Because I think you and your client are deceitful and have no intention of paying."

"Domenic, we can meet tomorrow and make the appropriate plans."

"Sorry, too late. I need the money today. If I don't have it today, I am shutting the plants down at midnight. If I don't have adequate insurance, I cannot in good conscience let people into the plants knowing that they might get hurt and there's no money to pay for their healthcare."

There was a long, silent pause.

Threatening to shut down production lines in the automotive industry is absolutely forbidden. It is something never to be uttered out loud. It's considered a lethal threat. When a main production line shuts down, it can cost the automotive company anywhere from $20,000 to $50,000 a minute. At that rate, millions of dollars in costs can accumulate quickly.

"My client can't pay today."

I hung up.

They immediately called back. The senior lawyer took the lead. He had lost his patience. He yelled into the speaker phone: "YOU ARE HOLDING A GUN TO MY CLIENT'S HEAD. THIS IS NO WAY TO NEGOTIATE."

I burst out laughing.

"Hey, I didn't ask to be Jimmy Hoffa. I'm not trying to form a union here. You made a deal—just honor the deal. Your client got parts for their cars. Pay your bills. These people worked in earnest for you, and now you want to cheat them. This isn't a gun. A gun is a single mom showing up at an emergency room with her kid on a Saturday night thinking she has insurance. Then two months later when she's unemployed, she gets a bill for $1,500—THAT is a gun. Pay your bills or you don't get your parts."

I hung up.

The phone never rang again.

No lawyers bothered me.

Thirty minutes later, $1.5 million was wired into our account.

Problem solved.

I got the employees their money, but it was a bittersweet moment. I wasn't entirely sure if I had used my wisdom or street fighting skills to resolve the matter. I thought I had grown beyond being so crude and blunt. I had hoped that when I returned to the crisis management world, I would be more calm and more clear in my decision making and judgment. I thought my time with the monks and nomads and Brent would have made me more sage and wise. But apparently that didn't happen in this situation. When push came to shove, I again jumped in and plowed ahead. The only thing I was focused on was the people in trouble. I felt like I could help them, and I didn't care what others thought of me, or what it would cost me in future lost income.

And this is how the next few years would continue. I dove into one burning fire after another.

By September of 2008, one of the biggest and oldest brokerage firms in the country, Lehman Brothers, collapsed, and the entire world fell with it. A cascade of personal and corporate debt engulfed the country, and my firm and I were right in the middle of all of it.

I worked endless hours, fighting to help as many people as I could. Each assignment became more complicated and more desperate as we moved deeper into the Great Recession.

In a brief period of time, I advised and restructured billions of dollars of debt. In a matter of 22 months, in addition to having dozens of other clients, I served as CEO and CRO (chief restructuring officer) for three different companies, in three different industries, all with revenues greater than $100 million, all with thousands of employees staffed across big portions of the United States and all in deep trouble.

By spring 2009, I was a partner in my firm. I had been given awards and recognized as a leader in the industry. If my soul had been looking for something greater to achieve, I think this was it. I was able to help countless people in need, and I was able to build a successful consulting practice. All of it was immensely rewarding.

It felt good to be able to help preserve job and communities. It also felt great to be in a position of authority where I could influence other decision-makers. However, it was also a place where you could never get too comfortable, regardless of your success. In the restructuring world, it is believed that with every promotion, you're one step closer to the door. In a world of panic, fear, and diminishing assets, if you can't find the money to repay the lenders or investors, those at the top get fired quickly.

By the summer of that same year, the 70- and 80-hour work weeks had finally taken a toll on me. My vision deteriorated significantly. I no longer felt comfortable driving a car, so I decided to move to New York City because it was the easiest city in the country to get around without having to drive. My firm had an office and several employees there, so I felt that it would be an easy transition.

I was legally blind but still working long hours and managing multiple clients in addition to managing our firm. Despite my positive attitude, it was still a persistent challenge to get through a day. I could not see someone's face if they were more than three feet away from me. Everything was a blur. I learned to walk and move methodically. Gone were the high-energy days of my younger years. I couldn't move fast because I would experience vertigo. Routinely, my head would spin, and I would bump into chairs, desks, doors. If I turned my head too quickly, the blur would feel as if someone had spun me in a circle.

At times, it was difficult to live with the physical impediment because I knew it was a problem that wouldn't go away. It was painful and debilitating, but I tried to be optimistic, so I adjusted to my circumstances. I learned to put most of my energy into listening carefully and feeling the energy in people. I also focused on information more intently. I became much better at memorizing numbers and events. I needed to remember facts and figures because I couldn't rely on my eyes to see them again.

When my eyes and vertigo were unbelievably bad, I would stay at home and take all my calls from my sofa, on my back. I would lie down, close my eyes, and just listen to the tone and nuances in everyone's voices. Their cadence and tone were as revealing as looking at the expressions on their faces.

This was a time when everyone was losing something. Business owners were losing, but so were accountants, bankers, lawyers, and millions of employees. Jobs, savings accounts, and homes were being lost. People were angry, scared, and frustrated. They looked for people to blame, and they grabbed anything they could to save themselves. I was in the middle of all this financial and emotional firestorm. It was my job to help them find reason and find a way out of this mountain of debt and loss. It was complex and unrelenting, but I was going to try as hard as I could to help as many as possible, regardless of what obstacles would be put in front of me.

It was August 2009, the third day of what would be many of the exact same phone calls I would receive beginning at 7:30 a.m. from Pat, a senior banker at one of the largest banks in the world.

"Hello."

"You piece of shit."

"Hi, Pat. How are you?"

"Go fuck yourself is how I am. You know what I want."

"Pat, I've only been on the job for two days. I can't give you an opinion on anything."

"You fuckhead. I don't know you. I don't know your stupid, shitty, pissy fuck-fuck firm. You're an asshole. You're nothing. You're nobody to me. I will ruin you. I will destroy your entire firm. You understand me, shithead? You're nobody to me."

Pat was not in touch with his feelings.

He thought he was uncomfortable, but really he was very frightened.

Each morning, as I sipped my coffee and looked out my window, I watched the river water pass and I let Pat insult me for a solid 20 minutes. I never answered back with anger or profanity. I kept a steady tone and tried to be constructive. Pat was a big man with a big job, and he thought he was going to lose $300 million. He thought he was giving me instruction, but all I heard was a frightened stray dog, cornered and barking for help.

"Pat. It's going to be fine. Just let me do my job. I promise you that you will be the first to know of any surprises. Just let me and my team do our job."

"Surprises? What surprises? I don't want any more surprises. I want those fucking idiots to file for bankruptcy today. You understand me? TODAY! Just get in there and tell them to file for fucking bankruptcy TODAY!"

"Pat, I can't say that. I have no basis in fact to make that recommendation. I told you that it would take six weeks to perform a thorough analysis of the company. There are a lot of factors and moving parts to consider."

"Who are you? Fucking shithead. Go fuck your facts. I want that company in bankruptcy, and I want all the assets liquidated immediately. Do it or I will have you fired. You're nothing. How the fuck did you get here anyway?"

"Pat, the bank group hired me. You're part of the bank group. They interviewed five firms. We got selected."

"I didn't want you. I don't know you. You're nobody. You know what? You go fuck yourself."

And he'd hang up.

Every day, for many days, 7:30 a.m.

As the weeks passed and my team dug deeper into the company, we learned that this wasn't a poorly run company. It just looked that way because the CEO and CFO were acting arrogantly and childishly.

As promised, I reported "surprises" back to Pat. It was a genuine surprise to me that the company was being run as well as it was. Despite sharing this good news with Pat, he was still not convinced that bankruptcy was not the best option. In his mind, if the current CEO and CFO were in place, they were a threat, so bankruptcy was the best option for him to recover the most amount of money. I knew I had to do something, or else thousands of people would lose their jobs.

I decided to cut through the labyrinth of lawyers and bankers and instead speak directly with the CEO and CFO.

Very plainly, I told them that they were a hair away from losing the entire company. But, for some reason, they found the news to be funny. For two years, they could not hit their sales or profit targets, but they still had a sense of humor. Why did they keep missing their targets? Because they kept creating unrealistic goals for the entire company. They believed that if you aim high and fall short, then you end up further ahead than just trying to be realistic. I understood their intentions but told them that this wasn't a motivational coaching seminar; it was a very big, multi-national company with thousands of employees.

I then explained to them that their missed projections meant they were in default of covenants on their bank loan. Those defaults meant the banks could pick up the phone and demand their loan be repaid today. If the company couldn't repay it, they would freeze all their credit and accounts, and they would be left with no choice other than repaying them or filing for bankruptcy. At that point, the CEO and CFO got serious. They assured me they would re-cast their projections with realistic numbers.

While they worked on new numbers, my team assembled a thorough written analysis of what liquidation or bankruptcy would look like in financial terms. As expected, a bankruptcy would cause Pat and the other bankers to lose more than half of their loan. Once this analysis was presented to Pat, he changed his tune about bankruptcy. In fact, he went entirely in the other direction. He realized he had been on a perilous path. Countless people would have lost their jobs, hundreds of millions would have been lost—and he would be the one taking the brunt of the blame.

We recommended that the bank group stay in the loan, and they did. Shortly thereafter, a private equity group came in and purchased 100 percent of the loan from the bank group. They got back every penny of their once very troubled loan. It was a win for everyone involved.

One morning, around 7:30 a.m., I got a call from Pat.

"Domenic, it's Pat. How are you?"

"I'm good. Just having a coffee."

"Domenic, I just want to say I'm sorry. I owe you everything. I would have lost everything. My job, my home, my wife. Everything. I don't know what happened to me. I lost my mind."

"That's OK, Pat. It happens to all of us."

"You don't understand. Because of you, I now look like a hero. I was that close to killing my entire career and ruining lives, but now I'm up for a promotion. Domenic, anything you need. Anything you need, just ask me. I owe you everything."

"Well, what I really need is for you to stop calling me at 7:30 a.m."

From there forward, Pat only had good things to say about me and my firm. He held to his word and sent a steady stream of work my way. Eight weeks earlier, all of that was unimaginable. I was just a nobody to him.

In the spring of 2010, on a Sunday morning, I read an article in the *New York Times* about the people of Haiti and how they were still in shock from the monumental earthquake that had occurred two months earlier. More than 200,000 Haitians were killed by falling rubble from the collapsing buildings, and in the weeks that followed, thousands of amputations were performed. Billions of dollars had been donated in aid for the country, but there still appeared to be a need for help.

I finished reading the article and immediately decided I should get on the first available plane and go there to help in any manner I could. I had worked in difficult situations for many years, I thought that perhaps I could use that experience in this situation. I wasn't entirely certain of what was in front of me, but I took it step-by-step and began planning the trip.

I looked online for hotels in Haiti. Surprisingly, there was one hotel that was still standing and operational. I booked one of the few available rooms. I then found an airline that was flying into the capital, Port-au-Prince, and I immediately bought a ticket. Then I went to a camping and outdoor supply store. I bought $3,000 worth of survival gear, water purification systems, bandages, and anything I thought might be useful. I stuffed everything into a giant duffle bag. My next stop was the bank. I withdrew $3,000 in $20 bills. The last place I needed to go was the bookstore. I bought four books on Haiti. If I wanted to help people, I needed to understand who they were and their history.

The next day, I taped stacks of $20 bills to my body. I had learned from my days in Moscow never to carry your money in one place. I didn't know what I was getting into, so it was better to be safe than sorry. I got dressed in my hiking clothes, put on my jump boots, put my hunting knife in the duffle bag, grabbed my books, and went to the airport.

The plane was half empty. Most of the people on the flight were in the medical profession, military, or journalism, or with a nonprofit. Shortly after we landed in Port-au-Prince, I knew this was not going to be an easy trip. Our plane sat on the tarmac for 20 minutes. In that time, I saw that the conveyor belt for the luggage was broken. All the luggage from planes was being unloaded and carried away one bag at a time. I looked to either side and saw planes from the United Nations, Salvation Army, and United States military. On the ground in the hangar, near the conveyor belt, were many soldiers and volunteers. I couldn't understand why all these people couldn't get a conveyor belt to work. If all that money and workforce couldn't get this to work, what else was broken?

I wouldn't have to wait long for the answer.

Pretty much everything was broken.

Outside of the airport, there were thousands of people bustling back and forth. It was a mix of sounds that ranged from crying to screaming. They were looking for food, water, work, and help in any manner. Most looked unbathed, gaunt, and weak. I had my duffle bag, but I had no idea how I was going to get to the hotel. There were no taxis, rental cars, or buses that I could see. With no options in front of me, I decided to just walk until I found a solution. As I walked toward the swarms of people, I was approached by a man who said, "Do you need taxi?" I immediately said, "Yes." He then grabbed my bag and said, "Hurry, follow me." I had no idea if he was a taxi driver. He could have just as easily been mugging me, but I followed him through the crowd, nonetheless.

In a matter of minutes, we arrived at his car, a Jeep Cherokee. He directed me to get in the front passenger seat. He threw my bag in the back seat and then slowly marched the car through the big crowd. They came to the window begging for help. First there was one, then there were five, and soon more than a dozen. I knew I couldn't help all of them, but I wanted to do something. One man was emphatic. He cried, pressed his hands against the window, and said, "Please, mister. Please. God loves me, too." That's it. That put me over the edge.

Yes, he was right, God loved him too. He didn't deserve to suffer. I then reached down to my left leg, pulled up my pant leg, and removed a stack of $20 bills that was taped to my leg. As I rolled down the window, the driver yelled at me. "Don't. Please don't. They will kill us. If you give one money, you must give it to all of them. They will fight us and each other for money because they are starving."

The driver made sense. The safe thing to do was not stop and lower the window. We could easily be overtaken by the crowd, but I couldn't just drive away doing nothing. I had to try. I rolled down the window and began handing out $20 bills to whomever I could. They would grab one and run away. The driver became nervous, so he drove faster and eventually the crowd disappeared. I understood where he was coming from as well. He, too, was just trying to survive.

As we drove to the hotel, it was readily apparent that the country was still in a state of despair and chaos. The roads were filled with rubble, fires smoldered, and street gutters were lined with dead bodies. Everywhere I looked, I could see rows of tents and makeshift campgrounds.

When we arrived, two armed guards stood in front of the gated and locked door of the hotel. I asked my driver if he would drive me for the remainder of the week. He agreed so I asked him to pick me up at 9 a.m. the next morning.

The hotel did have running water but only four hours of electricity per day because it was being produced by a generator. Part of the hotel had collapsed, but there were a few guest rooms available. Most of the people there were from other countries, looking to sell something that could aid in the rebuilding of the country. In addition to these salespeople was Anderson Cooper's production team from CNN.

Each day, over the next few days, I had my driver bring me around the city and countryside to visit campsites and makeshift hospitals. He would drop me off and wait in the car as I walked around. Whomever I came across, I helped them in the manner I best could. Depending on the circumstance, I gave them money, water purification lights, bandages, food, or camping gear. In one instance, I helped move the dead from a makeshift hospital to the morgue. Some people whom I met just needed help walking. In those instances, I offered a shoulder and fresh legs. It wasn't much, but it was something positive that hopefully brought each person a moment of relief.

On Saturday of that week, further into the countryside, I came across a group of young men and women who belonged to a Christian church group. There were about five people in this group. They asked me what I was doing alone so far away from the city. They informed me that it was not safe because gangs were now kidnapping foreigners and holding them for ransom. On the day of the earthquake, the principal prison collapsed, and thousands of criminals escaped. They formed "machete gangs." They walked around wielding machetes. They robbed young and old. And looked for police officers to kill.

In my entire time in Haiti, I hadn't seen one local police officer, and it's because they too were afraid of the gangs. When the police learned about the prison collapse, many of them burned their uniforms and denied being officers. Now, two months later, in certain parts of the countryside, foreign doctors and aid workers were afraid to visit because lawlessness ruled.

These young people in the church group informed me that they were growing increasingly frustrated with the slow rebuilding efforts and were concerned that many more people would die while they lived outdoors. They informed me that many were bathing and drinking from streams, and now children and the elderly were getting sick. Typhoid, malaria, and even cholera was developing in these communities. I listened to them attentively and still struggled to understand where the billions of dollars in aid pledged to the country had gone. At the end of our conversation, I told them to meet me in the same place the next day. I explained to them that I would bring them items that could help them with some of their problems.

The next day was Sunday. Easter Sunday to be specific. My driver brought me to the same spot as the previous day. Two members of the church group were already waiting for me. Before I could exit the car, they came to my window and told me that it was best if I left. When I asked "Why?" they explained to me that people were there to kidnap me. These criminals had heard about me and found out that I was coming back to the same place so now they were waiting for me.

Sure enough, as I looked farther out to the right side, about 20 yards away, I saw a man standing by a tree. When I turned to my left, there was another man who looked like a teenager, and he was sitting in a tree. Both stared toward me. My driver told me they were waiting to give a signal to other gang members that were positioned farther away.

I took a moment to consider my options, and then I decided to stay. In my mind, if I left, it would only send a message that would make others weaker. If I couldn't be brave in the face of this adversity, how could I expect others to overcome it? I also felt that this "gang" were cowards. If they had intended on kidnapping me, they would have already done it. I think they were trying to spread intimidation among the Haitians more than anything, but I didn't know. There was only one way to find out.

I got out of the car and grabbed my duffle bag, and the church group led me to a nearby house where one of them lived. I told my driver that if he didn't feel safe, he could leave. I would find a way home. I didn't want to put him in a dangerous situation.

I brought the group everything that remained in my bag. I spent the next hour showing them how to use the ultraviolet water purification system as well as how to clean and dress wounds on the skin. At the very minimum, I knew they could now get clean water to hundreds if not thousands of people for at least a month, maybe more.

My driver picked me up a couple hours later, and we returned to the hotel without any threat of violence.

The next day, I returned to NYC, and by nightfall I was admitted into the hospital. I was doubled over in pain and running a high fever. In my haste to get to Haiti, I had forgotten to get shots to protect me from all the very nasty airborne and waterborne viruses and parasites. I was eager to help others to the point I forgot about taking care of myself. It was a very dumb thing to overlook.

I spent the next couple of months unable to eat hardly anything. I existed on yogurt and water. With each gulp of water, it felt like shards of glass were going down my throat and cutting into my stomach. On several occasions, I met with an infectious disease specialist in the city. After a litany of tests, he could still not find what had made me so sick for so long. Eventually, I rebuilt my immune system and felt fine, but what made me physically ill would remain a mystery. It could have been an actual virus or just my body reacting to all the pain and suffering I had witnessed. It could have also been guilt. Every day I wrestled with the notion that I could have done more to help them. I wanted to return to Haiti, but somehow I couldn't find the time or strength to make another trip. I'm not sure why. Perhaps it was a level of pain that was beyond what I was willing or able to experience again.

13

MIRACLES

As I recovered from my trip to Haiti, my mother's health appeared to weaken. Her vibrancy had faded. Her bile duct kept clogging, and as a result she had to fight off persistent infections. With each new round of antibiotics, her immune system became weaker. Eventually, she underwent surgery, and doctors removed a stone that was causing the blockage in the duct. For a brief period, she regained strength, but the infections returned. With the bile draining externally, there was always an open wound that could be contaminated easily. Despite my parents' best attempts to keep everything around my mother as sterile as possible, she eventually contracted sepsis.

In the fall of 2011, my mother was brought into intensive care, and the doctors induced a coma while they flooded her bloodstream with multiple antibiotics to wipe out the sepsis. By the time I arrived back in Windsor, at the hospital, the entire family was in tears. The doctors had explained to them that the prognosis was not good. That sepsis is extremely dangerous and it kills more people each year than cancer.

This time, my mother hadn't asked for me. She didn't have time. They had her sedated before I could speak with her. But it didn't matter; I knew what to do. I sincerely didn't know what sepsis was, but I didn't care. One of the doctors tried to lower my expectations with a sober prognosis. I just nodded, put my arm around his shoulder, and said, "Thank you for your honesty...but I'm betting on my mother."

I knew nothing about her current medical condition, but I knew that crying and fearing the worst wouldn't help one bit. I also knew that my mother wasn't dead and probably could hear everything around her. I was also certain that all the commotion and talk of pain and death would annoy her. So, there was my answer—confidence. No fighting, no arguing, no crying; I would be confident in the medicine and her resiliency.

I then turned to my family and told them she would be fine—it was only an infection. I encouraged them to speak with her as if nothing was happening and she was wide awake. I told them to have conversations about everything other than sickness.

My mother had a lot of friends. News of her condition spread quickly. Each day, people from around the city came to visit her. And, with each of them, I shared the same directive: "Be positive, and no talking about sickness."

By the end of the second week, more than a hundred people had come to visit my mother. Additionally, we made dozens of phone calls to family members and friends in other countries whom we thought she might want to hear from. We called them and held the phone to her ear as she lay there sedated and let them share their good words. It was powerful and inspiring to see all these people come to support my mother and our family.

However, despite all the positive conversations, the meaningful prayers, and candles lit on her behalf, she began to deteriorate.

The doctors informed us that in a desperate attempt, they would administer an additional antibiotic to stamp out the sepsis, but it might be too much for her liver to handle. At this point, they felt either she would die of liver failure or sepsis.

The next day, as multiple antibiotics poured through my mother's bloodstream, I sat by her bed. I didn't know what to do. I had nothing to say. I just sat quietly, staring at her. At that moment, I heard what sounded like little girls playing. I turned my head to look out the window, and I saw two girls about the age of seven, dressed in cute, white summer dresses. They were holding hands and spinning each other 'round and 'round as they laughed and sang short jingles. I couldn't understand much of what they were saying, but it looked like they were having the best of times. I watched them go 'round and 'round laughing and giggling, but then I realized something was wrong. The girls outside the window were on the roof of the building next to the ICU. It was still the hospital building, but it was a part that was eye-level to the floor my mother was on. I struggled to figure out how two girls got onto the roof of the building.

Then, I saw it.

I saw them fade in and out of focus. It was as if their faces and dresses would briefly fade out of existence.

They were spirits.

It was my mother and her twin sister.

Luigina had come to comfort my mother.

I laughed and then looked toward my mother's spirit and said, "I knew it. I knew you weren't ready to die. Get back in here. Get back in your body."

I know she heard me, but she just kept on spinning around.

Now, I became upset and more adamant. "Get back in here. Enough playtime. Enough of this coma business. I'm busy and so is everyone else. We can't spend our entire life at the hospital waiting for you."

There I was, in a complete role reversal of my childhood, but this time I was the parent scolding the child. This time, my mother was on the roof, and I was pleading with her to come back inside.

And, just like that, the playful little girls went away.

My mother's body was still virtually lifeless. None of her diagnostics had changed. I was certain that I wasn't imagining what had just happened, but I wasn't about to tell anyone. I just thought I would resume being quiet, knowing that whatever happened, my mother was going to be happy.

The next day, a call was made to mom's older sister Renza, who lived in Italy. As children, my mother followed my Aunt Renza wherever she went, all day long. My aunt was patient with her as she followed and stopped to talk with every single person they encountered. Every walk and every task took so much longer because my mother loved to socialize. My Aunt Renza was the only one who had the patience to let her be completely free. We held the phone to my mother's ear as my aunt told her to stay strong and that they would see each other soon. It was the only call made that day. Made to the voice and person who helped her become so much of what she was in life.

A few hours later, against all odds, my mother's diagnostics turned and improved significantly. She was brought out of the deep sedation and was wide awake. She was not completely out of harm's way, but she was definitely on the path to recovery.

As the nurses worked to prop her up, she looked around the room. She was confused and a bit frightened. She didn't know where she was or what had happened the past two weeks. Not one thing. Not one conversation, not sepsis, not dancing on the roof—nothing. But it didn't matter. Somehow, she made it back again.

Over the next few years, my mother regained her strength and returned to a normal life. By this time, she had undergone so many surgeries that her body resembled a rag doll that had been stitched up and passed around from neighbor to neighbor. Her liver was only partially working. Her pancreas had minimal ability. Her digestive system was barely functioning because it was being crowded with her ever-growing cyst. Her home looked like an entire hospital. No fewer than four rooms were filled with medical supplies. Countless medications were regulating one thing or another. Digestive enzymes, pain patches, hormone supplements, antibiotics, and on and on. No fewer than a dozen bottles of one medicine or another sat on her bedroom dresser. Bandages needed to be changed twice a day. Bile needed to be drained and re-administered into the body once a day. All other medications needed to be taken around the clock, all day, and all night. She was in constant pain and constantly fighting for energy, but...she was alive.

For her, this was her normal life. She didn't think it was exceptional; she thought it was annoying and sometimes an inconvenience. She waxed and waned on how she felt from one day to the next, but still she carried on. She still cooked, baked, gardened, and volunteered with the church and charities. She kept finding reasons to be alive, to be entertained, to be helpful, to keep moving.

The times when she couldn't find the motivation, my father would find it for her. He was in effect the attending doctor, nurse, cook, janitor, and pharmacist, so being coach and motivator was easy for him. He gladly took on the extra work for no additional pay. And, when he'd run out of motivation, my sister and her girls would step in. They would find ways to get her to tell stories, to cook or bake with them. Just their youthful energy and presence would provide her with endless reasons to be alive and thriving. She loved being a grandmother, and she took great pleasure watching them grow.

And then, of course, when my sister and her family had exhausted their reservoir of motivation and no one else could find a way to get my mother out of bed, they would call me.

I had a different motivational style.

Generally, in these moments, I would phone her.

"Hello."

"What color suit should I wear to the funeral?"

"You're ridiculous."

"I'm thinking navy blue. I know black is customary, but I'm your son. I should look a little bit different than everyone else—right?"

"I'm in a lot of pain."

"I know. I understand. You can't do it anymore...so, you know, let's move it along. If you're going to die, please hurry up."

"Is that how you talk to your mother?"

"My mother? No, my mother apparently has died. I just want to move things along so I can spend time with my future stepmom."

"Your father's never going to marry anyone else."

"No. Not if you're alive. So, hurry up. Make a decision: Are you staying or are you going?"

"I'm really in a lot of pain."

"So what? Take some more pain medicine, get out of bed, and go do something productive. Either that or I'm going to start looking for dates for Dad."

"You really are too much."

"I learned it from you. Now, get out of bed. I'm busy. I have to take my navy-blue suit to the cleaners—just in case."

Before she could finish her next sentence, I would hang up. My father and sister thought I was mean, but I knew what it took to re-ignite a fire inside of her. I knew bathing my mother in pity would not work. I also knew inspiring her to a better and brighter future wouldn't work. This was a woman who had truly been through anguish and suffering. When she would hit rock bottom, there were only three things that could bring her back into the vibrancy of everyday life: drugs, anger, or jealousy. One of those would work, but I preferred to invoke all three for good measure.

By 2014, I had lived 12 years with extremely blurry, limited vision and incessant pain in my face. I managed to get around and still work, but now my vision was so poor it was time for me to have the surgery that I had avoided and dreaded. I was finally prepared to have two corneal transplants. In general, the procedure is straightforward, but post-surgery, there can be many complications. The cornea is similar to an organ and the body can reject it at any time, which means another transplant would have to be performed. It was delicate. At anytime after the surgery, for the rest of your life, if you hit your head, the cornea could become detached and cause infections and bleeding within the eye, creating even more damage.

Aside from the complications, the concept of the surgery was still unsettling to me. The notion of having to see through someone else's corneas was strange and disturbing to me. I wondered endlessly if I would still see the world in the same manner and if there would be a "residue" of memory from the person who had died. I'm not sure if my fears were rooted in actual science. Perhaps I had watched too many movies, but new eyes felt too personal to me. A part of me was almost comfortable with just continuing as I was. Just embracing the blindness. But, despite my worries, for many practical reasons, I had to have the surgery. I wanted to resume a full life. A life like I had known for so many years.

I met with several ophthalmologists, and all agreed that I did need the transplants, but then I met a surgeon in Beverly Hills, California who had developed a technique to restore vision without an actual transplant. Dr. Brian Boxer Wachler pioneered two different procedures for treating keratoconus without removing the corneas. One is called Intacs. This procedure reshapes the curvature of the cornea from within by flattening the bulge created by the disease. The other is called Holcomb CR-3 Cross-Linking, where a proprietary vitamin B2 formulation is applied to strengthen the cornea.

Dr. Brian (as he prefers to be called) explained to me that with these procedures, he would be able to restore most of my vision. To me, this seemed impossible. For more than a decade, I had searched for solutions, and I could not find them. And now, out of sheer luck, I met a man who said, "No problem...we'll have you brand new in no time." This seemed too easy and too fast. I was convinced he was a con artist. I took his literature and told him I needed to think about it.

Most people would have been overjoyed at receiving such good news, but I had concerns. I had watched my mother go through so many different surgeries that I knew there's no such thing as easy when it comes to the human body. I also knew that even the best doctors make mistakes. My greatest concern was that if something went wrong in the procedure, I would be living in total darkness.

My life was very blurry, but I could still see shapes and colors and distinguish one item from the next. I wasn't prepared to lose that. Once the cornea is gone, there's nothing there to help you see.

The next day, I took a deep breath and decided to take a leap of faith. I had to decide one way or another, and Dr. Brian's approach seemed the least invasive.

A few days later, I had the procedures. Dr. Brian had a calming and nurturing disposition. My eyes were examined with every machine from every angle. In less than 30 minutes, he completed the Intacs and Cross-Linking. I went home with bandages on my eyes. The next day, I returned, and he removed the bandages. He tested my vision, and sure enough, 80 percent of it had returned. I had taken a leap of faith, and an actual miracle happened.

I looked intently at Dr. Brian's face. It was the first face I had seen clearly in many years. I just stared at him as my brain processed all the fine details, the shape of his nose, mouth, pinkish color to his skin, his long ears. Then, I looked around the room, just pausing on each item, soaking in the new reality: big gray chair, small brown desk, eye-testing machines with lots of buttons. I was 47 years old, but I was viewing the world as if I was a child.

I got up from my chair, thanked Dr. Brian. I continued to look at each item as I walked out of his office, and then I passed a mirror hanging on the wall. I walked past it and then went back to look at myself. I couldn't remember the last time I had seen my face clearly. Up until then, my reflection just looked like a hazy image from a dream sequence.

"Oh my." I was a bit startled as I spoke out loud.

"Where did those come from?"

I was taken back by the wrinkles on my face and the gray hairs on my head. When I first lost my vision, I was a fresh-faced, brown-haired 35-year-old man. Now, I was looking at twelve years of aging without warning. It was like bumping into a friend from high school as a mature adult. You recognize the person, but it takes a bit of time to adjust to what they look like in the present moment.

"Oh well. Life moves on."

I spent the next couple weeks just staring at everything I came across. It took me much longer to do my grocery shopping because I could actually read the labels. It also took me a lot longer to get ready in the morning. I kept staring at the stranger in the mirror. Walking around my home also became a longer phenomenon. It was as if there was dust and fingerprints everywhere. I thought I had been a clean person, but I hadn't realized how much I missed. These were some of the moments I wondered if "blurry" wasn't better than 20/20, but they were only fleeting thoughts.

For so many years, I had gone to bed fearing that would be the last day with vision. Doctors had convinced me that at any moment, my world could be dark. I prepared for it over and over. But now, 12 years later, it seemed like a giant waste of energy. Every night, I should have gone to bed waiting for a miracle. Either way, magic did manage to find me, and I am eternally grateful for the gifted mind and hands of Dr. Brian.

Thank Goliath

During this period, my mother, too, resembled a walking miracle. She still had her day-to-day challenges, but otherwise, she carried on as usual, talking on the phone, visiting with people, sharing stories. She was still patient and listened to the struggles of others, but now her conversations were occasionally peppered with statements of the afterlife. In a subtle dramatic tone, she'd say things like, "I understand. I really understand what you're going through. I've touched the pearly gates five times. FIVE." Whenever I heard her say this I would interject and say, "I think it was only four." With absolute sternness she'd snap back, "It was five. I was there." Of course, I couldn't let this type of banter pass.

"Oh, really. What did they tell you? Sorry, lady, you've got the wrong address."

And she'd take the bait every time.

"Is that such a thing to suggest about your mother?"

"You know, they have better ovens at the other place."

"You're not funny."

"You could cook for all of the sinners."

"You're really not funny."

"They say that Big Guy with the horns has quite the appetite. He'd love your cooking."

"Five times. It's not something to joke about."

"Did you lose your key? Is that why you couldn't get in?"

"I don't know who raised you to talk like this."

"It was the same person they won't open the gates for."

Despite these easier moments when we had fun, we were all aware of one problem that was not going away—her cyst. We knew at some point, it would have to be dealt with again.

As expected, it continued to grow over the years. Doctors had figured out ways to slow its growth, but because of its precarious location, it could never be removed.

In the spring, my mother consulted with a new pancreatic surgeon, considered one of the best in Canada. Despite her previous great survival rate and resiliency, he concluded that she was inoperable. He claimed the cyst was too big, too complicated, and there were too many other things going on with her. It was just too much for him to even try, even if not trying meant certain death for her. However, he did offer some hope by suggesting that she consult with another doctor.

This new doctor, Dr. Sheung, was director of endoscopy. He was new to the hospital in London, Ontario. Apparently, Dr. Sheung was young, sharp, and full of promise. He was overseeing a specific type of alcohol ablation program, the only one of its kind in all of Canada. To most, it sounded very innovative and regal. To my family, it sounded just like what had been performed on my mother in Toledo, 13 years earlier.

Despite his busy schedule, Dr. Sheung found time to look at my mother's scans and files. With great confidence, he assured my parents that he could indeed help her with his one and only "endoscopic ultrasound-guided pancreatic cyst alcohol ablation." My mother was elated, "Thank you so much, Dr. Sheung. Just one question: When can we do the procedure? I'm in a lot of pain, and I would really like to do this as soon as possible."

Without hesitating, he answered her, "Absolutely. As soon as possible." My parents felt assured. They got in the car, drove home, and waited for Dr. Sheung to call with a surgery date.

One week passed.

Two weeks passed.

Three weeks passed, and Dr. Sheung was nowhere to be found. He didn't return phone calls. His secretary said he was remarkably busy.

By the fourth week, my mother could no longer take the pain. She was admitted to the hospital in her hometown of Windsor.

They briefly examined her but did not conduct a thorough diagnostic. They concluded that there was nothing more they could do or should do for her. They explained that Dr. Sheung was on the case now; she was his responsibility.

As she lay in the hospital bed, the pain in my mother continued to intensify. She'd clutch the sheets, she would double over on her side, she'd bite the pillow and kick her feet, day after day. When she'd ask the doctors in Windsor for more pain medicine, they would advise my father that they were concerned she was becoming addicted, and therefore more meds were not needed. In their eyes, addiction was bad, but death was acceptable.

It was now five weeks after meeting with Dr. Sheung, and still he was nowhere to be found. By now, the doctors in Windsor began telling my mother that she had to go home because they needed the hospital bed. They believed her pain was just something that she always had dealt with and was nothing new. And her fever and infection, well, that also was nothing new. Benedetta and Giacinto had dealt with these issues for years, so without question, they could handle this in the comfort of their own home without any additional medical supervision.

My mother refused to leave.

She was turning jaundiced and vomiting every time she tried to eat or drink anything. Yet, every day, a doctor in Windsor would come to her, on his rounds, look in her face, and tell her she had to go home.

At their wit's end, my sister and father called me and asked for suggestions. I told them I would be there the next day.

I walked into my mother's hospital room and saw a mangled soul. She looked like someone had thrown her off a moving train. We exchanged no hellos, no jokes, no questions. Like a homeless drug addict in the street gutter, she stretched out her hand toward me and said, "Please get me some medicine for the pain."

If you've ever wondered what it feels like to want to kill someone, just think of someone you love who is being tortured, endlessly and mercilessly in front of your eyes. Your choice is to watch them suffer or kill their torturer. That's the feeling.

I had that exact feeling, but I wasn't about to act on it. Killing doctors wouldn't help my mother. I needed solutions, and I needed them fast.

I stormed out of her room and down the hallways, looking for her attending doctor. In a matter of minutes, I found him. With great tension in my head and fists, I managed to calmly introduce myself and ask him to provide my mother with additional pain meds. Oblivious to the fact that I might squish him like a bug, his eyes rolled, and a gloss came over his face. "Mr. Aversa, your mother is being given an appropriate amount of medication to sufficiently manage her pain. We've been telling her this for more than a week. She really should go home and wait for her surgeon from London to phone."

Something inside of me snapped. I lost all sense of reason and just felt rage.

I grabbed the doctor by his necktie and pulled him within inches of my face. "You're going to do one of two things. You're either going to fix her or you're going to shut up. You and no one else on staff will ever tell her or my father that they need to go home. While she's here, you are going to give her more medicine for her pain. Have you bothered to read her medical history? Have you conducted any additional MRIs or CT scans to see what is happening inside of her? Do you think she's faking this pain? How big of an idiot are you?"

I saw that he was now genuinely terrified.

I let go of his tie and I stepped back. Shaken and red in the face, he looked at me. "I'm sorry. I'm just doing what I'm told. There's nothing we can do for her in Windsor, so by definition the hospital bed should be given to someone else."

Realizing that he was most likely telling me the absolute truth and that they could do nothing, I took a deep breath and said, "OK. Can you do one thing for me? Can you write down on a piece of paper what you just said to me?" He now resumed a more fearful look, "Why do you want that?" I knew his concerns. "I'm not going to sue you or have you reprimanded. I have to find a doctor that can help my mother. If I can't find one here in Canada, I will need to take her to the U.S. I will need a letter from this hospital that says you can't do anything for her so OHIP will approve the procedure and pay for it." He understood what I was requesting and wrote a letter for me in a matter of minutes. I thanked him and apologized for my less-than-gentlemanly communication style. I was embarrassed for losing my temper. I could have achieved the same result without physically threatening him. I was upset at the situation. but I'm not sure what came over me. I didn't know how I became unhinged. I thought I had resolved my issues with anger. I thought that trauma had been released in my sessions with Brent.

Either way, I didn't have time to dwell on it now. I needed to find someone who could help my mom.

I walked back to my mother's room. I looked at her and said, "Hang in there. We'll get this fixed. I'm going to do what I need to do." She stared at me and said, "Don't take long."

It was the first time she had ever put me on the clock. I didn't know what was happening inside of her, but I knew she didn't have long to live. I turned to my dad. "Keep asking them for pain meds. If they don't give them to you, get some from home and give those to her. They're not going to tell you to go home anymore, so you don't have to worry about that."

And I left.

My father didn't give her additional pain meds because he feared that something would go wrong. He was knowledgeable and intelligent, but he wasn't a doctor. He felt that he should follow the doctors' direction. He thought, *What if I give her additional pain medicine and it stops her heart or further damages her liver?* He wasn't wrong in his thinking. It was the responsible approach. I just saw things differently. I made my living by having to choose between bad and worse every day, all day. But there was no time to debate the matter. We needed to find a doctor that could help.

I went to my parents' home, pulled out my laptop and cellphone, and immediately started calling and writing as many people in positions of power as I could reach. I figured I would start at the top and work my way down until we had a solution. I began by calling the CEOs of the hospital in Windsor and London. Windsor's CEO was a thorough professional and accommodating. I asked him to please have the staff stop asking my mom to leave and to reconsider the pain medicine levels. He said he had been unaware of the situation but agreed to help and offered to call

Dr. Sheung to expedite the matter. London's CEO was distant but concerned. He wasn't concerned so much about my mother's health as he was the reputation of his hospital and Dr. Sheung. He offered to intervene and help in any manner.

I then called Dr. Vasili, the doctor who had saved her life in 2001. He was now living in Green Bay, Wisconsin. I explained the situation to him, asked if he could help. Without hesitating he said, "Absolutely. Just get her to me and I'll take care of whatever needs to be done."

Next on the call list was Dr. Sheung. I called him throughout the day and into the early evening. I left message after message but never heard back from him.

The next morning came and still no call from him. He was elusive. He did not allow his direct number or email address to be given to anyone unless he specifically approved. At this point, I knew if 10 phone calls and two additional phone calls to the CEOs of hospitals couldn't get him to call me, it was time to take a different approach.

I began by calling politicians for the London hospital district and the same for Windsor. I called the MPPs and MPs for each area (they are the Canadian equivalent of a member of Congress and Senate). For good measure, I also emailed each of them an outline detailing the urgency of the situation and all the parties involved. I was able to connect with three of them; each offered to help.

I then began calling law firms across the province, looking for representation. I wanted to be prepared to have someone appeal to a court if we needed that level of representation—and be prepared to litigate if we chose that path. I put two law firms on standby, and then I resumed calling Dr. Sheung.

By noon, he called me back. I didn't have time to reprimand him; I simply wanted to get her on his schedule immediately. It was at this point that Dr. Sheung began to stammer and struggle for words. He explained to me that now, he was uncertain his approach would help my mother. I was confused. He let all this time pass without any communication, while she suffered, and just now he realized that his one-of-a-kind treatment couldn't help her. What changed? How did he come to this new conclusion?

Turns out the only person Dr. Sheung spoke with before returning my call was Dr. Vasili. Dr. Sheung called him to discuss my mother's case. He got his name and number from me. I had left it on every message and with everyone I spoke with. I had told him to speak with him because he was intimately aware of all her details and had saved her in the past. I'm not sure why he made the call because he had been so confident in his diagnosis, but now it didn't matter to me. The only thing that mattered is that he was now telling me that it would be best if we took my mother to see Dr. Vasili. I told Dr. Sheung that was fine and that I needed a letter from him stating all those details. He had a letter written and emailed to me within the hour.

Now it was time to contact OHIP and get their approval. Unlike 2001, I decided to get their approval to move my mother to the United States before we moved her. She was in tremendous pain, but I was reassured by one of the politicians that they had already contacted OHIP, and approval was being expedited. The office of Percy Hatfield, MPP, specifically his constituency assistant, Chuck Gascoyne, was instrumental in leading the effort to move the approval through this big and cumbersome bureaucracy.

Chuck was so helpful that I didn't want to risk upsetting any of his relationships and undermining his efforts by taking the matter into my own hands. Things appeared to be working in our favor, so I wanted to maintain that goodwill. I didn't know what my mother would be facing once in Green Bay, which meant we might need a cooperative relationship with the insurance provider. As expected, not long after I sent the doctors' letters to OHIP, they gave approval for a procedure in Green Bay. It was limited in scope and extremely restricted in the amount of money that could be spent, but it was a "yes." It was a solution.

We made arrangements to fly to Green Bay the next day. Neither OHIP nor the Windsor hospital would provide us with a nurse or medical assistant to accompany my mother on the trip. Despite her weakened condition and obvious threat to her vital organs by her cyst, they told us that Canadian medical staff would not be covered by licensing and insurance in the United States, therefore could not be provided to us. Again, we were on our own.

We had to figure out the timing of her biliary drain, her nausea, and her pain meds with estimated time of the trip to St. Anton's Hospital in Green Bay. We had to make sure she would be as comfortable as possible for as long as possible. In certain circumstances, this trip might be easy. In this case, we had to pick her up at the hospital in Windsor, cross the bridge to the United States, and go through Customs and Immigration—a phenomenon that can rarely be predicted. It could take 10 minutes or 60 minutes or longer; you just never knew. We then had to drive 45 minutes to the Detroit airport in Wayne County, check in, go through security, go to the gate, board the plane, fly an hour and half, deplane, pick up luggage and rental car, then drive to St. Anton's. We tried our best to calculate all this travel time, and then we prayed everything would be on time and that my mother could hold on for the duration of the trip.

The next morning, my sister and father prepared my mother for the trip. I picked them up at the hospital at 11:30 a.m. My parents sat in the back seat, and I drove as fast as I could without rattling my mother. For my father and me, this was 2001 again, a race against the clock. My mother, his wife, was dying. We didn't know when or how, but we knew from her gasps of air that death was not far. Again, we were in a car, crossing an international border, desperately trying to reach a savior.

We drove over the bridge, reached Immigration. I handed the officer three passports. He bent down and looked at my mother. Without any questions, he said, "You're good." Even he could see that time could not be wasted. I took back the passports and hit the gas.

Once at the airport, we got my mother onto a wheelchair, and I instructed my father to go ahead without me. I needed to park the car. I told him if I wasn't on the flight to just go ahead, and I would take the next flight. We had time, but we didn't know what bumps in the road we would encounter. Anything could take us off schedule, so we couldn't take chances at wasting time. There were already too many issues to contend with. It was as if we were transporting a sliver of a human being. She was routinely vomiting into a bag we had for her, had turned a shade between yellow and white, writhed in pain, and barely had the strength to hold her head up. We just needed to get her there.

I made it to the flight and was one of the last people to board the plane. My mother closed her eyes and put her head on my father's shoulder. The time to taxi the plane was not long. We were up and flying within 10 minutes.

We arrived in Green Bay at 3.30 p.m. We picked up the rental car and drove as fast as we could to the hospital. As we entered

St. Anton's, they directed us immediately to the ICU. Dr. Vasili was ready for us and waiting with a team of doctors, nurses, and specialists. They put her into the bed and began treating her within seconds.

Dr. Vasili took one look at my mother and then back at my father and me. He lashed out. "I KNEW IT. She's malnourished. JESUS, look at her. What were they doing there? How is she still alive? The DAMN PAIN should have killed her by now. What were they DOING?"

For a moment, we felt like schoolchildren. We just stared at him and shrugged and shook our heads. He was already five steps along in his diagnosis, and we hadn't been there for longer than a minute. We knew she wasn't well, but not to the extent he was describing. He then looked at his colleague, a pain specialist. He, too, shook his head and grimaced in disgust. Dr. Vasili continued, "Let me tell you something. I'm telling you right now. This is gross negligence. It is DISGUSTING and REPREHENSIBLE. I'm telling you RIGHT NOW, I will testify in any litigation that you bring against them—ANY litigation! I know them, and I don't know what in God's name they were doing."

In 13 years of knowing Dr. Vasili, we had never seen or heard him raise his voice, lose his temper, or criticize another doctor. He was always courteous, forgiving, and supportive of the Canadian medical system. But today he was furious.

At this point, there was nothing else my father and I could do for my mother. It was now between her, Dr. Vasili, and God.

The next morning, she was in surgery for four-and-a-half hours. The following day, she had eight more hours in surgery. Dr. Vasili and his team found many problems that had not been addressed by any of the doctors in London and Windsor.

They found that the cyst was much bigger than anticipated. It was the size of a cantaloupe, and it was pushing her stomach up into her esophagus, pushing her duodenum to the point that it was so stretched, no food or liquid could pass. This was the principal cause of the malnourishment and the excessive vomiting. The cyst was so large and so menacingly positioned that it was pushing the ganglion nerve into my mother's spine. Dr. Vasili explained that this phenomenon was the primary cause of her searing pain. He said it was like a rock pushing a nerve up against a wall. To illustrate the point, he took my elbow and pressed it against the wall and kept pushing and moving it. As my elbow burned and pain shot up my arm, he said, "It's kind of like that, only worse. She was feeling that every day, all day."

They also found that her pancreas had stopped working years ago. We knew the remaining part of her pancreas was not functioning well, but no doctor in Canada had ever told us that it had completely stopped functioning.

Most critically, they found massive infection in her liver. Two-thirds of her biliary tree was blocked, and most of her liver was not functioning. Not one doctor in Canada had mentioned this or even suggested it as a possibility. This was the most surprising discovery for us because in the previous three years, since her incident with sepsis and induced coma, we had asked her doctors, "What is causing her infection? Why is she perpetually on antibiotics? Why is she constantly showing infection in her blood?" The response was always the same. "We don't know. The infection must be coming from the external drain tubes." Having no other answers presented to us we took this explanation to be accurate.

Dr. Vasili then showed us an image of her liver on a CT scan and explained it to us. Neither my father nor I is a doctor, but within seconds we could see the blockage, infection, and weakened condition of her liver. It was all there as plain as day. This, too, should have killed her years ago.

In two days, Dr. Vasili and his team at this small hospital in a town with a population of less than 100,000 people performed miracle after miracle. One by one, they discovered and treated every life-threatening issue within my mother. These were issues that some of Canada's best had not noticed, bothered to look for, or concluded were just too much trouble to even attempt to resolve. We thought she had been suffering for weeks, months, but in reality, it was years. Years of countless trips to the doctors' office and hospital. Years of waning energy, nourishment, and life force. Years of unnecessary and excruciating pain.

What can you say about these doctors and the medical system in Canada? What do you say in this circumstance where not one, but multiple doctors and hospitals made constant critical errors? Do you take the high road and praise all the good and hard-working people in the medical field? Do you turn a blind eye and focus on being grateful that now all will be well?

What do you do with a wide group of people who are inexplicably incompetent and negligent? Do you sue them? Sue who? You're suing the government. It would take many years, endless fighting, and a daily re-living of all these terrible events...to get what? Maybe a little more money than it took to cover legal expenses? With odds of less than 35 percent arriving on a settlement and less than a 1 percent chance of winning at a trial, the question was: Why bother? Why bother wasting more time in your life arguing with lawyers, administrators, and corrupt criminals posing as medical doctors?

In a just world, all these men would be stripped of their medical licenses and put in jail.

In my world, I would subject them to the same level of pain and suffering they put my mother through for the same amount of time. I would insert a balloon the size of a cantaloupe in their gut, remove their pancreas, and infect their liver. I would have them choke on their own saliva, regurgitate their food, become malnourished, and sweat in a fever as pain seared through their ganglion nerve. I would then stare at them from the end of a cold metal bed, with a look of complete judgment and disapproval as they begged for additional pain medicine.

Some people may feel that my world is too graphic and too primitive. For me, it's not graphic enough. I've only briefly described a moment in time for my mother. Imagine having to have lived in that manner for years. How would you feel about those who willingly let you or a loved one suffer in this manner?

Once the anger subsided, I was left speechless.

In the end, I had no words. My world doesn't exist because I would be in jail. Nor does a just world exist—at least not within the medical system in Canada. People put their head down, go on with their lives, thankful for what they have and hopeful they never have to be one of the tens of thousands of Canadians who are subject to horribly negligent doctors in the country.

My mother spent the next three months in Green Bay. She recovered under the careful, compassionate, and impeccably talented medical team at St. Anton's hospital. My father stayed by her side the entire time. He, too, was grateful for the generosity of the hospital and several of their patient outreach programs that provided him with financial aid for food and housing. And OHIP held true to their word and went far beyond the scope of the original approval. They recognized the severity and extent of her health issues that had not been addressed in Canada. The final invoice for all my mom's medical treatments was approximately $500,000 U.S., which they paid in full.

The following year was a bumpy road for my mother. When she returned to Windsor, the healing process was not easy. As her body tried to adjust to all the work Dr. Vasili had performed, there were aches and pains and much vomiting. Family and friends offered a great deal of assistance to her and my father. They helped clean, cook, do laundry, and of course be there for emotional support or a trip to the local hospital when she became dehydrated. However, eventually, as she had done many times in the past, she recovered. She spent the next few years living very comfortably and happy. Her life returned to normal. She gardened and spent time with her granddaughters cooking and at the beach. She traveled to see her family in New York and Italy. For her and my father, it was as if all the struggles of the past were long past them and now they could enjoy life without worry. Finally, their dreams of peace and good health had arrived.

14

AMEN

This time was different than the others.

This was 2021, the time of Covid.

This time we couldn't be with her. She was completely alone.

They locked us out. We were family, but we couldn't get past the front door of the hospital. We were allowed to call, but only two of us could be accepted on a pre-approved list. We were given passcodes for the phone. If we gave the wrong code, they wouldn't answer our questions.

We had grown comfortable with uncertainty and ambiguity, but this time we were completely in the dark with nowhere to go. We just had to sit in our homes and wait.

The previous two years had been filled with calm and good cheer. My mother was in a happy place. Most of her medical issues had been addressed, and she was living comfortably. Each evening, from her home in Windsor, she would get on FaceTime with her sisters in New York and Italy. They would talk, eat, reminisce, watch movies, and, many times, knit. They were in three separate countries and three separate rooms but as inseparable as they had been as children. Covid restrictions were burdensome, but for my mother and her sisters, it only made the conversations longer. There was no place to go, so they made the best of their time inside, with each other.

A year passed in this manner. Then the vaccines arrived and held promise for a return to normal life.

In March 2021, shortly after receiving her first shot of the vaccine, my mother contracted pneumonia. Her lungs had always been delicate, so my father felt it would be best to take her to the hospital. Once there, he was informed of the Covid protocols, which prevented him from entering with her. He was vaccinated but not allowed into the hospital. She assured him she would be fine.

She was admitted, and by the next morning, we were informed that in addition to pneumonia she had sepsis. No one was certain which infection had developed first; in the blood or in the lungs. However, everyone was certain of what needed to happen next.

Within the hour she was sedated and induced into a coma, put on a ventilator, and filled with antibiotics.

As a family, we had been here before. This time was a bit different, but we had been here. I reassured everyone that she would make it out again. I was certain of it.

However, I was also certain that I was struggling.

I was supposed to be happier.

I was supposed to be healthier.

I couldn't shake the pain. In the previous few years, I tried to shake it off, but it kept getting worse. Lights bothered me. My memory was fading. The slightest sound irritated me. My fuse grew shorter. I lost my temper easily. I grew upset at everyone and everything. One by one, I stopped talking with people. My laugh became smaller and eventually muted. If I heard something funny, my brain knew it should laugh, but I couldn't.

I couldn't sleep. I felt like a shadow of myself. I struggled with the simplest of tasks. I had to think about how to tie my shoes. I didn't know what was happening, but it was making me angrier by the day.

I didn't want to die, but there were days I was in a blanket of depression. In the past, I could snap out of it, but this time was different. There were times I felt that I was nearing the end of my life. I was overwhelmed with growing sorrow and pain. I didn't know which way to turn.

My mother and I had always found a way to overcome adversity, but at this moment we both appeared lost in darkness. We were 2,000 miles away from each other, and this time we couldn't even speak by phone.

There was nothing we could do.

We had to just sit and wait for what was next to come.

After the fourth week of an induced coma, the doctors informed us that my mom had overcome sepsis and pneumonia. She had once again defied the odds. Her lungs were still weak, so she remained on the ventilator. By this time, my father was allowed to enter the hospital and be by her bedside. Of course, within a week, the doctors in Windsor presented their typical pessimism. They were convinced that her lungs would never recover, and they suggested that my parents have "that" conversation. "That" being the conversation about unplugging her ventilator and letting my mother suffocate to death. Everything else in her was working well; her body was fine, and her mind was lucid. Yet, her attending medical team felt there was nothing else that could be done for her, so she either had to get better quickly or they were going to unplug her machine to make room for someone else.

And, once again, I was outraged at what I deemed to be criminal behavior. But this time, I was powerless. I couldn't be there in person. The border between the United States and Canada was closed to all non-essential travelers. I wasn't allowed to go see her or even enter the country. Apparently, when a family member is in Intensive Care, trying to come to their aid is considered "non-essential." Every direction I turned, I hit a brick wall. I couldn't find a path to help her receive better medical care. I contacted lawyers and politicians. I tried to get a judge to hear her case to have her moved out of Canada, but I got nowhere. Everyone had the same answer: "Covid rules. There's nothing you can do."

Apathy rained through the entire country. Everyone had given up and lost their sense of will after living through extensive lockdowns and regulations. I saw this type of phenomenon in companies that had been troubled for extended periods of time. It was "complaint fatigue." There were so many things to complain about that everyone eventually grew numb to hearing complaints.

In her sixth week of hospitalization, my mother was moved outside of the city to a smaller hospital. The government was expecting a "surge" of Covid cases, and they needed to make room for them, so all non-Covid cases would be sent to other hospitals or be housed in tents that served as makeshift hospitals. We were initially concerned, but it turned out to be a blessing. The hospital she was transferred to was located in Chatham, Ontario, about 45 minutes from Windsor. It was a smaller hospital that had less stringent Covid rules and a staff that wasn't suffering from burnout. In Chatham, my father could spend four hours a day with my mother, speak with her nurses and doctors, and be on hand if they needed any additional information. We knew her current health was complicated by previous issues, in particular her bile drain tube and her feeding tube. They were continuous open wounds that were highly susceptible to infection.

After a week in Chatham, she continued her journey on the road of miracles. Once again, she came back from the pearly gates. She grew stronger each day. She was now able to breathe for six hours at a time without the ventilator. Seven weeks earlier, the doctors in Windsor didn't believe she would live more than five days, but here she was again, fighting back and getting ready to live to her fullest. At this point, she returned to her daily routine on her iPad and FaceTiming her sisters, her children, and whomever she could reach. Her voice was weak from the months on the ventilator, but her eyes and ears were as active as they had ever been. She needed just a little more time with therapy, and she would be at home, in her own chair and bed, knitting and talking the evenings away with her sisters.

However, once again, the federal government independently decided that they knew what was best for her and that we had no say in the matter.

The "surge" never came, so the hospital administrators chose to move my mother back to the hospital in Windsor. They offered no reason for the decision. My father pleaded with them not to move her because she was doing well and needed just a little more time for her lungs to be fully functioning. His pleading fell on deaf ears.

They treated him, her, and us as if we were inmates in a prison. They wouldn't listen. They didn't have to listen, nor did they care.

They moved her back to Windsor in the early morning without notifying anyone in the family. She made the trip alone, in the back of an ambulance.

Despite not having a "surge" in cases, the county health administrators felt it was best to keep the heightened protocols in place. This meant neither my father nor sister nor any family member could be with my mother. Having 35 years of experience in watching doctors and nurses work on my mother, my father knew how things were supposed to be done and where mistakes could happen. The most vulnerable spots on my mother were those external tubes. If they were not flushed properly, they would easily attract bacteria and cause infection.

Over the years, he had watched over-burdened, stressed-out, federally funded nurses and doctors hurry through the cleaning process. My father knew that this was definitely a weak spot for my mother. He tried to contact her attending medical team in person, but under the new rules, he was not permitted into the hospital. He went to the front doors several times, hoping to find a sympathetic security guard that would let him in, but he got nowhere. He phoned the nurses and doctors, he left voice mails with instructions, and when they did answer the phone, they gave him the "ya-yas"—brushing him away and dismissing his concerns with "ya, ya, thank you, we know what we're doing."

But they didn't.

By the end of the week, she again had sepsis.

This time, she just didn't have it in her to fight back. She knew she would be alone again, on a ventilator surrounded by doctors that couldn't give her the attention she needed. If my father could have been by her side the entire time, she would have fought. After 55 years of marriage, she relied on him and his steady hand. She didn't need much to hang hope. Just a hint of reassurance from him would have fueled her for years to come.

Unfortunately, this time, she was done. She wasn't going to let doctors decide when she was exiting. They couldn't give her the quality of care she needed, but she could decide when it was time to go.

She informed her doctors of her decision and asked to see my sister and father. Surprisingly, they granted her this request.

They arrived within the hour and stood by her bedside. We knew this day would come; we just didn't know when. But my mother's strength and determination still prevailed. She wasn't going to leave with a whimper. She had one last point to make. Her final words were instructions. She looked at my sister and father and said, "Don't sit in the cemetery crying for me. Go live your lives."

She was one week away from celebrating her 75th birthday when she decided to make her exit. There was no last gasp. No panicked drama. She just closed her eyes and went. My sister and father honored her wishes and held their heads high as they moved along. It was time for a new chapter in everyone's lives. Everyone carried themselves to a new place in a stoic but warm manner.

Everyone but me.

I was angry.

I knew that things could have been done to save her. I knew this wasn't supposed to be the end of the line for her. A couple months earlier, she was as strong and vibrant as she had been in the previous 20 years. We were on the phone, laughing and exchanging barbs and jokes. I knew her. I am her son. I knew the life force in her. I felt her power in every beating I took. She was my Goliath. She was the giant who made me stronger and smarter than I could have ever imagined. She taught me persistence and resiliency. The same determination I had when I stood up against her is the same force that came to save her when she needed me.

Whether she planned for it or not, as a child, she had prepared me for my entire life. I was able to fight off criminals and death threats and save entire communities because of her. She taught me how to learn from adversity, how to overcome the giant, and how to grow from all of it. None of this was by accident. It was all a culmination that had been built upon itself to take us to this moment. I knew she could live longer. I just needed to get her out of Canada and into the hands of doctors who had saved her in the past.

I needed an answer.

I knew I could find one if I tried hard enough.

I smashed my fists into my desk. Over and over, and over. I just needed the clock to turn back a little bit. Just enough to give me time to get to her.

Over and over, and over.

Just one more chance. One more chance to save her.

I called to her, "Mom, please…just give me one more chance. You always gave me one more chance. Do it again. Just one more time."

I smashed my fists into the desk until they were numb.

"Mom, please."

She didn't answer.

It was then that I realized I couldn't smash through free will.

I had to accept that she chose to go.

If she wanted to stay, she would have said, "My son knows what to do." But she didn't. She told us to go on with our lives.

Thank Goliath

I answer the phone.

"Hello."

"What are you doing?"

"Working."

"Did you eat?"

"I did."

"What did you eat?"

"A salad."

"A salad? Salad is not food."

"What is it?"

"It's something that goes around food."

"We eat dandelion greens."

"Dandelion greens are not salad."

"What are they?"

"Nutrition."

"Mom, why are you calling me?"

"You should eat something with nutrition if you have to work the rest of the day."

"Is my diet the most important thing on your mind today?"

"Why are you on a diet? Is that why you are eating salad for lunch?"

"Mom, I'm busy. I'm not on a diet. Why did you call?"

"Do you know who died?"

"No. Who died?"

"Just take a guess."

"I have no idea who could have possibly died."

"You knew him. Take a guess."

"I knew him. Who died?"

"Spinelli."
"Who?"
"Spinelli."
"Who is Spinelli?"
"Joe Spinelli. You knew him."
"Joe Spinelli? I don't know a Joe Spinelli."
"Of course, you do."
"Who was he?"
"Do you remember that quiet boy you played soccer with?"
"Quiet boy?"
"He had brown hair, small boy, quiet. Nice boy."
"You just described everyone on the team."
"His father would drive you to the games once in a while."
"Who was his father?"
"I don't remember his name. He was a nice man."
"Mom, I'm sorry. I don't know Joe Spinelli, and I don't remember a small boy with brown hair that I played soccer with."
"Do you remember the pool?"
"What pool?"
"The pool. You used to go back to his house after the games to go swimming in the pool. You went there all the time."
"Are you talking about Adam?"
"YES, Adam. Nice boy. You went there all the time."
"I went two or three times."
"You had fun."
"Mom."
"Yes."
"What does this have to do with Joe Spinelli?"
"Joe lived next door to Adam."
"And from this you think that I knew him?"

"He would say 'hi' to you all of the time."
"I don't remember him."
"You know him."
"Knew him."
"I told you that you know him. I was right."
"Knew him. He's dead."
"He was a nice man. The ball would go in his yard. He never got upset. He'd bring the ball back to you guys and never complained."
"I don't remember, but that was nice of him."
"Anyway, poor guy, 63. He had cancer."
"Sorry for him. That's very young. Thank you for the news, but I have to go."
"Are you going to call his wife?"
"Why would I call his wife?"
"To give your condolences. I have her phone number."
"Mom, I don't know these people."
"It's a nice gesture. Her name is Annabella. Poor woman lost her husband at 63."
"I'm not calling her."
"It doesn't cost you anything to be nice."
"I have to go."
"OK, then just send a card. You want the address? I have it."
"Mom, why don't you send them a card?"
"Fine. I'll sign your name on it, too."
"I have to go."
"If you would stop with the diet, you would be in a better mood."
"Goodbye."
"One day you're going to die, and you're going to wish people sent you cards."

"What's her address?"

"No matter how old you are, you should always listen to your mother. I always make sure you do the right thing. Let me get my glasses and I'll give you the address."

Every few weeks, we had this exact same conversation. For about 10 years, she would call me to give me an obituary update. Each time, it resembled a TV game show. And each time, it ended with "let me get my glasses" before she would recite the deceased person's address to me.

I never sent one card.

She thought I did, and that seemed good enough for me.

I didn't know them, so I figured what difference would it make?

I should have sent them.

She was right, it doesn't cost anything to be nice.

I came to that realization within hours of my mom's passing. The notes, texts, emails, and phone calls poured in from around the world for the next few days. They came from people I hadn't spoken with in 40 years and even from those I didn't know. Mom made friends wherever she went her entire life, and now they wanted to offer their condolences.

It was challenging to be respectful, stoic, and sorrowful when again we watched inattentive, overworked, and highly protected doctors make mistakes that caused her undue pain and, this time, death. What they hadn't accomplished in the previous 35 years, they achieved this time with the help of federal protocols. However, as a family, we tried to rise above because we knew we weren't the only ones suffering. We knew that millions of people, around the world, had passed away in similar circumstances, alone, far from family and loved ones.

A week after her funeral, I felt lost. I wasn't sure what to do. I didn't want to sit and grieve. I also knew my mom wouldn't want me running from my problems. The best I could come up with was to put my thoughts down on paper, and perhaps that would help me come to terms with her passing. In the past, I would have called her to ask for her opinion, but she was no longer there. I thought about all of the conversations over the years and figured that maybe I would capture her voice by writing those discussions on paper. I knew above all, I just wanted to be alone with my memories. The next day, I packed a bag with clothes and some food, and I flew out to the middle of the desert in Arizona with the intention of locking myself in a dark, cold hotel room to begin writing what would eventually become this book.

An hour after I arrived, I settled in and set up my laptop. As I sat at the desk, in front of my computer, I felt a tickle behind my right ear, and then I heard my mother's voice. "Amen."

I looked behind me and to either side and saw no one.

I knew it was her. It was definitely her voice, and the tickle behind my ear is something she often did to me when I was a child.

I thought about the word "amen." I knew that it meant "so be it," but what did my mother mean by telling me "so be it"? Was it her way of telling me to accept her death and to move on? It could have been, but I was uncertain. I decided to search the internet for further clues or hints. I just typed the word "amen."

On the first page of my Google search I saw "Amen Clinics" and "Dr. Daniel G. Amen." I then searched his name and the clinics. The first and most prominent item to appear was a YouTube video, a TED talk by a man named Dr. Amen. I thought I was hallucinating. I didn't believe someone actually had the name "Amen." But I searched further, and it was legitimate: Dr. Daniel G. Amen, brain disorder specialist.

I watched the 14-minute video and listened intently to Dr. Amen describe how he and his team had scanned the brains of more than 83,000 people. For these scans, he used a technology called SPECT (single-photon emission computed tomography) to produce a three-dimensional image of the blood flow that is occurring in your entire brain. With the SPECT scan, he can accurately determine where there is weakness, trauma, and even cysts or tumors. Dr. Amen explained how the human brain is fragile and can easily be damaged and affect all other aspects of our lives without us being aware of the damage.

According to his years of research, many people developed psychological issues such as depression, anxiety, attention deficit disorder, hyperactivity, and social isolation because they had actual physical damage to the brain rather than some underlying mental or emotional issue. Tens of thousands of his patients were treated by other doctors for these psychological issues without ever having looked at the physical health of the brain. His motto was simple: "Fix your brain, fix your life."

He had my attention.

I took out a pen and wrote all the times I had been hit in the head and with what. I also wrote down every collision in a sporting event or car accident.

Aside from the countless years of being hit in the head with hands, fists, brooms and wooden clogs, there were years of playing soccer and butting heads with other players. On a couple of occasions, I was knocked out cold. Also on the list were several ski accidents where I hit my head either with a ski or on the ground. Then, of course, the time I flipped an actual Jet Ski in the water and the entire machine fell on my head and knocked me out. Fortunately, I was wearing a life vest. Lastly, there were the five car accidents I had been in throughout my life. Only one was caused by me, but it didn't matter. In several of the accidents, I solidly smashed my head against the driver's side window, which certainly caused some form of damage.

I looked at this long list that spanned most of my life. I realized that not once had my brain been scanned or examined in any manner. Despite concussions, stitches, severe blows, and car accidents, no one, including me, thought we should look at the actual physical brain to see if there was any damage.

I didn't need more convincing. I knew something was wrong. Over the past year, my thoughts had become darker. I struggled to remember information. Lights and sounds bothered me. I spent more time alone and became easily irritated and angry. I had difficulty concentrating. And, mostly, I was unhappy. On the couple occasions I shared this information with others, they told me I was aging. That I was just becoming a grumpy old man. I didn't mind the thought of being old, but I was only 54. This notion of aging and becoming progressively miserable was something that didn't make sense to me, and I was just unwilling to accept it as fact.

I immediately picked up the phone and made an appointment for the SPECT scan.

Two weeks later, the scans were performed on me, and the results were sent shortly thereafter.

A SPECT scan creates an image of the blood flow in every area of the brain. A healthy brain scan looks like a smooth, peeled cantaloupe. Blood flows evenly and actively in all areas. An unhealthy brain scan looks like a cantaloupe that has ridges, lesions, and holes. My scan looked exactly like everything I had experienced. It looked like someone had beaten me with a hammer and a baseball bat. A significant portion of the entire brain showed decreased blood flow and activity. Some areas had virtually no blood flow. The ridges, scalloping, and lesions carried throughout all the images. From every angle, it was clear that there was a lot of damage. It was alarming. The only inescapable thought in my mind now was whether all this trauma could be fixed.

A few days later I met with Dr. Morrow from the Amen clinic. Together we reviewed the scans.

Dr. Morrow jumped right in. "Domenic, you have a tremendous amount of physical damage to your brain. Being completely candid, these scans are as bad, if not worse, than the hundreds of professional football players I have treated over the years."

My heart sank. I was used to dealing and even delivering bad news, but this was figuratively and literally hitting me over the head. I focused on the scans and asked, "OK. Thank you for being direct, but what does that mean?"

He replied, "It means you have a lot of work to do. We can fix it, but you have to be dedicated to the entire program that we provide for you."

I nodded. "And, if I don't do all of it? Or, if it's not successful? What happens?"

Stoically he stared at me and said, "You will most likely develop dementia within three to five years. You will have a precipitous decline in your mental, emotional, and physical ability. If that occurs, we may be able to mitigate the decline but may not be able to repair it."

I thought "dementia." How did I get here? My mother just died and now I'm not far behind her? How is this happening?

Now, frustrated and confused, I asked Dr. Morrow, "Excuse me, but if my brain is as damaged as it is, how am I functioning today? How did I get this far in life? I used to manage thousands of people and process countless numbers and pieces of information in a highly stressful environment…and I was good at it. How could that be?"

Dr. Morrow smiled and nodded, "We wondered the exact same thing. Then we discovered the answer." He shuffled papers and pulled out a different image from the scans. He held it up and said, "Look here. This image shows a much healthier brain. It's smoother. This is an image of your brain when we put you through a test and it was required to focus. It appears that whenever you were required to focus on a task or subject, the blood flow increased dramatically in your brain. It increased so significantly that it was able to compensate for any damage. This is the reason you were able to perform at such a high level. However, when you're not focused, these other issues arise such as emotional control, depression, memory loss, irritability, sensitivity to light and sounds, inability to sleep."

I was somewhat reassured by his answer, but my mind went back in time and searched for answers. "Dr. Morrow, what was the primary cause of this damage? When do you think most of it occurred?"

Doctor Morrow put the images from the scans on his lap. "Domenic, certainly your work, decades of this intense pace and stress contributed. And, most likely some of the injuries from sports and car accidents caused issues. However, most of this damage was caused in your childhood. The brain and your body was not fully formed, so it made it more malleable and susceptible to damage. But, you are very fortunate. Somehow, your brain figured out a way to overcome all of this and get you here. Now, we have to fix it. We either fix it or it will finally reach the end of its limits."

I didn't think it was possible, but at the same moment, I felt both pain and relief. It was painful to think that my mother had helped create this mess, but it was also a relief knowing she was helping to clean it up. I wasn't angry. How could I be? My mother gave me the foundation and inspiration to build a wonderful life for myself and for others. I was now here, being given a chance to heal. To me, there was nothing further to discuss. I simply said, "Tell me what to do."

I dropped everything and began a five-day-a-week schedule of attending one form of therapy or another. The entire protocol included 3-4 hours in a hyperbaric oxygen chamber where high-dose oxygen is pumped into a pressurized chamber; 1-2 hours in a CVAC pod where there are rapid changes in air pressure, essentially mimicking high-altitude training; 1-3 hours of NanoVi, a device designed to help the brain repair damage from free radicals; 1-3 hours of Alpha-Stim, where microcurrent electrotherapy alternates on either side of the brain; 1-2 hours of neurofeedback, a technology that helps produce healthy brain waves; and lastly, working with a licensed naturopathic doctor to receive the proper vitamin and nutrient supplementation to feed the brain—a process that would help it through all of these therapies.

I didn't think it would be as difficult as it was. I was unaware that trying to repair a brain takes a lot of energy. However, by the end of the first month, I began to see improvement in all aspects of my mental and physical disposition. I was calmer, happier, and sleeping more soundly. I continued with this intensive schedule for four months and then tapered back in the fifth and sixth month. Each month, I made progress. My thoughts became clearer and more optimistic. My body felt lighter and stronger.

All of the hours in closed quarters with pressurized air gave me time to think about Goliath. The giant that challenged my mother and me, in every imaginable way, all through our life. Some people viewed Goliath as a curse and a threat to us. Some viewed it as just plain bad luck or pre-destined fate. I suppose that it could have been any of those things, but for me and my mother, we saw the giant as a noble teacher. Every time we faced adversity, it gave us a chance to grow and examine life more closely. It also gave us a chance to learn about ourselves, about others and how strong, creative, and resilient we are as humans and souls. It gave us a chance to reflect on mistakes, weaknesses, corruption, and sheer criminality of others. In both the good and the bad, we learned to rise above and find the good in everything. We believed in God. We believed in Love. Adversity, dressed as Goliath, gave us a chance to become wise, forgiving, and noble. Rather than letting it crush and destroy our faith and hope, we chose to learn from it and share that knowledge with others.

Throughout this process, I also realized that adversity had one final lesson for me. In my reflection and rumination, I realized that as a child, I had learned to survive regardless of whatever giant I might confront. I spent decades living in this manner—in a state of survival. Not only could I survive in extreme situations, but I taught others how to do the same. If you needed help, I was there for you. I would fight for you, your company, your community until the very bitter end. I would face scorn, ridicule, bullets—nothing frightened or deterred me. Every bit of my being, especially my brain, was designed to survive in the face of adversity. One way or another, I would find a way to help you. My mother had this same foundation of survival. She helped build it in me and with others.

Despite possessing this fortitude, I now realized that surviving was not living. Surviving was not living a life of wisdom and high spiritual expression. It was just hanging on. It was the bare minimum of human existence. I now came to understand that our souls can do much more than just survive. I had to accept this final piece of truth: Until I healed all the underlying physical damage, I could never properly heal the emotional and spiritual components within me. Going through this therapy allowed new pathways of blood flow to develop, and old ones to be repaired. It improved the actual flow of blood, air, and nutrients to my brain. All of this, in turn, influenced the cognitive functioning and every other physical aspect of being a human. It's as if I rebuilt my entire body. It felt like I had gone back to my childhood and got a chance to start a new life, with truly a clean slate. In this new state of being, the memories and experiences of the past would remain with me, but the bumps, bruises, and pain would be left behind.

Had my mother not passed away, and had she not come to me in the middle of the desert, I may have not addressed any of these problems. I may never have found Dr. Amen.

With this last whisper, this last gesture and final miracle, she pushed me out of survival mode and into a place of healing. She knew that as I healed, I would find the joy that I once lost.

Even in death, she was one step ahead of me.

ABOUT THE AUTHOR

As an entrepreneur and operational turnaround expert, Domenic Aversa is sought after by both global business leaders and government agencies. He has actively assisted companies in dramatic transition for more than 25 years.

He has served as an educational speaker and managerial advisor on international business development, recession preparation and insolvency issues for many business and academic institutions. Audiences have included the Harvard Business School and the Sloan School of Management at MIT.

Domenic captured his business experience in the world of crisis management in his first book, *Corporate Undertaker; Business Lessons from the Dead and Dying.*

He is a member of the board of directors for the non-profit, Michael's Gift (www.michaelsgift.org). The organization is dedicated to the healing of spiritual, emotional and physical trauma.

He currently resides in California with his wife, Nirvana, and his two cats, Carnelia and Truffles.

www.ingramcontent.com/pod-product-compliance
Lightning Source LLC
Chambersburg PA
CBHW071230070526
44583CB00017B/2119